THE NEW BARBARIAN MANIFESTO

HOW TO SURVIVE THE INFORMATION AGE

IAN ANGELL

KOGAN
PAGE

This book is dedicated to my three Guardian Angells: my late mother Eluned Angell, my father Roy Angell, and of course my wife Mary Angell.

First published 2000
Reprinted 2000

Apart from any fair dealing for the purposes of research or private study, or criticism or review, as permitted under the Copyright, Designs and Patents Act 1988, this publication may only be reproduced, stored or transmitted, in any form or by any means, with the prior permission in writing of the publishers, or in the case of reprographic reproduction in accordance with the terms and licences issued by the CLA. Enquiries concerning reproduction outside these terms should be sent to the publishers at the undermentioned addresses:

Kogan Page Limited
120 Pentonville Road
London
N1 9JN
UK

Kogan Page Limited
163 Central Avenue, Suite 4
Dover
NH 03820
USA

© Ian Angell, 2000

The right of Ian Angell to be identified as the author of this work has been asserted by him in accordance with the Copyright, Designs and Patents Act 1988.

British Library Cataloguing in Publication Data

A CIP record for this book is available from the British Library.

ISBN 0 7494 3151 2

Typeset by Kogan Page Limited
Printed and bound in Great Britain by Clays Ltd, St Ives plc

Contents

Part VI   The winners

Part VII   How to become a winner

Preface

You may find the writing style of this book rather strange. You may even think that it reads like a sermon, preaching 'hellfire and damnation'. It is intended to be strident – after all it is a manifesto. But don't let the tone put you off. There is a good reason for this choice of style; for although much of the book foretells an age of doom and gloom for the many, it also contains a message of salvation for the few. Please persevere because the book does hint at how you and yours can join the latter elite band.

I want to convince you that a 'brave new world' is being forced upon unsuspecting societies by advances in information technology. This is a brutal and brutish world, a world of barbarians, where the certainties of the 20th century, its power bases and its institutions are collapsing. With illustrations from around the world, but particularly from Britain and the United States, I will show that this is no nice neat tidy transition, but a severe and total dislocation with the past. Individuals, companies, communities and countries will either be catapulted into a new prosperity, or relegated to poverty, obscurity and extinction.

The message of *The New Barbarian Manifesto* is quite simple. The way that a society arranges its economic production feeds back into social behaviour and eventually reshapes that society's norms. Advances in new technology are amplifying forces that are highly disruptive to economic performance, and are consequently undermining societal stability. The impact of these forces on the creation and ownership of wealth means that our 20th-century socio-economic institutions must either mutate or die. The 20th century, the century of the masses, is over. Like all mass cultures, it has eventually degenerated into the natural state of societal entropy, the gradual running down to disorder and chaos.

This book is structured to enable you to understand these forces and use them to advantage, with pointers to becoming a winner in this new age. In the introduction and in the first three chapters, collectively called **Impact of the superhighways**, I will discuss the new forces and also the rejuvenated old pressures now unleashed by information technology. In the next part, **Work and employment**, I will show that the nature of work has changed fundamentally, and that every state will face the major problem of finding employment for its unemployed and unemployable citizens. In **Assault on the status quo**, I will focus on two particular 'virtues' of today's 'advanced' societies, namely the redistribution of wealth through taxation, and universal suffrage, and will expose their degeneracy. The consequential breakdown of our society is then mapped out in the next part, **Transition**. The following part, **Recognizing the new order**, will show how to see through the societal rituals that blind us to the disintegration happening all around. The penultimate section will use the new insight to identify **The winners** (and losers), and the final chapter will show **How to become a winner**, how to be a 'new barbarian'.

We all have two choices: follow 'new barbarians' and advance to an uncertain future, or obey 'old barbarians' and their fundamentalist gospel of a false past. The new barbarians represent the winners in the new economic reality, leaving the losers to circle their wagons around old values and rituals, easy prey for the old barbarians. The outcome of their coming battle will be a world of three zones. The first world is the libertarian realm of new barbarians that supports the rights of the individual, not of the tribe. The second world is an uneasy compromise between old barbarian ideologies and the modern world; its mode of governance focuses exclusively on the rights of the collective. Might is right in the third world, a place of terror and repression. Putting it simply, the three worlds are an open society, a closed society and no society.

If trapped in the two lesser worlds, we will be forced to conform to old barbarian rituals. Therefore, we must throw in our lot with the new barbarians. The alternative is to be left to the mercy of the masses, forced to accept the mind control of religious, political and ethnic bigotry – or suffer the consequences. The history of every human society has been of the tension between the individual and the collective, between the self and the tribe, between private aspirations and social norms. Today we are again faced with the three evils of socialism, racism and religious intolerance. We must flee to the first world of 'smart regions', to prosper in a climate of individualism and of intellectual and financial freedom. Should we fail to escape in large enough numbers, then a new Dark Age will engulf us all.

Welcome to the future. Welcome to the 'brave new world' of *The New Barbarian Manifesto*.

Ian Angell

Acknowledgements

I would like to thank all the graduate students of the Information Systems Department at the London School of Economics over the past decade, particularly my PhD students and those MSc students who attended the course on 'The Global Consequences of Information Technology', and on whom I 'tried out' the ideas expounded in this book. There are two friends who merit a particular mention. First, there is Stephen Mooney, with whom I developed that course, and with whom I shared the teaching during the first three years of its existence. It was he who brought to my attention many of the quotations used in this book, particularly those of Jane Jacobs and Ayn Rand. Our discussions greatly influenced my thinking and inspired me to write this book. Steve is an incorrigible optimist, who believes that new technology will bring about a better world. I have fond memories of our long and animated conversations, where his sunny outlook so contrasted with my terminal cynicism. I look forward to reading his book on the coming Information Age! Of equal importance to my view of tomorrow's world is Bernhard Straub, with whom I hammered out my position on ritual and morality that forms the backbone of this book.

I know it is invidious to single out any others from the many who helped and inspired me, but nevertheless I will thank Zhang Bingxhun, John Gauntt, Gus Hosein, Fernando Ilharco, Wendy Jacobi, Oleg Kalnichevski, Deepak Kanungo, Rodrigo Magalhaes, Eve Mittleton-Kelly, Kreg Nichols, Selwyn Seymour, Ido ben Shaul and Jimmy Tseng. I can only hope that the others, far too many to name, will forgive me for their omission.

Then there are the friends who read various drafts and gave me the most constructive comments: Dan Atkinson, Brendan Barns, Rowan Bosworth-Davies, Pat Crimmin, Neil Gregory, Rachel Hanig, David Kingsley, and of course Pat Lomax of Kogan Page who edited the final version.

Last but not least, there is my wife, Mary, who has had to live with this book for the best part of a decade.

Introduction

It was the best of times, it was the worst of times, it was the age of wisdom, it was the age of foolishness, it was the epoch of belief, it was the epoch of incredulity, it was the season of Light, it was the season of Darkness, it was the spring of hope, it was the winter of despair, we had everything before us, we had nothing before us, we were all going direct to Heaven, we were all going direct the other way.

The first words of *A Tale of Two Cities*, used by Charles Dickens to depict the French Revolution, ring hauntingly true today. For today we too are on the brink of another revolution, possibly an evolution, a new social and economic reality. Only recently have we begun to realize that the changes in the 'Information Age' will be just as significant as those of that other revolution, the Industrial Revolution, which has shaped all our todays. Human society is entering a totally different tomorrow. It is undergoing fundamental global changes that will either catapult individuals, companies, communities and countries into a new prosperity, or relegate them to poverty, obscurity and extinction.

Trotsky was right when he said history is 'the natural selection of accidents', and our world today is full of accidents just waiting to happen. Everywhere, cynics are preying on the perfectly natural human fear of the unknown. Today that unknown is more unknowable than ever. It is all too common for us to respond: 'I don't want vague visions of the future; I want specific answers to my problems, and I want them now.' But there are no easy answers in times of uncertainty. The situation is far too fluid for that.

In the shadows I see the very nature of employment, of work and the workplace, of institutions, of society, of politics and even of capitalism itself, mutating. 'Are these the shadows of the things that Will be, or are they the shadows of things that May be, only?' (Charles Dickens again, *A Christmas Carol*). The survival of the fittest will decide who will win the inevitable natural selection. These mutations are confronting each other in the political power vacuum left by the fall of communism, and by the increasing impotence of liberal democracy, as the utopia promised by science and technology has turned into a nightmare for the 'Common Man'. Global plagues, nuclear proliferation, chemical and biological weapons, overpopulation, mass migration, unemployment, uncontrollable capital markets, pollution and poverty have left us with a world full of frightened people.

Welcome to the future. Welcome to a world as different from today as today is from the pre-industrial age. Welcome to the *Brave New World*. But why new? New, because a new order is being forced upon an unsuspecting world by advances in telecommunications and mobile computing. We are on the verge of a new revolution, an Information Revolution, that is taking us out of the Machine Age, into who knows what – into that brave new world. But why brave? Brave, because this is not a world for the timid. None but the brave will win here. This is a brutish world where the socio-economic certainties of the 20th century, its power bases, its institutions are collapsing. The world as we know it is transforming. Everything is changing, and I really do mean everything: politics, economics, business, society as a whole. And I really do mean change: not the nice tidy change that the management gurus sell in their 'change management seminars'. This is not a nice tidy transition – but a severe and total dislocation with the past.

Information technology and other new technologies have provoked profound structural changes in the world economy, and these are concocting unimaginable levels of complexity. This complexity is manifesting itself as market instability, political turmoil and civil unrest, increasing rage and violent actions amongst previously passive people, as well as 'immoral' behaviour on a gigantic scale. In fact we are witnessing the possibility of a wide-ranging and complete systemic breakdown in many societies. As the problems run totally out of control, we will need to identify the trends if we are to have any chance of stopping the rot, let alone of prospering in these totally unstable conditions. In this book I want to expose the fault-lines that are appearing everywhere, and the awesome effects they will have on everything we do.

Today, each of us has a simple choice: stick our head in the sand and hope the problems will all go away; or try to understand the situation and make the best of it. It is pointless bemoaning the unfairness of it all. The die is cast and there is nothing anyone can do about it. We must make sure that we are standing upright, on the right side of the gain line. We need to make the future work for us, for our families and those we care about. To that end I hope this book will be of some help.

For 'when we lose the comfortable formulas that have hitherto been our guides among the complexities of existence… we feel like drowning in the ocean of facts until we find a new foothold or learn to swim' (Werner Sombart). The drowning media are clutching at straws. That is why they give so much exposure to the views of politicians drowning alongside them. Many of today's commentators are deeply pessimistic. They see only chaos ahead, and some ignore the problems in the hope that they will all go away. They see chaos because they are interpreting events in terms of the very control structures and institutions that are failing. They are reflecting an increasingly uncertain tomorrow in the wildly distorting mirror of yesterday's defunct certainties. They want the world to be the way it ought to be, as it was yesterday. But yesterday doesn't work any more. The very past success of our institutions has made them decadent and degenerate, and has spawned systems of such complexity that now the old certainties are beginning to fail.

The forlorn hope is that the few optimists out there may be right, and that the flow-tide of chaos can be turned back by re-imposing the old order, by reasserting strong social, political and economic control – that 'the will of the people will prevail'. But these controls, our institutional rituals, are failing.

Uncertainty, as always, precedes the transition to a new order – and new ritualized controls. Humanity has always lived in such a state of continuous and unremitting transition. Change never goes away; however, there is the not-so-small question of scale. Sometimes the sheer immensity of change merits the label 'revolution'. I am convinced that the future will brand our present age as a time of revolution.

The solid ground on which our Western societies were established is now shifting, as the basis of their power has become degenerate, and is disintegrating. Increasingly, we are losing faith in the nation–state. We know something is radically wrong, but we are blinded by our misguided societal rituals, and are unable to recognize just what the real problems are. We are so wrapped up in our own particular problems that we fail to see the big picture. When we look around at the growing nightmares in Western society – drugs, unemployment, crime, terrorism – it is easy to blame them as the causes of social collapse. This is a fundamental mistake. These problems are the **effect** of the break-up of the underlying order, **not its cause**. They are the consequences of our power structures now become impotent – a classic symptom of social collapse, the first stages of a revolution.

Societies all around the world have arrived at just that same state, where their certainties no longer drive away doubt. The rituals of communism are now discredited worldwide, and those of democratic processes increasingly look remote. In Britain, the once solid rock of monarchy is ridiculed, discounted to a butt for puerile media curiosity. The dignity of the US presidency and the Oval Office is diminished by a stream of sexual innuendo. Our societies are without viable norms and standards. They have become decadent, ready for collapse. Natural selection is left to decide whether these societies will degenerate into complete collapse, or mutate into different newly stable survivors.

In a strong society, degenerates and mutations alike are destroyed by the normal homeostatic processes and rituals of a vigorous power structure. However, when that power base has itself become decadent and unstable, it cannot purify itself. Consequently degenerates and mutations will prosper. They will poison (in the case of degenerates) or change (in the case of mutations) the system. This vocabulary of biology, valid in observing the behaviour of organisms, is highly relevant for interpreting changes in social, political and economic structures! Remnants of old orders can survive, and possibly older orders can be regenerated, but only if they mutate to cope with the new conditions. Confronting a rapidly approaching new order, it should come as no surprise that we are losing confidence in the meaning of the vocabulary of our social norms. We no longer know what the words mean. Terms that slip off the tongue like 'money', 'work', 'family', 'community', 'the people', no longer mean what they used to. Standards of 'justice', 'morality' and 'fairness' become moveable feasts. Consequently societal leadership, half-heartedly claiming justification in these outmoded concepts, is doomed.

Apparently oblivious to, or ignoring, the societal collapse taking place around them, Western politicians espouse political correctness, all the while failing to see in it the excesses of a popular 'ideological thuggery'. But the masses will not win in the natural selection for dominance of an increasingly elitist world. Naturally, the politicians don't like it. For the past two centuries 'the values of the weak prevail[ed] because the strong have taken them over as devices of leadership' (Nietzsche). But no longer! Aggressive opportunists – barbarians – are carving out the new order, as when money markets manipulate national currencies and pour scorn on the pleas of finance ministers, or when drug barons flood the world with narcotics. There are trillions of dollars in hot money sloshing around the world's financial markets. Money from the black economy, narco-dollars and ill-gotten gains from arms and other forms of smuggling in addition to tax-flight capital, is flooding into 'cyberspace'. The Triad involvement in the arms trade alone nets them $500 billion annually (Kerry, 1997). This money is, in effect, gambling against national economies, and profiting from the numerous mistakes of inept politicians. The huge losses are covered by the poor, and getting poorer, taxpayers. On Black Wednesday, 16 September 1992, British ministers 'ran around like headless chickens' while still claiming to be in control, moving interest rates up and down like a yo-yo. (On that day the Bank of England spent £20 billion in its futile attempt at defending the pound. Interest rates were raised to 15 per cent, all in vain. The pound ultimately crashed out of the European exchange rate mechanism.) It fooled no one. Politicians may promise and posture, but now the global markets decide.

The markets need movement to make their profits. Rumours, not politicians, drive movement and start the cash registers ringing. The markets are in control, not politicians, although the press contribute to the notion that government is: it is easier to accept information from 'close friends' of the senator/minister than to go looking for real stories. The spin doctors may actually start rumours in the interests of their political masters, so that the market-makers don't even have to invent rumours any more. Unfortunately the volatility (or chaos) is getting out of control. Even the smart players can get burnt in the arbitrary positive feedback of a market rout.

Meanwhile, the democratic politicians are 'eunuchs in the harem' of *realpolitik*: they see everything, they've read the books, they think they know how it is done, but they simply no longer have the equipment to play the game. Governments give every impression of 'being in office, but not in power' (Norman Lamont). Yet impotent politicians worldwide want to appear moral in their power-broking. They seek justification for their actions in an infinitely flexible 'international law'. But their position is not based on morality or justice, and never has been. Power is intrinsic in the institutions of the time, and that alone gave them their position. Only now that power is in terminal decline. It comes as no surprise that they are thoroughly bewildered when the consequences of their actions finesse, even reverse, their best intentions. But they should care! 'Professional people have no cares, Whatever happens they get theirs' (Ogden Nash).

Politics has become a profession, an end in itself, and in these cynical times, decadent politicians display little sense of either pride or shame. More and more they are seen as self-seekers, losing all the respect of those they represent. Despite this, most of the populace still believe that politicians are a necessary evil; but for how much longer? 'When buying and selling are controlled by legislation, the first things to be bought and sold are legislators' (P J O'Rourke). As Giuliano Amato, the ex-prime minister of Italy shrewdly points out: 'Corruption is greatest where it is found out.' Politics is like business; it is business, a shady business. As usual Groucho Marx hit the mark: 'The key to success in business is honesty and fair dealing. If you can fake that, you've got it made.' Nowadays, under the microscope of information technology, they can't fake it. No one believes politicians any more, or even cares. Shake hands with today's politician, and count your fingers afterwards! Or was it ever thus? At least in the days of British prime minister Walpole and the 'rotten boroughs', before the Great Reform Bill of 1832, politicians used their own money to buy votes. Now, they use ours.

Politics is being taken out of the hands of politicians and back into business, and into the community. Single issues are politicizing previously apathetic citizens. In Britain, politicians encounter public fury when, for example, they try to encourage the growing of genetically modified foods, or force through the building of motorways against popular wishes. The 'legitimate trade' in exporting live animals to continental Europe has been vilified, and few see anything wrong with screaming mobs attacking the lorries. Surprisingly, it is not only the 'peasants' who are revolting – even the law-abiding middle classes are taking to the streets and fighting with police. Vigilante groups are springing up everywhere as police desert no-go areas. What more obvious evidence do we need that our comfortable world is coming to an end?

In the United States the rich are hiding themselves away in ghettos behind high security fences. It seems hardly a month goes by without hearing of some lunatic with a gun on a murderous rampage. Wherever you look, support for, and faith in, law and order are breaking down. In Japan the subway system is attacked with nerve gas. French farmers burn lorries carrying livestock, because their work practices are threatened. French seamen blockaded Calais because a British firm employed Polish crewmen (Duval Smith, 28 February 1995), each at a quarter of a French seaman's wage. The all-powerful I G Metall, the largest German trade union, has promoted an 'alliance for jobs', cutting overtime and limiting pay rises in the (vain) hope of increasing (not just protecting) the jobs of its members (*Reuters News Service*, 22 March 1996). Yet all this will not dent unemployment trends. There can be no job security in the Information Age.

All around the world defenders of workers' rights still feel totally justified in attacking the imagined wrongdoing of employers. Governments are being tempted to levy excessive taxation, both national and local, to fund the dependency culture and its underpinning of increasingly labour-intensive public services and expensive technology-bound health services. Meanwhile in California, Proposition 13 has lit the blue touch-paper for taxpayers all around the world to organize and fight back!

These apparently unrelated incidents are all symptomatic of the collapse of the old order. We can all compile a myriad of similar examples. This book will look further into these and other events. But will this degeneracy lead to decline and fall, a collapse into anarchy? No! The future will work, for some. Will it be 'the best of times' or 'the worst of times' for us? Will we, our families and friends find 'the spring of hope', or will it be 'the winter of despair'? Is 'everything before us' or 'nothing before us'? Whatever happens, it will be natural selection, and not the politicians, that will decide whether we are all going 'direct to Heaven' or 'direct the other way'.

Part I

Impact of the superhighways

1

Information superhighways

So what is precipitating all this change and uncertainty, and why is it all happening now? The answer to both these questions is quite simple: a new order (which to many will be disorder) is being forced upon an unsuspecting world by advances in telecommunications and computing. The many stresses and strains in today's societies were just lying dormant, waiting for a catalyst to trigger a chain reaction. That catalyst has arrived, and it has created an explosive mixture that is unleashing unstoppable global economic and political forces. The certainties of the past are being blown apart by information technology; the future is being born on the so-called 'information superhighways'.

Very soon these electronic telecommunication networks, covering the world via cable, satellite and radio, will enable everyone in the world to 'talk' to everyone else (at least everyone who can afford it). Global commerce will force through the construction of multimedia highways, and anyone bypassed faces ruin. As always, wealth will be focused in 'strip development', and those off the beaten track will be abandoned to obscurity. Throughout history highways have brought wealth to the towns along their length – this was true for roads, canals, railways, seaports, motorways, airports. The superhighways will be no different. This comparison with other transport systems is useful. Even though the building of those systems did prove highly profitable, the real money was not to be made there, but in the businesses and jobs that emerged out of their existence. Profits from building the information technology infrastructure will pale into insignificance when compared to those made from the information content roaming the superhighway. The best way to understand the lessons that past transport systems have for the superhighway is not to focus on the rail and road systems themselves, but to see what industries and artefacts were created and destroyed by the goods being transported. Those transport systems gave birth to such diverse progeny as the petroleum industry, mail-order, the suburb, commuting, museums, tourism and so on. In fact most of what we consider to be jobs (or society) today could not have existed without these earlier transport systems. It is sobering to realize how we tend to forget all about the previous lifestyles superseded by newer systems.

Unfortunately, many of the jobs that are tied into these now-old ways will also disappear completely. According to Alvin Toffler in his book *The Third Wave*, the way we use these older systems will change radically. The three wavefronts he refers to are the agricultural revolution (around 8000 BC), the Industrial Revolution (17th and 18th centuries), and now the Information Revolution. 'We, who happen to share the planet at this explosive moment, will therefore feel the full impact of the Third Wave in our own lifetimes. Tearing families apart, rocking our economy, paralysing our political systems, shattering our values, the Third Wave affects everyone' (Toffler, 1980).

Power and control

Information systems running along the superhighway will change everything, which is why politicians see it as so important to control the superhighway – a vain hope. Is it any wonder that US vice-president Al Gore led the developed world's politicians in a scramble to ensure that their own particular countries were ahead of the game? Ministers from G7, the group of the world's seven leading industrial nations, met in Brussels in February 1995, at the invitation of the European Union, to raise awareness of the superhighway. Their aim was to create an international (that is a G7) strategy that would ensure that political short-termism, meddling and indecision would not block development. And who would achieve this? Why the very same indecisive short-termist politicians meddling in its development.

Their discussions were coloured by the fact that the United States is far ahead in the race to create an information economy, thanks to a deregulated, competitive but tame telecommunications infrastructure, and strong bipartisan support from both Republican and Democrat parties. It could be argued that US advantage happened because the politicians weren't looking at new technology. Only when computing's importance became apparent did they make their first tentative steps at control, as in the antitrust action against

Bill Gates and Microsoft. US politicians had a much better understanding of telephones, hence the break-up of the AT&T monopoly in 1984 giving birth to the Baby Bells. They had over a century of experience since that day in March 1876 when Alexander Graham Bell was granted US patent number 174465 for a device that transmitted sounds over electric wires. European politicians, by contrast, have always been preoccupied with the clumsy process of creating what they believe to be controllable technical and regulatory preconditions, whether they understand the consequences of the technology or not. It is no accident that the United States talks of an information economy, whereas Europe argues on about an information society.

Of course all the politicians involved in the Brussels meeting were hoping that an equivalent number of new jobs would be created to replace those being destroyed by the superhighway, and they were intent on ensuring that as many as possible would come to their particular country. French politicians claimed to see the ogre of American cultural imperialism raising its ugly head, and stressed the need to preserve Europe's (namely their own) cultural identity. At the same G7 meeting there was some high-minded talk about a global university to educate people from developing countries; but no one mentioned who was going to pay for the service, or who would be paid for creating the educational material. Few believed such insincere promises, knowing that aid to poor countries has been steadily decreasing over the last two decades (Chote, 8 April 1999). The discussions were actually about setting up the infrastructure that would allow G7 countries to carve up all the new jobs between themselves, and ensure that the world's economic backbone stays in North America, Europe and the Pacific Rim.

Pious words abounded, concerning the availability of public information on the Net and the democratic nature of the information society. The rest of the G7 countries are likely to imitate the US attempt at bridging the 'information gap' between the political centre, in the US's case Washington, and the rest of the country. By supplying the population with electronic access to the data, politicians believe that 'the people' will be lining up to read what the politicians want them to see. They call it 'extending democracy'. In fact these sites may well be of enormous value to those with a professional interest in government output, but to most people they are about as noteworthy as a party political broadcast.

The cynic would say that the jobs these politicians are most intent on saving are their own. However, all such attempts to control technological development are misguided, as are the politicians' attitudes. What a splendid shame that the consequences of their best intentions will be the end of their own political power: but much more of that later.

Employment effects

All the while, computerization is deskilling, and far worse displacing, a large proportion of today's jobs. A conservative estimate from the British banking sector is that in the 1990s more than 150,000 bank employees (almost a third of the workforce) will have been made redundant, and more than half a million across Europe, which, unfortunately for continental bank clerks, is lagging behind Britain in the 'rationalization' stakes. The vast majority of these losses were precipitated by technological innovations such as the automatic teller machine, and by the need to restructure banking procedures in the face of international, particularly US, competition. However, many more financial sector redundancies are to come when electronic money is accepted by the richer sections of society, and fully automatic banking becomes the norm. The job losses lurking just over the horizon for some other business sectors, particularly in retailing, could be far, far worse.

Members of every sector in society, even those who are still lucky enough to have jobs, are finding it difficult to come to terms with this collapse of employment; a situation accurately summed up by radical US author Jeremy Rifkin in his mistitled book *The End of Work* (1995) – it should have been called *The End of Workers*. To quote Nobel Laureate Wassily Leontief, the role of humans in production will diminish 'in the same way that the horse in farm work was eliminated by tractors'. From all sides of the political divide, it is commonly accepted that Karl Marx was quite correct in his analysis of the power struggle between capital and labour. Capital needed labour, both as a healthy efficient workforce and as a market for the goods produced; but his 19th-century arguments were fundamentally misplaced by an understandable, yet ultimately fatal, oversight. Succeeding generations of Marxists thought that physical labour would always be needed to run the factories and machines. By organizing labour, and by threatening its withdrawal with other forms of mass violence, they believed industrialists would ultimately be forced to secede ownership of production to the masses. Marx didn't, he couldn't, envisage the computer – the ultimate extension of automation and the nemesis of semi-skilled labour. The Machine Age is dead; long live the Information Age! The ministers from G7 also epitomize the Machine Age. Their thinking still has not yet grasped the new realities, and their jobs, along with those of so many of their voters, will go the same way as the age they represent.

New freedoms

We are entering a new elite cosmopolitan age. Information technology, the collision of the previously disparate technologies of computers, telephones, consumer electronics, television and radio, has increasingly liberated the elite few from the restrictions of physical space and from the tyranny of the masses. It has freed them from the constraint, the mind-set and the moralities of the collective. It has set the individual free to roam the higher dimensions of 'cyberspace'. This new freedom will have profound and astounding implications for everyone on the globe. Together with rapid international travel and greatly increased mobility, information technology is undermining the very essence of political governance and its relationship to commerce, and is even changing commerce itself.

The electronic dimension of cyberspace has been expanding steadily for many years, and the pace of change is accelerating with the global linkups between telecommunication and mass-media conglomerates. These mergers and acquisitions are being sold to the public on the basis of superior entertainment channels. Visionaries like Rupert Murdoch of News Corporation, Ted Turner of Turner Broadcasting System (now part of Time Warner) and Bill Gates of Microsoft are carving out global media empires, giving them power far greater than the press barons of the past could ever have imagined. Is it any wonder that politicians worldwide are raising the alarm about what they see as cultural imperialism?

Problems for governments

What the politicians are really complaining about is their loss of control over national destiny. They gave up on the financial markets years ago. But now satellite telephones, television and the Internet have also limited the state's ability to impose total control over the press and media and other knowledgeable elites. Governments no longer have time to choreograph the release of sensitive or critical reports. The population can get access at the same time as they do, as was the case of the Starr Report being released over the Internet. Or consider the role played by fax, radio and satellite television in the abortive coup against Soviet president Mikhail Gorbachev by the communist old guard in August 1991. Gorbachev himself was kept up to date with events during his confinement by listening to the BBC World Service (Dowden and Castle, 26 March 1995), and the whole world saw Boris Yeltsin standing on a tank defending Moscow's White House. Soviet control over the national media proved impotent to stop it. Yet governments can and do use the technology. It is claimed that Dzhokhar Dudayev, then president of Chechnya, was killed by a Russian guided missile launched 150 miles away that homed in on his mobile satellite telephone (Muradian, 5 May 1997). The telephone was literally the death of Yihya Ayash, 'the Engineer'. Israeli agents tracked down his mobile phone, and managed to place a small bomb in the earpiece when it was sent to repair the 'faults' in reception caused by the same agents (Goldberg, 7 January 1996).

However, in general governments have lost the plot. Their secrets are no longer secure; whistle-blowers can distribute material on the Net highlighting malpractice; before the Internet, they didn't know where to send their evidence. Forget the fiction of journalists protecting their sources; there are very few journalists who wouldn't hand over their informants when intimidated by governments. But now details can be launched into cyberspace for anyone to pick up, without risk of betrayal. That having been said, hackers in the pay of the state will quickly sabotage any site, once identified. This is what happened to disgruntled MI5 agent David Shayler when he threatened to publish on his Web site information about the British secret service's attempt on the life of Colonel Gadaffi of Libya (*Sunday Times*, 2 August 1998).

In the autumn of 1993, the overly paternalistic court in Ontario sought to limit press reports of the sordid Bernardo/Homolka murder trial, but this proved futile when regular reports appeared on a computer bulletin board based in the United States (Cathcart, 19 February 1995). The British press were very circumspect about the 'Camillagate' tape-recording of a sexually explicit conversation between Prince Charles and Camilla Parker-Bowles. But when it was leaked to an Australian magazine *New Idea*, faxes between Australia and Britain soon became red-hot. The Chiapas guerrillas used the Internet in a propaganda war against the Mexican government, telling the world of army atrocities, all of them fictional (Fineman, 21 February 1995).

Pornography is being beamed into British households on the Internet despite government edicts. From the very earliest days of the French Minitel system, about 15 per cent of its traffic was euphemistically described as 'pink'. One survey of Usenet discovered that 94 per cent of the pictures sent were sexual in nature (Brown, 30 April 1995); many of the images were illegal in most parts of the United States. Another survey revealed that more than 20 per cent of all Internet searches included a visit to a pornographic Web site (Neligan, 25 June 1998).

However, it is important not to gain the impression that governments are impotent in stopping the free flow of information. They have a vast arsenal of weaponry at their disposal, including proxy servers: powerful computers that intercept and filter all Internet traffic entering and leaving their jurisdiction. Governments around the world, such as China, are already using this technique to stop their populations accessing forbidden data. However, in using such methods it is impossible for them to pretend that their citizens have freedom of choice. Then there are draconian measures, such as those imposed by totalitarian regimes like Iran, punishing all who listen to the radio or own a satellite dish. In Myanmar, the government can impose a maximum 15-year prison sentence for owning an unauthorized modem (Woods, 21 October 1996). The Chinese government found engineer Lin Hai guilty of subversion and jailed him for two years. His crime? Delivering 3,000 Chinese e-mail addresses to a dissident offshore magazine Da Kan Kao (*Big Reference*) that subsequently 'spammed' them with anti-government propaganda. Subsequently Lin Hai was awarded the '1999 freedom of cyber-speech award' by the Webcasters' Coalition for Free Speech (Williams, 16 February 1999).

Britain banned renegade MI6 operative Richard Tomlinson from using e-mail and the Internet as part of the terms of his probation (*Sunday Times*, 2 August 1998). He had been released after six months of a year's jail sentence for threatening to publish his memoirs as a spy. However, countries are fighting against a tidal wave of technology. The Net, fax, telephone, radio and television increasingly allow individuals to bypass government censorship. Even as early as 1990 there were more than 2 billion portable radios and a billion televisions in the world (*Economist*, 2 May 1992). Governments think that they can use nationalized broadcasting stations to control their populations, but of course radio signals seep in from abroad. One hundred countries deliberately broadcast their propaganda across frontiers, not counting the private stations pouring out capitalist advertising. Television, on the other hand, is much more difficult to pick up from abroad, particularly when governments ban the use of satellite dishes. However, back-street workshops are getting very much more sophisticated, and they soon will be able to turn out cheap camouflaged dishes made from spare components.

In June 1998 a Munich court found Felix Somm, former head of CompuServe Germany, guilty of disseminating pornography and neo-Nazi propaganda. His crime was being head of an Internet Service Provider (ISP) that had inadvertently given Germans access to such proscribed material. He was sentenced to a suspended two-year jail sentence and a fine of 100,000 deutschmarks. Even the prosecution lawyers thought this excessive, and likely to damage badly Germany's chances of playing a major role in the exploding global marketplace for electronic commerce (Naughton, 7 June 1998). Wealth generation comes with innovation in science and technology, and countries that ban or interfere with such innovation, whatever their reasons, must lose out economically. In tomorrow's world it will be the innovators of technology and their agents who create wealth. Their recognition of their own scarcity value means that they now consider themselves as self-governing in a world of choice, rather than as members of any particular nation–state, or even of any particular company. Indeed they will be using telecommunication technology to sell themselves on the open market, the open global market. Thanks to the cyberspace of international computer networks, the global economy is now a reality.

Cyberspace and the Internet

Wherever we look today, we see cyber-this and cyber-that: apart from cyberspace there are cybercafes, cybercash, cybercorps, cybercrats, cybernauts, cyberpunk, cybersex (also cheekily named teledildonics), cyborgs (cyber organisms), etc. This prefix, the first two syllables of the Ancient Greek word κυβερηντης, meaning steersman, was lifted initially by American mathematician Norbert Wiener (1961), when as part of his research, he created the terms 'cybernetics', the science of systems of control and communications in animals and machines, and 'cybernation', meaning control by machines.

The term 'cyberspace' itself was invented by William Gibson in 1981 in a short story called *Burning Chrome*, but it is exemplified in probably his best-known novel *Neuromancer*, a classic example of the cyberpunk genre, in which science fiction meets sex, drugs and rock 'n' roll. Despite, or perhaps because of, this pedigree, and its attraction to a generation of 'nerds', the term 'cyberspace' has stuck. Gibson is a master of his craft. Even when we strip away his extremely unlikeable and violent characters, and deny his portrayal of technology used as a magic wand to deny the laws of physics, we are still left with a background scenario that is a terrifyingly convincing portrayal of a sick future society glued together around communication technologies. His society is dominated by global corporations through their control of information superhighways. The elite stays sinisterly in the background, while Gibson concentrates his stories on the dispossessed, a society that is a nightmare caricature of today's US inner city. Like the sci-fi masters of the past, particularly Jules Verne and H G Wells, it is his ability to paint the complex yet convincing backdrop, rather than the principal story itself, that sets Gibson's work apart.

Although Gibson coined the term 'cyberspace', today's popular and fanciful interpretation of the Internet has more in common with Neal Stephenson's 'metaverse', described in his 1992 novel *Snow Crash*. Here 'avatars' are personae programmed to inhabit a three-dimensional magical universe. It is worthwhile taking a closer look at this belief of magic in technology, because this form of mysticism is responsible for much of the popular misunderstanding of cyberspace. It is quite incredible what is being claimed for cyberspace: 'virtual reality will allow you to put your arms around the milky way, swim in the human bloodstream or visit Alice in Wonderland' (Negroponte, 1996). But the hyperbole goes very much further than this. The ultimate and extremely silly conclusion is in *Lawnmower Man*, a film based on the Stephen King novel, where a computer scientist uses virtual reality to turn his retarded gardener (the eponymous lawnmower man) into a genius. The conclusion is that glorified computer graphics can 'expand' a stupid human mind to genius level. Such *Star Trek* 'mind-melding' owes more to 1960s drug culture than to any potential power in computer technology; although it must be said that the cynical promotion by the computer science establishment throughout the 1980s of that equally foolish idea, biddable artificial intelligence, has added some credibility. Research into artificial intelligence did of course have the backing of financial capital. Capital had automated away the need for physical labour; if it could also sideline intelligence then it would be independent of people altogether.

Of course, to many, cyberspace is synonymous with the Internet, the world's biggest and somewhat anarchic network of computers, which uses standard telephone lines, and joins government offices, businesses, universities, schools and homes, giving them a cheap form of instant electronic mail and access to an enormous amount of data. Internet was originally set up as Arpanet in the late 1960s, by scientists at the US Defense Advanced Research Projects Agency, a few universities and the RAND corporation. The network was only ever used for research, and as a means of sharing scarce computing resources. The Pentagon never integrated it into their command and control system. However, like Pandora, once they had opened up the opportunity, they couldn't put the lid back on the box.

The Internet boom, as we now know it, started in the early 1990s when access restrictions were lifted. This was boosted when the Clinton administration promoted the system as an 'international information infrastructure'. It is claimed that new users are joining at the rate of 1 million a month, and that early in the new millennium the total number will exceed 100 million. However, critics claim the number of 'non-trivial users' is orders of magnitude less. Whatever the real number of Internet users, the Net is unquestionably a vast open forum for the exchange of ideas and information that reaches into huge numbers of upper-income homes worldwide, where 'surfing' the Net is a popular intellectual pastime. It was inevitable that businesses would muscle in on such an inexpensive way of accessing a prime market, particularly with the popular easy-to-use tools of the World Wide Web simplifying the navigation of cyberspace.

Nowadays Internet is seen as a way of expanding business. Not only does the Net deliver an enormous market for goods, it also makes the updating and delivering of brochures, and responding to customer queries, almost instantaneous, all at a cost significantly cheaper than other marketing modes. In the next decade a substantial number of customer queries will come this way. The Net will be where the rich will shop – an evolutionary multi-media extension of *Yellow Pages*. But no link, no customers! It is this aspect of cyberspace that is going to redefine the retail trade totally, and hence the nature of work, thereby ushering in unemployment on a vast scale.

With the advent of digital signatures, trusted third parties and other socio-technical innovations that make electronic business more secure, we will see an explosion of shopping on the Internet, and the nature of employment in retailing will have changed for ever. Digital money (also known as cybercash, or e-cash) will be sent to suppliers over the Net to cover the cost of smaller transactions, so-called micro-purchases, particularly buying low cost value-added data services on the Net itself. The potential of electronic shopping is enormous, and we can expect 'particularizing' of products, with customers transmitting a unique description of a product, such as a car or curtains or wallpaper, over the Net directly to the factory for production, bypassing the middleman. To a certain extent this so-called 'disintermediation' is already happening. It is having dire consequences for insurance salesmen and travel agents, and soon it will devastate any company in the retail sector that does not totally reorganize itself to take advantage of the new phenomenon.

Obviously cyberspace is far more than just the Internet (or intranets, extranets and other variants), and it will be far more down to earth, but nonetheless earth-shattering. It is not some mystical dimension of the intellect; cyberspace is firmly grounded in the three dimensions of physical space. What is different is the way in which we communicate and travel in that 'three-space'. Cyberspace is not a different dimension, but a change in the modes and rates of communication of people and their information artefacts. Put simply, cyberspace is a different interpretation of the world in which we live. It is no 'virtual reality'; on the contrary it is a very, very real reality. The technology that drives cyberspace is far more than just computer networks: international jet travel, television satellites, smart weapons, video, fax and telephone, compact discs, and so much more. Cyberspace isn't new. It has been around for decades. International tourism, the couch potato, pop-culture, Operation Desert Storm and the eurodollar market are all diverse examples of the many social phenomena emerging from cyberspace. Cyberspace is the innovative ways in which all the communication technologies can be used down here in three-space. It is not so much changing the world we live in, rather how we live in that world, by unifying the way we think about these sundry technologies under one label.

First and foremost cyberspace is about business, and this is why the 'nerds' who developed the Internet culture are furious at what they see as a takeover of 'their' Net. The nerd world of self-indulgent 'virtual reality' is over. Make way for 'the suits' who can afford to pay for the very real business opportunities furnished by telecommunications. In this new era each company must develop expertise in communication networks, including local area networks and links into global networks, not just the Internet. Electronic Data Interchange (EDI) connections over international networks will be critical to every niche supplier to the global market. There is a downside of course. Some suppliers fear loss of control over 'their' information, and a worry that the 'Chinese walls' within an EDI system will leak data to competitors – as Virgin Atlantic found to its cost when some BA employees allegedly hacked into its flight reservations system and diverted customers on to BA flights in the so-called 'dirty tricks campaign'.

But in the Information Age communication of business data is the very nature of commercial enterprise. Information systems are the very core of business. They are no longer seen as a mere set of applications. Each supplier, each customer is going to have to come to terms with this new paradigm if it wants to stay in business. For business is being on the superhighway; it is adding value to what flows along the highway; and it is taking information from the highway in order to add value to what business is doing.

So all's well with the world and we can sleep easy at night. Cyberspace is where business will make the world a better place for all of us, and where people can chat constantly to one another! Or is it? What if a terrible and terrifying ghost is lying in the machine? What if this vision of cyberspace is merely our world viewed through rose-tinted glasses supplied by Silicon Valley? What if, while we are all surfing the Net, the economic order outside cyberspace is actually falling apart? What if, while hiding in cyberspace, we refuse to see the brutality of the ensuing social collapse that is happening all around us?

2

The new barbarians

Cyberspace looks so exciting, so positive, so constructive. Why then do I insist that the changes set in train are dystopian? Surely it is progress, another step on the yellow brick road to utopia? There are still a few utopians out there, full of confidence for the status quo, who will support this claim. Francis Fukuyama, in his book *The End of History and the Last Man* (1992), declared that liberal democracy has triumphed.

'The end of history'?

Like Hegel and Marx before him, Fukuyama saw the perfectibility of the political system, hence 'the end of history'. The Soviet 'evil empire' had fallen with hardly a shot being fired, and the Berlin Wall likewise. Around the same time as Fukuyama's book was published, the then US president, George Bush, foresaw a democratic 'new world order' starting with the end of the Cold War and the fall of communism. A glow of optimistic wishful thinking, encapsulated in terms like 'peace dividend' and 'human rights' proved to be merely a quixotic illusion, a chimera that now lies shattered before economic reality. The 'peace dividend' does not compensate the redundant of the world's defence industries; the state of California alone lost 300,000 jobs with house prices dropping as much as 50 per cent in value over the five-year period from 1990 (McCrystal, 21 April 1996). Subsequently the whole world lives in fear of nuclear terrorism, as renegades in Russia's unemployed military–industrial complex sell nuclear weapons on the open market; not forgetting the proliferation of chemical and biological weapons, arsenals that even Third World countries or religious cults can develop.

Smug claims of a complete victory for enlightened liberal democracy sound singularly hollow before a narcotics epidemic in our inner cities, the various military adventures in the Third World, the rabid nationalism of 'ethnic cleansing' in former Yugoslavia, the genocide in Rwanda and the hypocrisy of national boundaries slamming shut against the mass movement of populations. In numerous United Nations conferences, such as Rio, Cairo and Copenhagen, representatives of what are optimistically called 'developing countries' demand aid, trying moral blackmail on the conscience of the West, previously softened up by television pictures of starving children. Unfortunately the competition among television reporters, their heart-rending portrayals of famine, death and disaster in search of an Emmy or Bafta, has become counter-productive. After the success of Band Aid, Bob Geldof was the first to recognize that 'compassion fatigue' had set in. Can anything be done for countries whose internal conflicts set them on a course of self-destruction, and whose leaders are cushioned by Swiss bank accounts stuffed full of aid dollars? Third World conditions will not recede into the past as a bad memory; far from it. Perhaps there is even a growing realization that Third World conditions could be the future awaiting many in the West. Parts of Second World Europe are already exhibiting Third World morality: £600 million of the £3 billion donated for the rebuilding of Bosnia has 'disappeared' into the pockets of corrupt local officials (Key, 18 August 1999).

So is it the 'end of history' as Fukuyama says? No, of course not! The few remaining optimists are deluding themselves. It is unchained capitalism and not democracy that has prevailed. Perhaps today's fashionable version of democracy will be the next to fall. The forces presently attacking today's peculiar form of global governance could actually be ushering in the end of the 'Open Society' (Popper, 1992). International financier George Soros, student of Karl Popper and self-proclaimed champion of the Open Society, certainly believes in the danger, and has been travelling the world warning of the threat to Western capitalism (Soros, 1998).

If our present situation sounds hauntingly familiar, it should do. In AD 358 Rome, a long-standing civilization based on organizational skills, commerce and technology, confident in its superiority, fell to the barbarian hordes that were once its servants. The taxation needed to subsidize the bread and circuses, the Roman equivalent of the welfare state, had brought the empire to its knees. But a decadent Rome didn't just disappear – choice fragments were looted and reformed into new orders. Similar collapses have occurred throughout history and around the world: Ancient Greece, Renaissance Italy, Ancient China, Aztec America. Today the socio-political order of our civilization has become degenerate, and is on the verge of collapse. What will happen to us, now it is our turn?

Friedrich Nietzsche predicted our future over a century ago:

'but now there are coming

new barbarians { cynics experimenters conquerors } union of spiritual superiority with well-being and an excess of strength

I point to something new: certainly for such a democratic type there exists the danger of the barbarian, but one has looked for it only in the depths. There exists also another type of barbarian, who comes from the heights: a species of conquering and ruling natures in search of material to mould. Prometheus was this kind of barbarian'.

(Nietzsche, 1967)

Opportunities to come

It is ironic that Nietzsche (1844–1900), who in his lifetime was attacked for having pro-Jewish sympathics by many anti-Semites including Richard and Cosima Wagner, should later be labelled by the uninformed as a Nazi philosopher. This was mainly the result of his racist sister Elisabeth, some 30 years after his death, deliberately selecting parts of his writings so that, out of context, they fitted Nazi propaganda. This is particularly the case with his theories of the Übermensch – the ultimate conclusion of his new barbarian theory. To Nietzsche, his superman was not of the Aryan herd, nor any herd. He points at '"the German *Reich*", as the *decaying form* of the state': he was referring to Bismarck's Reich, but the sentiment is still clear. Nietzsche despised all mass movements: 'the sum of zeroes is zero'. Nietzsche's hero is a 'free man', who drives forward with individualistic ideals, and who is consequently a threat to the herd. His superman is a spontaneous emergence of a new type of individual, from a new aristocracy of choice. Such individuals can and do appear anywhere on the globe, and are *Beyond Good and Evil*. Nietzsche's work could never be a philosophy for a mass movement like national socialism, which in his words is where the 'herd unlearns modesty and blows up its needs into cosmic and metaphysical values'! I apologize for deliberately labouring this point here, but it is crucial to the thesis of this book: mass movements are from the now-defunct Machine Age, an age past – whereas I am claiming that Nietzsche's writings give a philosophy for the individual to win in the Information Age.

Our new millennium will be a watershed. It will be a time of amazing opportunities, emerging through the heroic actions of individuals and organizations: heroic, that is, in the classical sense. Some of these opportunists, who will loot our decaying civilization, will claim the right to call themselves by Nietzsche's title of 'new barbarian'. Others from the depths will be old barbarians plain and simple – throwbacks to darker times. This book not only celebrates and recommends today's new barbarians, identifying the environment in which they operate, but also warns against the old barbarians. The new barbarians will value and enhance the best in our society, but the philistines will drag us back to an age of superstition, ignorance and stupidity.

Both new and old barbarians will amputate the degeneracy eating at the heart of today's Western societies. The new barbarians are the imaginative outsiders, individuals and organizations, who have the vision to see novel and simplifying interpretations of the complexity in our society and then take what is best. This 'vision is the art of seeing the invisible' (Jonathan Swift), that which may not be seen because of the arrogance of self-centred ritualistic behaviour. We will also face the revitalized old barbarians of race and religion, labour and capital, freed from the domination of the present. They will reassert themselves; and therein lies chaos and darkness, the end of Enlightenment.

I see the future in this 'new barbarian' hypothesis, although I would stress the hypothesis is not in itself a specific predictor of things to come. It is an account of a societal mechanism that drives transition and has recurred throughout human history, but particularly during times of turmoil, complexity and uncertainty. It is a mechanism whereby opportunists sweep away old moribund institutions, not in anarchy and chaos, but with new ideas, new moralities, new rituals and new power structures, subsequently laying the foundations for new institutions: a new order.

However, this new order will be born of conflict, mitigated to a certain extent by a predisposition toward human virtues. But such virtues are based on strength, not weakness. 'I have often laughed at the weaklings who thought themselves good because they had no claws.' (Nietzsche) There has to be a disposition to confrontation – and even to welcome it. 'One is punished for being weak, not for being cruel' (Baudelaire). Through conflict, the new barbarians will be tempered in the flames of economic and political competition. As they succeed and create their new order, where will we fit in? Will we fit in?

Implications for democracy

Democratic politicians won't fit in. They are perpetually surprised by the amoral opportunists who profit from treading a different path. In vain, our representatives try to legislate against them, although they have often succeeded in the past (witness the United States against Leona Helmsley of 'only the little people pay taxes' fame). But such politicians are just whistling in the wind of change. Mrs Helmsley was right. Soon it will only be the little people who pay taxes; the new barbarians will have a choice.

What is going on? How have the politicians lost control over the course of events? The old certainties are falling apart; politicians dabble on the world stage but don't know what to do. Their myth of control is laid bare. All around us, institutional rituals and procedures that have stood the test of decades, centuries even, are crumbling. The glue of the old order is now coming unstuck; our ritual games no longer paper over the cracks.

The new barbarians do not accept that the utopian ideology of modern-day liberal democracy has triumphed once and for all. As in imperial Rome, the new barbarians see 'bread and circuses' for the masses in the triumph of a universal franchise: welfare systems, entertainment, television, sport, pop music. Democratic processes remain merely to keep the masses under control during the death-throes preceding decline and fall. The new barbarians see only opportunity. For they recognize modern-day democracy for what it is, a once-proud individualism that has been hijacked by the old barbarians of collectivism. They know democracy in its present form will continue for the time being, but it is of no consequence to them. They know that their battle will be against the old barbarians, who will rally around the flags of revitalized religious intolerance, racism, socialism and capitalism.

Democracy is itself barbarism, an old and now degenerate barbarism. The barbarism of the many against the few, barbarism become respectable through being the norm, but barbarism all the same – a barbarism that claims its legitimacy from 'ideologies of difference' based on religious and ethnic prejudices, and political populism, on tribal moralities that stress 'us' against 'them'. These anti-individual old ways must be confronted by the new barbarians who hold no loyalties to the herd. New barbarians are cut free from the constraints of national boundaries by the new communication technologies. They have no herd morality, or as they would say no 'slave morality'. Their world is *Beyond Good and Evil* (Nietzsche, 1968).

Barbarians old and new

Make way for the barbarians (old and new), the opportunists awaiting their chance to hijack the future, and form a new order. The seeds of this new order are already here, they have always been here and they have already germinated. But are they friend or foe? They are the individuals, and transnational enterprises and companies that hold no herd loyalties. They are the press and media barons, the market manipulators, international businesspeople, international terrorists, 'downsized' states, criminal conspirators, drug barons, neo-colonialist non-governmental organizations, economic mercenaries, financial plutocrats, religious and political fundamentalists, amoral individualists: the new you and the new me? They are the power brokers, now cut free from the constraints of national boundaries by the new communication technologies. They are the virile, vigorous and vital opportunists who will strike at the very heart of the power base of impotent politicians and other trivialisers of our age. The barbarians know that their time is coming, for natural selection is on their side; history is on their side.

Barbarians, old and new, are already here; they have breached the walls of liberal democracy. They are the very reason for the uncertainty of our time, but blinkered by a present obsessed with past uncertainities, their growth remains shrouded to many. In the course of this book I shall celebrate some controversial insights into future trends and likely scenarios, and launch new and imaginative ideas that anticipate new orders. I shall indicate the winners and losers, the new social structures, philosophies, moralities, rituals and ethics. I ask you to interpret today's news stories from this perspective, and to follow through with your own forecasts about new institutional, societal and political stabilities so that you too can succeed.

To succeed, we must join these barbarians who care nothing for the polite society of the 20th century, for its arbitrary logic, its models and moralities, its philosophies, its politics, its genteel manners and bourgeois sentimentality – for its degeneracy. The barbarians are at the gate. Our Rome is burning! The barbarians know that societal evolution is not benign. Evolution is 'nature red in tooth and claw'. It spawns carnivores as well as herbivores. The carnivorous barbarians care nothing for democracy or the rules of parliament, that representative of herbivores. Grass eaters beware, the jackals are circling; the hyenas are laughing.

3

Globalization and localization

The first example of the barbarism that will undermine the status quo has already emerged out of the new freedoms bestowed by global telecommunications. Seeking short-term returns, speculators decimate the value of national currencies and wipe out whole industrial regions. The 'globalization' of commercial enterprises (not merely their 'internationalization') and their 'mobilization' has totally changed the relationship between these companies and national governments. Individuals, companies and communities are setting up large transnational commercial networks that pay absolutely no heed to national boundaries and barriers.

Global enterprise

The successful commercial enterprise of the future will be truly global. It will relocate (physically, electronically or fiscally) to where the profit is greatest and the regulation least. The umbilical cords have been cut; the global company refuses to support the national aspirations of the country of its birth. This new business paradigm was expressed most forcibly by Akio Morita, causing uproar in Japan, when he announced that Sony was a global company and not Japanese!

Global companies are setting themselves up within 'virtual enterprises' (Davidow and Malone, 1992), at the hub of loosely knit alliances of local companies, all linked together by global networks: electronic, transport and human. These companies assemble to take advantage of any temporary business opportunity, and then they separate, each moving on to the next major deal. Production and distribution are co-ordinated across different countries according to cost, within quality limits. Apart from local products, local companies also deliver local expertise and access to home markets for other products created within the wider alliance. Such enterprises are project-based, and developed around complex networked information systems: the information system is the virtual enterprise, it is the headquarters – there is nothing else – and it can be based virtually anywhere in cyberspace. In cyberspace the apparent size of the firm can be amplified far beyond the physical reality. You are what you claim to be. You are what you can deliver via the telecommunication networks. That well-known cartoon of two dogs sitting in front of a personal computer says it all: 'On the Internet nobody knows you're a dog.' Nobody knows, and nobody cares... provided you deliver the goods.

The very presence of these vigorous global enterprises can enliven national economies, but they can just as easily destroy them. That presence need not be physical; it can be electronic. The slightest rumour can spark off currency speculation that can focus funds sufficient to wreck the fiscal policies of all but a few countries. Look no further than the 1993 sterling and lire crises, or the 1995 Mexican peso crisis, or the summer 1997 collapse of Far Eastern currencies, such as the Thai baht and the Malaysian ringgit, which fell like dominoes (Alexander, 31 August 1997). The baht dropped by 25 per cent in value, and the Thai government lost more than $12 billion in their futile defence of their currency. All countries now find they have decreasing control over their affairs, caused by a whole range of social, political and economic factors unleashed by new technology.

Speculators in the money and derivatives markets, who precipitate these crashes, are not all 'foreigners'. Many often seriously damage the economies of the very countries where they themselves are resident. For the speculators too are not in control of events. Once the feeding frenzy has begun, even high-roller pension funds have no choice other than to join in, and push to the edge the industries and the countries of the very pensioners they serve. If they try to stand out against the stampede then they too will be trampled underfoot along with national economies.

Finance ministers too haven't learnt the lesson, or possibly they won't admit that they are no longer in control of national economies. Economically wrong decisions, made on the basis of political expediency, or large spending programmes on prestige symbols of national pride, will be punished severely by the money markets. In fact the markets pounce on this kind of irresponsibility by politicians, because it gives them a no-risk opportunity of profiting at the taxpayers' expense.

The sheer volume and the variety of trading of financial products and instruments determine that the fiscal and monetary policies of national governments, even in conspiracy with other governments, have very little positive influence. Exchange rates can no longer be used to balance the flow of goods between countries. Any manipulation of these rates by governments will draw the wrath of the markets down on interest-rate levels. It doesn't even need a conspiracy among the high-rollers. The big players are always on the look-out for acts of governmental folly. Although they are independent of one another, they tend to make similar analyses. Their every move is followed closely by the rest of the market, thus perpetrating a coherent attack on a national economy.

My colleague Lord Desai (24 October 1995) says 'corporations rule the world'. Because of capital mobility, the state no longer has the power to shape its own macroeconomic policy. 'A Brave New World is being created out there. Not, as one hoped, by one-world idealists or UN diplomacy, but by global CORPORATIONS for the simplest of all reasons – profits. The state can either play along with them or have delusions of grandeur. The cost of delusions will be severe and will be paid not by politicians but by the citizens.'

'Of the 100 largest economies in the world, more than half are corporations not countries… The top 200 firms' sales add up to more than a quarter of the world economic activity… their combined global employment is only 18.8 million, which is less than three quarters of one per cent of the world's workforce' (Anderson and Kavanagh, 23 October 1996). The world's 359 largest corporations account for 40 per cent of global trade. The share of that trade among the world's 48 least developed nations (10 per cent of the global population) has fallen by half to 0.3 per cent in the last 20 years (Brittain and Elliott, 12 June 1997). There are 1.3 billion people surviving on less than a dollar a day. Even in the West, 100 million people are living below the poverty line.

No frontiers

The barbarians of global enterprises think nothing of pushing a nation's economy to the brink, and beyond. They do not identify with any particular country, and consequently they walk away from a country just as easily as they enter it. Benjamin Franklin recognized their type more than 200 years ago: 'Merchants have no country. The mere spot where they stand on does not constitute so strong an attachment as that from which they draw their gain.' What is different today is that, because of the superhighways, merchants large and small have the ability to move both themselves and their assets rapidly away from government predators. Nowadays the cost of entering the global market is as low as the price of Internet access. This means any one of us can become a merchant and, once free from government power, we can use our combined financial muscle to strip the assets off even the largest national economies.

Companies think globally because they can communicate globally, and because the shareholders, the executive, the capital assets and the employees are spread out across the globe! Transnational corporations have no choice. They must operate close to important clients in rapidly changing markets on the other side of the world, because their uncompromising competitors are already there. Today's accepted wisdom is that the shrewd global company knows that it cannot control far-flung enterprises from a single home-based corporate headquarters, or run it with executives of a single nationality.

Ultimately commercial enterprises will institutionalize a new individualistic and self-interested culture, and cut themselves totally free of today's flag-waving nation–state. When a particular state's policies go counter to a company's economic self-interest, then that company's executive and shareholders will show no loyalty. Wealth has no loyalty, only self-interest. The company will move lock, stock and barrel to the other side of the world if it makes commercial sense. And there is no lack of states eager to attract the business. In the spring of 1997, Ericsson and other large Swedish companies including Volvo and Astra voiced the possibility of leaving Sweden because of its high taxes – not corporate taxes, because these are relatively small. The drip, drip, dripping effect of penal personal taxes was driving talented Swedes abroad, making it impossible for Ericsson to recruit the quality staff they needed. It is no use repealing the last tax hike; that's like blaming the last straw for breaking the camel's back. Ericsson and the other companies have had enough, and they have the example of Ikea, the Swedish-owned furniture business, which based itself in the Netherlands for tax purposes (Burt, 6 July 1998).

Chasing profits across the world

Shareholders too have become an international rather than a national community. They no longer invest in any national interest. If proof of this statement were needed, we need only look at how rich Germans, perceived by many to be of the most loyal nationality, are sending huge sums of deutschmarks to the British Channel Islands. A number of factors have set shareholders free: most countries now actively encourage inward investment.

There are many tax havens to act as intermediaries. Global telecommunications mean that there is immediate reporting of international stock market data, and local representatives can be contacted quickly. If necessary, easy air travel means that the owners of this liquid wealth can check in person. This is supported by instant access to their financial capital, and the ready availability of lines of credit (for the credit-worthy).

Such shareholders have one clear and overriding objective: a profitable return on the investment risks they are taking. Hence, they too willingly pledge their loyalty (in other words their money) to freewheeling companies. Increasingly, that profit has itself become a particular form of information, existing in cyberspace, flowing through the world's financial markets at a rate unimaginable just a decade ago. Who knows what form money will take when this trend culminates with money becoming separated from national economies, and out of the clutches of national politicians?

Against this background, companies will move to politically stable areas with a ready supply of educated workers, and most importantly with preferential taxation and regulation policies. The fund management arm of Lazard Brothers, the merchant bank, moved from London to Dublin in the spring of 1996, just in case an incoming socialist government should consider a 'wealth tax' (Pratt, 19 May 1996). The multimillionaire composer, Sir Andrew Lloyd Webber, and other British showbusiness celebrities threatened similar moves; as it turned out they didn't actually leave, but there is still time (Hind, 22 February, 1997). In 1998, Mick Jagger and the Rolling Stones cancelled a pop concert tour of Britain because it would have incurred a big tax bill (Atkinson, 13 June 1998). The enterprise of companies and individuals, not countries, creates wealth – it has always been thus. Now, with the aid of global telecommunication systems, these individuals and companies can fly the nest, and they are scouring the globe looking for agreeable regions where they can profit from trade with a minimum of interference.

International trading now includes new forms of barter and exchange on the global networks, particularly in superior scientific and technological expertise and knowledge. Money, which is merely a means of facilitating economic transactions, has itself become electronic information. What constitutes money can no longer be monopolized by national governments or supranational groups. 'The cause of waves of unemployment is not "capitalism" but governments denying enterprise the right to produce good money' (Hayek). In the digital age every company, every city, can issue its own electronic currency. The real issue is not 'dollar bills, but Bill's [Gates] dollars'. 'Money does not have to be created legal tender by governments. Like law, language and morals it can emerge spontaneously. Such private money has often been preferred to government money, but government has usually soon suppressed it' (Hayek).

However, in the age of Internet can government keep suppressing it? Mervyn King, the deputy governor of the Bank of England, has stated that companies that settle their debts using electronic transactions outside of the formal banking system are in effect denying central banks the power to control national economies (Denny, 27 August 1999). Hayek's vision of *The Denationalization of Money* can now become a reality (Hayek, 1976). Internationalization trends inevitably lower the transaction costs of money, and make taxation of profits and regulation of the process almost impossible – a real competitive advantage for any virtual enterprise with a moveable centre of gravity, and for those merchant new barbarians who are willing to trade their expertise in this electronic market.

To a certain extent this is already the case in some countries where the dominant notes of exchange have another nation's label printed on them. Since January 1994, $500 million per week are being shipped in $100 dollar bills to Moscow. The number of dollars in Russia now has a face value greater than the total circulation of roubles. Since it costs four cents to print each bill, the US treasury makes a profit of $99.96 for each note not presented in the United States (Kerry, 1997). This seems to contradict Gresham's Law: 'Bad money drives out good.' (Gresham's law is the observation of Sir Thomas Gresham, who around AD 1560 was purchasing Spanish coinage in Antwerp on behalf of the English Crown.) However, that law is only valid when government can enforce acceptance of bad money in exchange for the good, hardly the case with the Russian mafiyas.

New ways of trading

At a time when so much heat and so little light are being generated over a single European currency and monetary union (in essence solving yesterday's problem of reducing the transaction cost of continental trade), new currencies are springing up everywhere, all made possible by new technology: beenz – a new universal form of credit on the Net; supermarket loyalty schemes; air miles; to name just a few. For with technology bringing down the transaction costs of exchange with the existence of digital cash, it is of little consequence for traders whether there are one or one thousand currencies in circulation. Community token-exchange schemes are issuing currencies – there are already more than 300 in Britain alone, and the number is rising fast: acorns, bobbins, cockles, cranes, groats, naaris, strouds, trugs (Winnett, 26 March 1995). These LETS (Local Exchange Trading Schemes) started in Canada in the early 1980s, where communities with a shared sense of trust – for that is all it takes to create a currency – developed their own financial systems, with cheque books and other instruments to pay for goods and services in and around the locality. The idea was first introduced in a depressed mining community of the Comox Valley (Linton, 1999) to kick-start the local economy where there was trust in the community, but no trust between the banks and the community. Social pressures are enough to ensure that debts are repaid. Banks can't think in this way: they work on creditworthiness through formal employment, or on ownership of capital goods. For those who are not creditworthy, their transaction costs go up, and hence, so does their cost of borrowing.

LETS cut across all this untrusting formality. LETS need trust. Trust needs a sense of community. A closed community can play this non-profit game for the mutual benefit of all. Every member starts with zero IOU tokens, and keeps track of debits and credits by double-entry bookkeeping. Usually measured in hours of work, they assume that an hour's labour is the same no matter what the work, although some of the more sophisticated schemes have introduced agreed multiplicative factors to pay for more highly skilled work. LETS schemes are usually fairly small scale, and so the state usually leaves them alone: national currency and LETS existing side by side. This is because these schemes are usually started in very poor communities. But what if the rich get the idea? What if LETS turn into global exchange token schemes (GETS), and become the mechanism for company money? The tally money or truck money of the early British Industrial Revolution could reappear. Then the buying and selling of goods and services within the company community become a form of transfer pricing, invisible to taxation authorities. It should come as no surprise that tax authorities are looking at LETS with increasing concern. This explosion of new currencies delivers the self-evident potential for evading taxation and duty. Furthermore it does raise the amusing question of whether the tax payable on a transaction made in acorns should be paid in acorns.

Such schemes are relatively new in the West, but Chinese family businesses, spread across the globe over the years by the many diasporas that have affected that large nation, have been using 'chop shop' money for generations to bypass the national financial regulations of their host countries. Otherwise known as Fei-Ch´ien (flying money), a complete underground banking system based on trust has developed within the worldwide Chinese community. There are, after all, 40 million Chinese living outside mainland China, an enormous trading community. The worldwide Asian community too has its corresponding 'hawala' or 'chiti' banking system, with origins set down long before Western banking was developed, and which was regenerated in Britain to bypass the exchange controls that used to be in force. In the United States it is known as 'stash house'. Whatever its name, new technology has rejuvenated this ancient mode of token exchange, and it is causing serious problems for legitimate money systems. Earlier this century the hawala token was a torn playing card or bus ticket, or even a painted cube of sugar. Nowadays tokens are likely to be deposited as container-shiploads of blank video-cassettes that sail continuously between hawala bankers around the globe. Very soon their electronic tokens could go off-planet.

Across the EU, both the tax and the excise authorities are realizing that they lose revenue whenever dematerialized goods or services are bought over the Internet, as when software paid for by credit card is downloaded from America. They are even talking about placing a blanket tax on the volume of information flow, bit by bit, as if, like whisky, its value can be measured by volume, rather than by what value it adds to a business – a much trickier act of measurement (Acey, 25 March 1996). The information rich leverage far more from their information than do the information poor, and so such a 'bit tax' will fall disproportionately on to the shoulders of the poor. And where will the tax authorities stop? Perhaps they will tax conversation? But they do that now in Britain, with the VAT (a tax on sales and services) on telephone charges. What happens when competition drives down these charges to an insignificant level? The painful lesson is that the taxes designed for the Machine Age cannot be collected on products from the Information Age.

Nor can taxes be collected from the international elite of global companies, which needs no nationality. Such companies are stalking the world looking for talent and profit; in the Information Age this pairing is indivisible. In particular, the intellectual products of science and technology are in very high demand. Conversely, organized semi-skilled labour, the power base of the Industrial Age, has been sidelined along with its collectivist ideologies and trades unions. Now each nation, each collective, must compete in a global marketplace for the wealth-generating services of virtual enterprises, without which they are doomed. Soon, only old barbarian global military action will be able to threaten highly mobile new barbarian entrepreneurs. But put under any threat, this elite will simply stop producing, leaving the state to fall behind in the global marketplace anyway.

New barbarians see their first step to freedom down the road to the virtual enterprise, in so-called outsourcing or facilities management, the farming out of office and support jobs and peripheral production facilities, leaving the company to concentrate on the core business. They will experiment with many such radical ideas that sound sacrilegious to the old ways of thinking. But to these barbarians, nothing is sacred. Once a company has made the decision to outsource, probably distributing the work around local suppliers, there is no turning back. It is only a small step in cyberspace to place these tasks elsewhere in the country. Why not elsewhere in the world? Head Office now becomes a mere focal point of executive control, and the company will move work to countries whose governments actively support and encourage their presence.

Corporate migration is exploding: Nestlé has moved jobs from Scotland to France, while Hoover has moved from France to Scotland. In Germany, major corporations in the pharmaceutical and automotive industries have reacted to what they see as excessive employment regulations at home by moving their factories abroad. The US-owned Dana engineering firm moved its entire factory from Kassel to Yorkshire (Norris, 22 February 1999). Every company is considering a move to the United States. No longer tied to a single location, companies are free to ring the death knell of organized labour and trades unions, leaving workers defenceless.

In their death throes, trades unions are orchestrating worker unrest across the world, from France to South Korea. This only reinforces the companies' view that they have made the right decision. There has even been talk of the European Union passing legislation to ban 'social dumping', which is dragging down the wages of their masses to Third World levels. Some governments are trying to coerce companies into placing employees (the voters) before owners and shareholders. Such thinking is from an age long gone! Surely now even the governments of nation–states have realized that they need their people employed. This need has completely undermined any control they may have had over employers. In order to save jobs, the British government offered BMW more than £150 million not to close down its Longbridge factory, inciting Ford and other car companies to ask for handouts. They paid the Chung Hwa Picture Tube, the Taiwanese television company, with £80 million in grants and incentives, to open a factory in Scotland (*Financial Times*, 16 November 1995). It took more than £200 million to attract Korean electronics giant LG (Lucky Goldstar) to South Wales (Barnett, 23 November 1997), only for their best plans to fall apart because of the 1998 financial crisis in the Far East.

The benefits to the companies are clear. Apart from grants, foreign companies have invested heavily because they can send their products across Europe under a 'Made in EU' label. They are using European bases as 'aircraft carriers' with uncomplicated access to the single European market. Some US states, such as South Carolina, are using the same tactic, of grants and entry to the huge American market, to attract inbound investment. In 1987, General Motors received over C $200 million as payment for not closing down its Sainte-Therese car-assembly plant in Quebec. The politicians who pay this money see it as a long-term investment. They believe that for every worker directly employed in these factories, five indirect support jobs will be created, supplying components, design skills and so on to the factory. All these workers can be taxed, and this will repay the grants and even leave a profit for government coffers. The reality, however, is somewhat different. Many of these factories are merely 'screwdriver operations', where workers assemble prefabricated components that were designed and built elsewhere. And that elsewhere is where the indirect employment will be situated. In terms of the national tax-take, these schemes are just variations on Soviet style non-jobs. It is doubtful whether the taxes raised and the social security savings made from these factories, and their direct and indirect workers, will ever repay the government's outlay.

New job creation

At least most American states know that real jobs can only be created by business, not by government interference, and this goes some way to explaining the low US unemployment figures. In Britain the government insists it will create 500,000 new (non-) jobs; in France the government will create 700,000 new (non-) jobs. However, politicians cannot indefinitely keep buying votes and still fend off the inevitable. As British politicians call their £5 billion 'New Deal' programme a success, their attempts to draw the long-term unemployed into work are failing. Even the official figures show at least a 40 per cent drop-out rate from the scheme (O'Reilly and Carr-Brown, 25 October 1998).

Jobs are migrating, but it is not just factory production and low-grade office work. Hi-tech jobs too are on the move. Highly skilled workers are to be found in developing countries, and their work is of comparable quality to that of Western workers, but at a fraction of the cost. The town of Bangalore in India boasts programmers with a worldwide reputation for inexpensive quality software. Texas Instruments, Ericsson, AT&T, the Target discount chain, IBM, Microsoft, Robert Bosch and many more companies have taken advantage of the business opportunities on offer. It has taken a mere decade for Bangalore to come from nowhere, to become a major player in a hi-tech niche market. All it takes is talent, and that talent can be bought at salaries at 15 per cent of US levels (Taylor, 8 April 1999).

International 'teleworking' has become a reality, with routine data-entry operations subcontracted to remote sites. Developing countries with good telecommunications infrastructures and cheap labour are favourite locations for this practice, now common among credit-card companies, airlines and other businesses with large data-entry requirements. Often such activities are being promoted as beneficial to the recipient country, by providing work, foreign currency and a transfer of technological skills. However, local subcontractors can be veritable sweatshops, conducting what is tantamount to computerized slavery.

For most of the 1990s, countries, regions, counties, towns and communities have all been offering major inducements to attract migrant corporations in their direction. It is not just the developing world that is scrambling for employers. Agents for the various Development Agencies in Britain have been travelling the globe telling all and sundry of their incentives. Billboards and TV adverts shout out the merits of towns like Pontypridd, Livingston or Milton Keynes. Magazines like *Fortune* carry multiple-page spreads telling readers why they should relocate to Denver, or Portugal.

Yet many national politicians still haven't grasped the new realities. Even in the United States, some corporations are fleeing their native soil, and foreign companies are being frightened away. In the midst of globalization President Clinton said he wanted foreign companies to pay their fair(!) share of taxes (that is more taxes). This would put the United States out of step with the rest of the world, which is frantically trying to attract inward investment by foreign corporations. It makes no sense to invent obstacles to transnational corporations, when the United States has numerous competitive advantages; some of the lowest labour costs in the developed world, high productivity and good labour relations and investment gives entry to one of the largest markets in the world. With sensible taxation policies the United States would be the natural first choice for any mobile corporation. BMW chose to move production facilities from Germany to South Carolina. Alabama attracted a Mercedes-Benz factory against strong competition from neighbouring states by offering incentives to the tune of $300 million (*Handelsblatt*, 4 October 1992). But foreign transnationals will move out if taxes become excessive. Both federal and state governments must realize that other countries, and states, competing for these big plants, are actually **lowering** their taxes. The people of South Carolina, Alabama and other states will not be pleased to find their hopes of employment dashed by Presidential pronouncements.

Even 'national' companies will be considering an 'escape clause'. Consider Microsoft. The US government, frightened of the power of Gates *et al* (governments use the pejorative term 'monopoly'), want it broken up into more controllable (by them) pieces, hence their court actions grounded in the arbitrary antitrust laws.

Whether they like it or not, national and local politicians will have to learn the hard lesson that they need the corporations far more than those enterprises need them.

Part II

Work and employment

4

Where do we work?
Do we work?

A line is being drawn between information rich and information poor, whether they be countries, communities, companies or individuals. Highly mobile virtual enterprises are developing totally new business practices. Using the networked portable computer and the mobile phone, they are turning office workers into 'teleworkers'. According to the Gartner Group there will be 130 million telecommuters worldwide by 2003 (*Canada Newswire*, 9 June 1998). As early as 1995 AT&T employed 35,000 teleworkers and they claimed savings of $1 million every week (Currid, 1 October 1995). Effective use of the superhighway now necessitates the integration of information technology across all aspects of office management.

The office of the future

The successful 'office of the future' will be a radically different animal: the 'virtual office'. The producers of office equipment are themselves facing up to this profound change, and what it means for their businesses. They asked well-known business consultant Charles Handy (1994) to predict the office of the future. He concluded that it will be structured like a club, with most of the space allocated for employees to socialize with colleagues and thereby reinforce organizational bonding. Such socializing will include sports gatherings and entertainment outings, but also a serious 'conference component', with companies bringing their teleworkers together to discuss company policies and direction, as well as introducing them to new management practices.

The working parts of the office will just be nodes in a telecommunications network. Front-office workers will spend much of their time on the road. Linked via the telephone system, their cars and homes are extensions of the office. All the data required for conducting business will be communicated to and fro between the employee's portable computer and a file-store. The file-store itself may even be outsourced, and so it need not physically belong to the company.

Should physical office-space be needed for the odd face-to-face meeting, then it can be time-shared. On arrival, employees are given the key to any appropriate office or desk (the 'hot office' or 'hot desk'), which needn't even be the same on each visit. What little paperwork they need, which is still not computerized, is brought in containers from a depository to their temporary desk, to be returned when they leave. There is no need for the physical location of the office to be fixed, or even owned by the company. The all-knowing company information system will have noted the exact location of each and every employee, and messages for her will be delivered directly, just in time, no matter where she is in the building, no matter where she is in the world. I say she, not because of political correctness, but because the workplace (whatever that is) is becoming increasingly feminized. In Britain women already take up 44 per cent of the jobs. Because of the changing nature of work, and the freedoms delivered by home-working, the Henley Centre predicts (Ghazi and Jones, 28 September 1997) that women will take on 80 per cent of all new jobs being created in the next decade.

With innovations such as the virtual office, the paradigm 'land is wealth' is being subverted by the impact of telecommunications. Companies will simply desert a factory or office if the demands of workers are excessive – as Timex did when it abandoned its Dundee site (Rougvie, 15 October 1993): in with the helicopters, take out all the valuable equipment, ignore the demonstrators and leave the local authority with useless property. Today, knowledge workers and their intellectual property are the wealth of a country or organization. In the Information Age, the value of offices and factories, with a few exceptions, will enter free fall, as demand for space will become a small fraction of the supply. There are going to be very bad times ahead for the owners of office blocks. The exceptions are properties located in economic hot-spots, which will be considered in Chapter 6.

New barbarian organizations do not get tied into long-term office leases. They know there are going to be bargains galore around the corner. They will hire office space on very short time scales – perhaps even for just a few hours. Since the office or desk is where they plug into the network, it can be anywhere, even shared with other companies. 'Just-in-timeshare' information systems will keep track of everything. We are already seeing the first signs of this trend with hotels, railway stations and airports supplying temporary office space. It is already a common enough practice for the business community to have coined the word 'hotelling' for it. But why pay rent at all? Why not hold your meetings in the lobby of the best hotel in town, and all for as little as the price of afternoon tea? Why not meet at Starbucks?

Teleworking

So-called 'teleworking' has come a long way in a relatively short time. The first teleworkers were small businessmen and women operating from home, often because they could not afford the overheads of an office. They used the most basic computing and communications facilities. But the mobile telephone changed everything. Companies very soon realized that offices are where telephones are housed. Much of the work could have been done anywhere, but each worker is constrained to sit by a handset bearing a unique telephone number, close to a filing cabinet stuffed with paper. In future, work will still follow the phone number, but now mobile office workers are 'road warriors', taking their telephone numbers with them, anywhere. The contents of filing cabinets can be digitized and put in a networked file store, also accessible anywhere from a laptop computer. Organizations can communicate easily, effectively and cheaply with geographically remote locations. Teleworking, in all its various guises, is now being considered seriously by every company.

Teleworking only really took off during the recession of the early 1990s, when companies chose the barbarism of the bottom line and reduced their fixed costs, rather than attempting to sell into sluggish markets. Staff numbers were reduced, and company functions outsourced to freelance operations, large and small, on a pay-as-you-need basis. It was only a short step from such piecework to teleworking. In fact companies were unknowingly setting up the infrastructures necessary for teleworking because they had to support the information needs of senior managers when they were travelling on business trips. The same infrastructure can be used by every teleworker. The salesforce can now go straight to the customer. They no longer need to call into the office each morning; their schedule and other necessary up-to-the-minute information can all be downloaded on to their 'portable'. Nowadays every commuter train is stacked with users of laptop computers, frantically talking into their mobile phones. Teleworking while travelling or during those long boring evenings in hotels means that companies get extra work from their employees at no extra cost – now that really is an efficiency gain.

Companies soon appreciated that much of their office space could be shed, since it is a substantially underused resource; even non-teleworkers are away from their desks as much as half of the time. That office space is often situated in very expensive property, and is only nominally occupied from nine to five: less than half the day! Once companies set off down the road of cost–benefit analysis, they soon discover that the total overhead costs per employee may be more than twice the salary. Teleworking delivers enormous gains by cutting back on office rent. No office means no heat and light, insurance, support staff, cleaners or security. It is also generally accepted that teleworkers have more than a third more time to work, due to less travel and fewer interruptions. Studies repeatedly conclude that working at home is measurably more productive than at the office, often by more than 20 per cent (Vallely and Wolmar, 18 July 1995). Far from being a destabilizing force, companies have realized that teleworking minimizes the negative effects of the 'industrial action' inevitable as unions lash out in their death throes. The closer companies look, the more attractive teleworking becomes.

Cost and time savings are not the only attractions. Companies find that any rarely used skill, as well as commonly available skills, can be bought cheaply and efficiently over the Net, without tying the company into long-term commitments. One obvious example is retaining the services of teams of translators, some in the most esoteric languages, who rapidly translate requests for product information or invoices, an increasingly important business need in the global economy.

It came as a great surprise to some companies that many highly specialized teleworkers actually perform more effectively out of an office environment, particularly when the work requires intense concentration. New technology can send massive files around the world in minutes, and so work such as computer-aided design (CAD) at a distance is now a feasible proposition. Design teams can be organized around 'groupware' at short notice in worldwide video-conferences, so that a company's best brains are brought to bear on specific problems with a minimum of disruption. It makes no difference whether those brains are in the office, or half-way up an alp.

It is not a straight decision between whether employees work at home, or commute to the office. 'Telematics centres', an idea originally expounded by Alvin Toffler (1980), variously known as 'telecottages', 'telecentres' or 'televillages', are springing up everywhere, and offer an acceptable and practical compromise. These centres can be purpose-built communities, or they can form, almost by accident, around various service companies. One well-known example of this spontaneous growth in the United States is Kinko's Copy Centers. Kinko Inc. expanded from neighbourhood college-campus copy shops to global retailer on the back of such informal communities. As people queued for copying, printing and other computer-related services, they struck up friendships with other customers waiting in line; a community of Kinko users appeared; friendships evolved. Some would go down to the Kinko store just to socialize, even if they had no copying to do! Often these new friends also discovered that they were potential customers for each other's services. Acting on the basis of their new-found friendships, and in their spare time, they exchanged advice and bartered services among themselves. In each transaction the recipient of the service didn't need to dip into their hard-earned savings; and the seller was paid with a promise of reciprocation as and when needed, very much like a local-exchange token scheme but without the tokens.

Telecottages, as their name implies, generally serve rural areas, and they are often dependent, at least in the short term, on external funding from various training and enterprise councils, local authorities, development agencies and from local firms and telecommunication companies. These small businesses are designed to make state-of-the-art technology, networks and applications readily available to local people, namely the underemployed and the self-employed, as well as to other small businesses with limited IT budgets.

Telecentres are similar in many respects to telecottages, except that they are run as businesses to provide a variety of facilities for urban teleworkers. By taking advantage of such facilities, redundant middle and top-ranking executives have used a small part of their redundancy money to set themselves up as self-employed consultants, rather than face the indignity of re-entering a shrinking 'meat market'. Large organizations are developing their own telecentres as an office of the future for mobile staff to drop in, and 'just-in-timeshare'. In essence both telecottages and telecentres are telecommunes. All the facilities needed by a modern company, such as fax machines, photocopiers, modems, scanners, electronic mailing, global video-conferencing facilities, instant video and data transfers, and all the latest business application software, can be rented as and when needed.

Telecommunes provide the aforementioned translation services, subcontracted labour for large data-entry projects, programming, and the brokering of information skills such as writing technical manuals, newspaper and magazine articles, and various subscriber 'information agencies'. These include 'clipping services', where every mention of a particular company in the press is located and passed on to that company; and 'reference services', where appropriate articles are gleaned from the plethora of journals, indexed and delivered in a common format. There are 'facilitation services', where agents familiar with a particular customer's information tastes filter the information overload on the Net. They deliver a focused product, such as a customized newspaper, or recommendations for an evening's television viewing chosen from the thousands of channels available. But it is not all 'new industry'. Telecommunes are also used by more orthodox businesses, such as architecture, accountancy and management consultancy practices.

A novel form of telecommune is the televillage, which may be a purpose-built group of homes ranging from small flats to family houses set around a hub that contains the village's electronic core and a few small offices. All houses are connected to a fibre-optic ring so that the residents can work from home, from a bureau or from the telecentre itself. February 1997 saw DualStar Technologies Corporation announce the completion of their CyberBuilding™ system for The Grand Millennium, a condominium residence and hotel facility located at 1965 Broadway, Manhattan. Apart from delivering the hi-tech infrastructure, the building also has a CyberCierge℠ offering hands-on support for residents (*United States Business Wire*, 10 February 1997). Such 'smart buildings' are popping up everywhere.

Telecommunes are in fact new communities based on principles of enlightened self-interest; they are convinced that 'small is beautiful'. They see themselves as part of a revolutionary movement, and they are already flexing their political muscles, insisting on being treated as a special tax category. Telecommunes are far more than just small local service bureaux. Key services supplied to the lone teleworker are: training in the use of new technology; giving skilled advice on a variety of business issues such as registration for the ISO9000 quality standard; supplying access to the very latest technology; and acting as hot-spots of ideas and the feedback of shared experience. They can also act as an electronic marketplace and 'hiring fair', where freelance teleworkers can come to sell their skills and be recruited.

Of course there is a downside to home-teleworking. Working from home can cause a great deal of stress. Many teleworkers find it difficult to separate their working and domestic lives, often uncomfortably balancing work commitments with the care of children or sick and elderly relatives. Cut off from office life, home can begin to feel like a prison, and teleworkers often experience a sense of isolation, both personally and professionally, leading to a lack of motivation. Breaks are essential. No one can work permanently on his or her own and remain effective. Socializing is very important, hence Charles Handy's prediction that the offices of large companies with teleworkers would be used as clubs.

However, for freelance workers, time away from teleworking involves both financial and opportunity costs, and so there is an inclination to work every possible minute. Consequently, to be effective they need to know about time management and other new management and interpersonal skills to complement the information skills they are selling over the superhighway: being assertive, balancing the workload, and prioritizing tasks, particularly having the confidence to turn away new business when there is too much work on.

There is the extra pressure caused by the wide range of tasks they now have to perform, which in an office environment would have been undertaken by other company employees: winning new business, delivering the goods or services, sending invoices, collecting payment, paying sales taxes, buying computer equipment, faxes and photocopiers, and even making sure of sufficient supplies of office stationery. Cash flow is of course a major source of stress: not getting paid or being kept waiting for payment, and the ever nagging doubt that present successes may be short-lived. Although more expensive than working from home, and not as comfortable or secure as the home environment, the telecommune has proved its worth by helping teleworkers deal with these pressures: supplying encouragement, supervision and both psychological and technical support, enabling human networking, and subcontracting any excessive workload to other members of the telecommune.

Telephony

Already highly successful, with the advent of desktop interactive video, teleworking will become the norm. Video conferencing is available, but it is far too expensive at present. With costs tumbling thanks to the Net, managers will soon be able to see workers at the end of a telephone line, and the last barrier to universal acceptance of teleworking will be down. But it doesn't all have to be rocket science. Take for example computer-assisted telephony, the simple coupling of computer systems with the telephone, the nucleus of most company communications with its customers. With the credit card making a trio, this has become the most effective selling environment ever devised. Within seconds of receiving a phone call, a screen shows relevant information to an operator, and assists that operator in rapidly entering details of the transaction. With caller identification – the phone number of the caller is automatically provided – the database can display the caller's file on screen before a single word is spoken. Hotel chains have been doing this for years, but only recently has the wider business community recognized its added value. Voice recognition systems, extending today's irritating button-menu systems, will take down customer details and go through standard follow-up procedures once a sale has been made by a human operator. Of course the operators can be teleworkers working from home, anywhere in the world. ICL, the British computer company (actually 84 per cent owned by Fujitsu of Japan, and 16 per cent by Northern Telecom of Canada), runs its mainframe help line from Poona in India.

Customers appreciate dealing with a well-informed, efficient and helpful person on the other end of a phone line. They want their dealings to be painless, and most importantly, quickly finalized by simply giving a credit card number. This is an ideal form of shopping in the cases where the customers know what they want, whether this be theatre tickets, flowers or, far more importantly, financial products. In Britain, First Direct has revolutionized the sale of insurance policies by selling only over the telephone. Automated voice-ordering systems enable mail-order companies to service a rush of orders, say in response to television advertisements, many of which would otherwise have been lost without the expense of taking on extra staff. When the buyer also has access to multimedia devices, making computer-assisted telephony a two-way process, then the whole nature of shopping will have changed. Possibly linked to cable television as with interactive digital television, specified product lines can be displayed in the purchaser's home, and teleshopping will have come of age.

Employment implications

The effect of these changing practices is not a simple transfer from office work to home work. There are profound second and third order feedback effects just waiting to explode. In Britain, 20 million workers commute to work. Many predictions claim that more than a third of these jobs can be teleworked, either wholly or in part – this is typical of most advanced economies. A new type of worker is appearing, the 'self-employed portfolio worker', working for a number of different companies, being paid on piece-rate, as and when consulted. Unfortunately much hi-tech low-level home working or from call-centres is poorly paid. Conservative estimates place half a million Britons working in call-centres by the new millennium (Palmer, 27 January 1999). These tele-operators are under enormous stress and the burn-out rate is high. Many are paid low wages per transaction and they are under constant electronic monitoring being treated little better than battery hens. With employers no longer tied to a single location, the workers are defenceless. Those lucky enough still to be in work will have to work harder, for more hours each week, for less pay, in less-secure jobs: and they had better be grateful for it. Even those service workers still employed live under the enormous stress of job insecurity. Companies will use fewer workers to cover the same workload.

Imagine the loss of jobs caused by the millions fewer commuter journeys each week; and this is not taking into account the reduction in the number of jobs supporting soon to be ex-commuters: the coffee lady, the cleaner, the security man on the door, the receptionist, canteen staff, porters, janitors, electricians, plumbers and carpenters. In fact all the jobs that support the workplace of the 'Machine Age', Toffler's second wave, will become endangered in the Information Age. The haemorrhage of commuters will precipitate an enormous loss in revenue for the railways and also for businesses that rely to a great extent on the passing trade of commuters. What about shops in railway concourses and automobile service stations? Furthermore, with the loss of jobs comes a 'triple whammy' for governments: lower tax revenue, increased social security payouts and the need to support deprived areas financially.

True there will be some, mainly social advantages, particularly for the well off. The roads will be far less congested: no more rush hour. A much-publicized recent report (*M2 Presswire*, 17 April 1998) stated that the average car speed in London is ten miles per hour, the same as in the days of horse-drawn traffic. London, in common with New York and all major cities worldwide, is in ever-present danger of gridlock. This danger will be removed. The use of far less fuel will mean less pollution; cars will last longer and there will be fewer road accidents. This is bad news for car makers, service stations and repair shops, but good news for insurance companies. In no case is it good for jobs. With road traffic flowing freely there will be no major road-building schemes and no demonstrations about the destruction of the environment.

The really clever companies will have customers as well as employees tapping directly into their systems. Nobody thinks twice these days about using an automatic teller machine (ATM). Once the security problems of electronic fund transfer are overcome, full-service Internet home banking is just around the corner. This will give us far more than just the most superficial transactions seen at present. We have already seen that the ATM revolution has caused a huge number of layoffs in banking, but home banking will bring another wave of job losses, and drive down the wages of those still employed. Now thanks to information technology, the threat of global competition and aggressive management strategies, everything has changed. Like direct-sales insurance companies, the bank of the future is an office in cyberspace, serviced by teleworkers. After all, 'we need banking, but we don't need banks!' The high-street bank will disappear. Only those people on the Net, and with satisfactory credit ratings, will have access to banking services. The rest, society's poor, will be left to the mercy of loan sharks.

This model ('disintermediation') is invading travel agencies and estate agencies. Unless these agencies can reinvent themselves, so as to add value to their customers, then more jobs will disappear as cut-price tele-operators with low margins start cutthroat competition. Worse is to come, and soon.

Even low cost teleworkers will not be able to compete on price against voice-activated computer programs, which can interact with callers in spoken English (or any other language). Systems, already up and running in the US banking sector, can automatically complete highly sophisticated financial transactions.

However, job losses in this sector will pale into insignificance when compared to the impact of multimedia teleshopping: not today's teleshopping, where frantic salespeople scream at the TV viewer about carpets, kitchen and bedroom furniture and so on, but truly interactive shopping. With a mouse, the customer chooses goods from a multimedia database of pictures of all the goods available in the store, together with prices and discounts. The order is sent via the Net to the warehouse, where it is boxed for delivery to the customer's home at the time indicated. The whole transaction is paid for automatically by credit card or by e-cash.

This new mode of purchasing will have profound effects on shopping centres – to survive they will have to sell themselves as social events, and as a place to find those 'special purchases'. What will happen to newsagents when newspapers and magazines are delivered electronically over the Net? Supermarkets will be particularly badly hit as groceries and run-of-the-mill products are ordered over the Net. What happens to the hundreds of thousands of people serving on the checkout tills? It is no surprise that supermarket owners run 'singles evenings', and commission polls that claim that most customers think of sex while shopping.

The result of all this teleworking is that the rich get richer, and the poor get poorer. Because of the superhighway, large numbers of workers will lose their jobs. In political circles there is a belief (or perhaps a pretence) that the inevitable huge number of soon-to-be job losses will be counterbalanced by new jobs created with new technology. A direct comparison is being made between the Industrial Revolution and the Information Revolution. However, the Industrial Revolution took more than 50 years to start sorting itself out, and even then the social conditions of the workers were not ideal. That revolution merely changed one type of physical labour for another. The Information Revolution is going to need intellectual muscle. The nature of jobs is going to change radically. Do the people who held factory or low-grade office or retail jobs have what it takes? The jury is out, but the very best I expect is a couple of lost generations – two generations of trouble.

There is certainly going to be far more part-time and contract employment. According to some colleagues at the London School of Economics, during the economic recovery of 1992–96, less than a third of the jobs created in Britain were full-time (Ghazi and Jones, 28 September 1997). The rest were part-time, temporary, casual and self-employed. The Henley Centre predicts that by 2010 the majority of jobs will not be full-time. One in eight workers is now self-employed (Barker, 26 May 1995). Twenty years ago 43 per cent of employment was in businesses with more than 500 people on the payroll. By the early 1990s downsizing and outsourcing brought it down to 34 per cent, and by year 2000 around 27 per cent. And Britain is typical of a global trend.

Major employers will shift the responsibility for ensuring the legal rights of the workforce on to the subcontractor, leaving the major company free of liability. Companies will finally be able to kill off trades unions. They will be able to shaft troublesome workers. Managers don't even have to look employees in the eye – they fire them by fax or e-mail. Financial obligations too will be pushed down to subcontractors, who increasingly will be lone teleworkers. If a company can re-site its teleworkers to 'the sticks', moving from high cost areas to low cost, then it can just as easily move abroad to countries with less stringent legal requirements and employment regulations. Traumatic shifts in the relative wealth of regions are in the offing. Such shifts, taken together with inevitable lower wages and rising unemployment, will also have a dramatic effect on the domestic housing market.

Caribbean countries are already using 'regulatory arbitrage' and low wages to attract telejobs from the United States. In Britain, regions like Northern Ireland are stealing jobs from London, which is hardly surprising with wage levels for computer staff at 80 per cent of the UK average and a substantially lower cost of living. Even the British Home Office was at one time seriously considering subcontracting to the Philippines a large but straightforward data-entry job of computerizing 3 million criminal records (Campbell, 30 June 1992). It wasn't the question of cheap labour or any moral dilemma that killed off the export of this project. Ultimately questions about the security of such highly sensitive personal data, and some adverse press comments, frightened the Home Office into accepting a higher bid from a British company. The taxpayer footed the bill again.

5

Knowledge workers versus service workers

What is going to happen with the fallout of jobs caused by new technology and the feedback of its second order effects such as teleworking? Peter Drucker (1992), the famous management guru, has a very interesting forecast. He says that humanity is polarizing into two employment categories: the intellectual, cultural and business elite (the mobile and independent 'knowledge workers'), and the rest (the immobile and dependent 'service workers'). Because of Drucker's stature in business literature we are now stuck with the label 'knowledge', and this is causing a great deal of misunderstanding by over-stressing the thought-process in work. The term 'talent worker' captures far better the spirit of Drucker's meaning, and that talent must be focused on wealth creation. Drucker himself is quite clear that knowledge in, by and for itself achieves absolutely nothing.

In a similar vein, Robert Reich (1991), formerly President Clinton's Secretary of Labor, believes that in the Information Age there will be three categories: 'symbolic–analytic services' (knowledge workers who are problem identifiers, solvers and brokers, and who have unique or at least very rare skills); 'in-person services' (such as hairdressers, school teachers, university professors, general practitioners, lawyers, accountants and shop assistants, all of whom deliver a particular service on an individual basis, and who have to differentiate themselves on price as well as quality); and on the bottom rung of the ladder are 'routine production services' (such as factory workers and truck drivers who make and deliver products anonymously). The latter two groups roughly correspond to Drucker's service workers. Included among the symbolic analysts are business gurus, sports stars, pop singers, film and TV celebrities and any unique 'talent' that sells itself and its products across the cyberspace of the global telecommunications media. I would also add two further categories: security and the underclass – but more of that later.

Changes in routine production jobs

A company cannot survive without its knowledge workers, but its routine production services and office work can be either replaced by robots or exported elsewhere on the globe where wages are lower. The movement of whole industries is nothing new, although previously import tariffs meant that jobs did stay within national boundaries, and vastly inferior channels of communication did limit travel to relatively small distances. The wage differentials in 19th-century England caused the hat-making trade based in London to move lock, stock and barrel to Luton. The subsequent savings for manufacturers were substantial. The two towns were separated by a mere 30 miles along reasonable roads, so that delivery times to the capital were short. However, they were worlds apart in terms of the cost and availability of labour. Today, thanks to international trade agreements and superb international distribution and telecommunications systems, neither national boundary nor distance is a problem. Once again wage differentials can precipitate the complete migration of an industry.

Wages of routine production jobs are already beginning to converge worldwide to Third World levels, although moralizing politicians in the developed countries are using the fact of 'inhuman' working conditions in the Third World for their justification of protectionist import controls, in their attempts to stem the tide (*South China Post*, 15 April 1994). But large corporations will ignore their pleas. If the US presidency can't control corporate America in its feeding frenzy over the China market, what chance do the rest of Western politicians have? The only force holding back business is China's state-tolerated piracy of intellectual property rights. Human rights don't fit into the equation.

Does it matter? Sentimentality has a habit of backfiring. When US senators passed the Child Labor Deterrence Bill blocking imports into the United States of any product made by children, the effects were unexpected. In Bangladesh children who earned a pittance in factories were thrown out of work, and reduced to scavenging and prostitution (Steele, 31 October 1997). 'The road to hell is paved with good intentions.'

The trend to export jobs is apparent everywhere, and there are small as well as large companies on the move. British Polythene Industries closed its factory in Shropshire with the loss of 150 routine production jobs, and switched the annual production of supermarket carrier bags to Xinhui, Guangdong province, China. BPI's payroll bill was cut by 90 per cent, and raw materials were also cheaper. Not that the extra profit went to BPI – increased global competition meant the supermarkets took that and passed it on to their customers. In 1992 the London International Group moved the manufacture of surgical and kitchen gloves to Malaysia with the loss of 650 jobs in Britain (Norris, 7 February 1995). Guess Inc., the makers of jeans, moved jobs to Mexico, Peru and Chile, with the percentage of their clothes sewn in Los Angeles being cut from 97 per cent to 35 per cent (http://www.citizen.org/pctrade/taa97acs/KEYTAA.html). Corgi Toys, a British institution, makes its toys in China. Such companies simply have no choice if they hope to remain competitive.

The new barbarians who run modern global companies, the knowledge workers with attitude, take full advantage of 'social dumping', and the consequential and substantial lowering of wage levels. There is a slightly less extreme, but nonetheless profound, knock-on effect of dragging down the wages of in-person service workers, a sector that is itself being increasingly automated. The banking sector is at the leading edge of job losses here, although losses will soon become increasingly apparent in other parts of the financial sector. The retail industry and the non-specialist mass teaching of schoolchildren and second-division undergraduates are also candidates for computerization.

The real generators of wealth

It is now abundantly clear that knowledge workers are the real generators of wealth. They always have been, only now they realize it. For their knowledge is the basis of innovation, and innovation underpins the creation of alternatives – not only alternative products but also alternative procedures. Alternatives deliver new competitive advantages, and destroy the old. It is the never-ending story, that all advantage is temporary and transitory. Without the ability to innovate, a company or a country is doomed.

At last the knowledge workers have come to realize this. The income of these owners of intellectual and financial wealth will increase substantially. They will be made welcome anywhere in the world, no matter what their age, race, sex, colour or creed. In an attempt at 'right-sizing', companies and countries will be scouring the globe, competing with each other to attract this top quality 'people product', dragging them off the planes if necessary.

Knowledge workers now have a choice. They can stay with the nations of their birth, providing of course that the price is right, or they can join the new barbarian hordes of 'economic mercenaries' somewhere else, thereby ransacking the old order.

From October 1994, foreign 'entrepreneurial investors' with £1 million at their disposal can bypass the usual entry rules into Britain, on condition that they invest £750,000 in government bonds, shares or corporate bonds and intend to make their main home in Britain (Ford, 25 May 1994). But Britain has been slow off the mark, and the scheme has been an acutely embarrassing failure. There has only been a handful of enquiries, none leading to immigration. The world's migrant rich have real doubts about settling in Britain for a number of very good reasons, not least the arrogance of the 'Anglo Saxon male' mentality that runs most of its institutions (Burke and Leppard, 5 February 1995). Canada's guidelines allow people with C $250,000 (C $350,000 in some provinces) to settle, provided they have a proven business track-record (Hogben, 29 December 1995). New Zealand's strict measures for all potential immigrants are waived if the immigrant invests £240,000. It is only a matter of time before intellectual capital, such as scientific and technological expertise, will be included on the balance sheet in all these countries when the financial calculations concerning the costs of immigration and emigration are made. In the United States, there is a fast-track immigration policy for businessmen and women who can offer $1 million and guarantee to employ 10 people. Six hundred millionaires emigrated to the United States in 1993 (Syal, 29 May 1994). Furthermore, the H1-B programme hands out six-year visas to skilled foreign hi-tech workers to help the growth of US companies. In 1998 the limit of 65,000 was raised to 115,000 to help cope with the 'millennium bug' problem (MacMillan, 2 June 1999).

Paradoxically in 1993, some 697 US citizens renounced their citizenship, many to avoid the tax rises imposed by both the Bush and Clinton administrations (McMenamin, 16 June 1997). The Clinton administration tried to impose an exit tax of 35 per cent on expatriates' assets more than $600,000, but it was stopped by Congress. However, the situation changed dramatically with the Illegal Immigration Reform and Immigrant Responsibility Act, which forbid those who give up US citizenship for tax purposes from visiting the United States. The Act categorizes tax-exiles alongside war criminals and terrorists. And how do officials recognize a tax-exile? It is presumed that everyone with an annual income more than $100,000, or a net worth of more than $500,000, has expatriated for tax purposes.

Meanwhile, small countries everywhere are being tempted to aid and abet capital flight. In 1995 the Seychelles' government passed an Economic Development Act, designed to attract badly needed foreign capital. Described as a money launderer's charter, the Act provided diplomatic immunity to anyone who would invest $10 million in a government-approved investment scheme, promising to protect the money from the scrutiny of any outside authority. An international outcry forced the government to rethink their plans (Kane, Levy and Haynes, 14 January 1996).

However, if only passports are required, look no further than Ireland. In 1990 the Irish Minister of Justice signed certificates of naturalization for 11 people: eight Saudi Arabians and three Pakistanis (Flynn, 4 October 1997). The passports were allegedly handed over personally, to the most notable new citizen Sheikh Khalid bin Mahfouz (a good Irish name!), by the Taoiseach Charles Haughey. The passports were in return for an investment of £20 million in Ireland, and they have been causing scandalous ripples for the Irish government ever since. Was this an isolated incident, or was it a policy decision? John Dorrance, former head of Campbell Soups, and worth well over a billion dollars, left the United States and acquired an Irish passport in 1994 to become the Republic's wealthiest man (Taylor, 7 April 1997).

Unless they change their ways, the other countries in Europe won't escape a haemorrhage of their wealthy citizens. Many of the above-mentioned 600 immigrants to the United States came from Europe. Disaffected Europeans are not only fleeing to the United States. The sport and film industries are showing knowledge workers the way, with numerous role models such as Michael Schumacher and Sean Connery. Tax havens like Monaco and Switzerland have been offering the super-rich an escape route for years. The trickle of tax-exiles could soon become a flood of knowledge workers. Only a few, like tennis champion Steffi Graf, will stay as hostages to their fortunes out of a naïve sense of patriotism, with the tax authorities hovering like vultures over her and her family. Graf ended up paying three-quarters of a million dollars in return for the German state agreeing to drop all tax evasion investigations of her affairs (Jago, 13 June 1997). Her father Peter took complete responsibility, and was sentenced to three years and nine months in jail on six charges of evading tax on more than $7 million (Bild, 25 January, 1997). Not that being a tax exile makes you completely free of tax officials. Another tennis champion, Boris Becker, shrewdly left Germany for Monaco at the age of 16 to get away from penal taxation, but the authorities never give up when they smell money. They raided offices across Germany to see if Becker had spent long enough in their country to make him liable for taxes (Boyes, 30 July 1998).

In Britain, champion jockey Lester Piggott was sentenced to three years jail over a £3.5 million tax fraud. In 1983 he agreed to 'settle' his tax bill, at which time he stated he had only three bank accounts. He persisted with this story until 1986, when he admitted to having three more large bank accounts. Subsequently he was found to have a further 14 undisclosed accounts (*Accountancy*, December 1987). He was caught because he settled his tax bill with a cheque drawn on one of those undisclosed accounts!

Economic liabilities

Every country wants healthy tax revenue levied on the wealth created by knowledge workers. However, nobody wants more service workers, as they are increasingly seen as economic liabilities. As long ago as the 1930s, John Maynard Keynes was aware that 'we are being affected with a new disease, namely technological unemployment. That is, unemployment due to our discovery of means of economizing the use of labour.' Jeremy Rifkin (1995) estimated that the jobs of three out of every four Western workers could now be done by computers. He confirmed that 1.8 million jobs in manufacturing disappeared in the United States during the 1980s. In Germany during a 12-month period between 1992 and 1993, half a million manufacturing jobs went. Over the 25 years up to the mid-1990s, employment in manufacturing in rich countries fell from 28 per cent to 18 per cent (*Economist*, 26 April 1997). On current trends it could be down to 10 per cent within 20 years. Comparisons with the impact of technology on agricultural employment are sobering. In 1860 farming made up 50 per cent of US jobs; today it is 3 per cent. Rifkin gives a depressing, but very convincing, prediction of the coming mass unemployment, identifying a severe and total dislocation with past work practices. The traditional job, the job for life, is gone for ever. Most of society will be trapped in a perpetual search for casual, part-time or contract jobs. Manpower, the employment agency, is fast becoming the largest private employer in the United States, with well over three-quarters of a million 'temps' on its books (*Economist*, 18 January 1997).

There is a growing realization that service and production workers are a net loss both to the state and to the company. They cost far more than they generate. They are surplus to requirements. In modern Greek, the word for work, δουλεια, is the same as that for slavery, with only a small difference in pronunciation. The Ancient Greeks believed that exchanging physical labour for money was demeaning and morally degrading: the activity of the mentally deficient, suitable only for slaves – tools that talked. What goes around, comes around!

Companies just cannot afford to keep a permanent and overpaid service workforce in conditions of intense global competition. Whenever possible they will adopt technologies that displace labour and, where that is not yet feasible, they will do all they can to replace job-holders by contract workers. Those service workers still employed will now be expected to add far more value to the company, unlike in the past where service work meant just turning up. Companies will be reducing the wages and staffing levels of service workers, and it is no accident that most Western companies are presently instigating major 'downsizing', 'delayering' and 'outsourcing' programmes. In the 1980s, General Electric downsized 104,000 of its 402,000 workers. General Motors had a workforce of 800,000 in 1979, which was reduced to 450,000 in the early 1990s. IBM dropped from a workforce of 406,000 in 1987 to 202,000 in 1995. Between 1990 and 1993, 85 per cent of the Fortune 500 companies reported they had delayered management (Ross, 11 April 1994). The theory is that such flattening of management structure changes the organization, so that administrative overheads are low while the potential for brokerage of the company's information and human resources is high.

Add value or perish

Middle management too is under threat. Under the euphemistic banner of Business Process Re-engineering (BPR), companies were making redundant up to a quarter of their managers. Then in 1996, BPR and its associated outsourcing suddenly lost favour. This was not really surprising because the downsizing had been approached in a very mechanistic way, and had created enormous internal problems for companies. Nevertheless, the reduction of superfluous employees at all levels was necessary. Technology hit first the workers, and then middle management; senior management is next for pruning! Companies simply have no choice. They must ask, and answer, some very brutal questions concerning which employees, managers and workers are resources and which are liabilities. Acting in this way, they are not being callous, unscrupulous, unprincipled or immoral. 'Nature is not immoral when it has no pity for the degenerate' (Nietzsche). The motto for everyone is: 'Add value or perish!' There is no room for sentimentality in this brave new world.

Of course this portrayal could be wrong. After all, the statistical propaganda that came out of the Clinton administration in the United States, riding on the back of an economic boom, claimed that it is possible to buck the trends outlined. What should we believe? Most governments claim that things are going well, and that it is all because of their good management. In 1992, the Bush administration claimed that many of the new jobs 'they' were creating were 'high paid'. This included jobs that paid a mere $6 an hour (Dawson, 15 April 1992). Clinton's Council of Economic Advisers claimed that between 1993 and 1996 the majority of jobs paid between 14 per cent and 17 per cent above the national average (which might have been expected to raise the national average and disprove the figures!), and that over two-thirds of new jobs were in managerial or professional occupations. This was a time following an excess of downsizing and outsourcing. Large numbers of ex-employees were re-employed as self-employed consultants. Can these really be categorized as new jobs? Added to this is the fact that in the 1980s downsizing had gone much too far, and companies had to rehire people to cope with increased demand in the now booming economy.

The US economy may have grown substantially over the last two decades, but the average earnings of 'non-supervisory' employees, around 70 per cent of the workforce, have declined from $8.42 dollars per hour in 1978 to $7.41 in 1994 (in 1982 dollars) (Luttwak, 6 May 1996). Furthermore, American companies are shrinking, whether the measure is in number of employees, sales or value added (Brynjolffson *et al*, 1989). More lies, damn lies and statistics? The trick in misusing numbers for political purposes, either pro or con, is to choose the starting date of counting very carefully, and the economic cycle will deliver figures that can demonstrate either case, no matter what the underlying trends. 'It's not the figures lying, it's the liars figuring' (Mark Twain). So whom do we believe?

Increasingly a large number of people, some reports say as many as 10 per cent of the workforce, just can't take the pressure and insecurity, and are considering 'downshifting' (Ghazi and Jones, 28 September 1997). Many are finally realizing that however much they earn, they end up spending it. They are thinking of giving up the rat race for a simpler lifestyle, placing quality of life before high earning. Linked with other employment trends indicated above, it means that an increasing number of people will have much more frugal spending habits, and this will feed back as a decline in the economy, hence more unemployment.

Impact of Third World population growth

These trends are all happening against a background of exploding population in the Third World. Ninety-five per cent of the world's population increase is in developing countries (Kennedy, 1993). Ironically information technology, more specifically television, is telling the whole world that the 'grass is greener' in developed countries, and showing the disaffected how to get there. In October 1997 thousands of Czech and Slovak gypsies seeking asylum turned up at Dover. It was all sparked off by a Czech television programme that reported that the British asylum and benefit systems were easy to manipulate (Ford and Lee, 21 October 1997), which they are. Two months earlier, Canada was on the receiving end of a similar influx of Czech gypsies who had sold all their possessions to buy a one-way ticket there. A television documentary told of a Canadian government programme that gave free housing, money and job opportunities to refugees. No such programme existed (Simao, 29 August 1997).

To combat such inevitable mass migrations, state barriers will be thrown up everywhere to keep out alien service workers. Each state has a surplus of its own to support. It is already happening. Canada is to impose a C $1,000 tax on people seeking landed immigration status, thus sending out a message that is likely to reduce applications from poor service workers, but increase applications from richer knowledge workers (*Daily Telegraph*, 1 March 1995). New Zealand requires aspiring immigrants and their families to pass a tough English language examination that will separate the educated from the uneducated (*Straits Times*, 2 August 1995). In 1994 California passed proposition 187 that barred nearly 2 million illegal immigrants from schools, welfare services, and all but emergency health care (Whittell and Rhodes, 11 November 1994), although a federal District Court overturned it in 1997 despite continuing widespread support in the state (Lesher and Weinstein, 30 July 1999).

Even more sinister pressures are in train. A 1998 survey by the South African Centre for Policy Studies uncovered increasing xenophobia in their country, which is rather ironic given its recent deliverance from apartheid. Three foreign workers, blamed for taking jobs from locals, were murdered in Pretoria (*SAPA news agency*, 13 October 1998). Fidel Castro coined the phrase 'demographic warfare' when in 1980 he expelled 125,000 Cubans in the Mariel boatlift. About 11,000 were genuine refugees; the rest were mentally ill, criminals and other undesirables that Castro wanted to offload on to the United States (Cornwell, 20 October 1994). The Khmer Rouge claimed that Vietnam was trying to annex Cambodia by flooding the country with Vietnamese immigrants (*BBC Monitoring Service*, 3 September 1994). Ethnic Albanians and Serbs in Kosovo swapped claims that each was involved in demographic warfare: swamping the region with new immigrants, or denying medical rights to disfavoured ethnic groups (*Reuters News Service*, 29 May 1992). The 1999 Nato action in Kosovo simply reversed the ethnic cleansing of a million Albanians, by cleansing 200,000 Serbs.

How long will it be before there are 'differential rights' for 'differentiated citizens', identified in a database and policed by smart cards? How long before the notion of 'human rights' is as outdated as the divine right of kings? Civil liberties campaigners are showing themselves out of touch with the Information Age, when they oppose what they see as attempts at forcing whole populations to carry identity cards. There will be no force – it is not a question of opting out; only valued members of society and economic merce-naries will be invited to opt in. No card? Then no benefits and no rights. States will reinvent the Ancient Greek status of the 'metic', conferring limited rights on aliens who are neither citizens nor slaves. Maybe democracy can only work in a city-state, as in Athens where it developed and of course where the vote-less slaves did all the work? And where women did not have a vote.

With information technology destroying large numbers of service jobs, will a catastrophic split in society be prevented by creating sufficient new jobs to replace them, in or out of cyberspace? Where are these jobs going to come from? The hope is still that jobs lost in manufacturing will be replaced by jobs in transaction processing – one for one, or better. What is the reality? In mid-March 1997, Microsoft, Intel and Cisco combined had a market capital-ization of $270 billion, two and a half times that of General Motors, Ford and Chrysler ($103 billion combined). Yet the worldwide employment roll of GM is 647,000, Ford 345,000 and Chrysler 114,000, each individually larger than the combined rolls of 80,000 for the hi-tech companies (*Economist*, 29 March 1997).

As the production processes of manufacturing companies become increas-ingly automated, their employment rolls can only go down. Those fired from this sector will find that far fewer jobs are being created by the new compa-nies. According to the Bureau of Labor Statistics, more than 8 million jobs in the US manufacturing sector have been lost over the past two decades (Holmes, 23 August 1999), and consequently average salaries have dropped by 10 per cent in real terms since 1978. Much of the new employment being created is in dead-end service jobs.

Technology is the problem

Worse is to come. Many of the jobs currently available in transaction pro-cessing will themselves become lost to computerization as systems become more advanced, as with computerized voice recognition systems. Blind to the trends, politicians still use the abracadabra words 'training in new technol-ogy' and 'jobs through growth' for the huge number of soon-to-be unem-ployed. If only it were that simple! Or is it? In 1994, an OECD report claimed that 'the current wave of technological change, if anything, has been mod-estly beneficial for jobs. The demand-boosting effects have more than offset the job-destroying ones.' They take the line that if economic growth is strong, if there are free markets in labour, goods and services, and if educa-tion and training are of high quality, then jobs will follow.

When will politicians and their lackeys ever learn that technology is the problem, not the solution? Today, productivity is delivered by a technology needing only a few machine minders. National economies are no longer able to grow themselves out of unemployment. Growth has been decoupled from employment; it is created from the talent of a few knowledge workers, not from the labour of low-grade service and production workers. Neither does it come from arbitrary education programmes, nor from throwing capital investment at it. Growth is delivered by entrepreneurs, but only if they are given the incentives, and otherwise left alone to get on with business.

Critics of this elitist position claim that the reasoning is flawed. They say employment is not a 'zero-sum game', that the elitists have fallen foul of a well-known economic fallacy, 'the lump of labour'. They say the amount of work available is not fixed. Although fewer workers are used in a particular production sequence, the technology increases the rate of production, lowers costs and prices, and hence increases demand and real incomes. With innovation continually delivering novel goods to the market, a virtuous circle of job creation is initiated. That argument may have been valid under the factory metaphor of production; however nowadays, not only is there a reduction in demand for labour, but also there is an increased supply from the developing countries. Furthermore, the fabrication of the new products themselves needs far fewer workers, and consequently the gearing of job creation has to be far higher. All of which goes to show that this fallacy is no longer a fallacy.

More older people living longer

But for a fallacy, listen to the forecast of the US Bureau of Labor Statistics (*Economist*, 11 February 1995) that between 1992 and 2005, the fastest-growing occupation in the United States will be home health-care, tending the sick in their own beds. Across the developed world, the proportion of elderly people in the population is growing. The Bureau sees the elderly as customers for in-person service work, not only in health-care, but also in home help, tourism and financial services. CNN even airs advertisements from financial advisers recommending that it is best to 'die broke'. Good news? Not if you are one of the many 'youngsters' depending on granny leaving you a bequest in her will. Forget the new car or deposit on a house. By the time she dies, the cupboard will have been stripped bare by the carers. Governments too will see a shortfall in their revenues from death duties. If this sounds callous and trivial, think again. The situation is changing the distribution of wealth across society. Feedback effects are polarizing wealth and will have profoundly nega-tive effects on taxation, on purchasing habits, on the housing market and other markets for consumer goods.

However, for most of the elderly in the population this image of a 'crin-kly'-led boom for service industries is total fantasy. Many of the elderly are living on the edge of poverty, and they are getting poorer by the day as their meagre savings drip, drip, drip away. The economists who make statements about a booming health care industry have never felt the shame, guilt and sense of failure of being unable to pay for their own funeral. And if the elderly can't afford to die, how can they pay to live? They become dependants, a drain on wage earners, either directly within the family or indirectly from government. The number of elderly poor swamps the number of rich. Rather than being a source of jobs, the elderly could be creating a sink for employ-ment. And it is the taxpayer who will pay for those who can't afford to be ill. This was clear to the ordinary US voter and to their representatives, when they rejected Hillary Clinton's health-care schemes.

Jeremy Rifkin says that rich societies don't actually need workers: 'There will be a small elite running American corporations and the rest of the work-ers will be left to do unmeaningful work as a result of computerization and automation.' So if there are no jobs in the private sector, then perhaps we can rely on the old standby of job creation, the public sector. The whole Soviet bloc has travelled this path to extinction in the failed communist experi-ment. The public sector doesn't create real jobs, but non-jobs; and there are more than enough non-jobs ('pensions in waiting') in that sector already. Even the rhetoric of government, if not their actions, has already recognized this fact. But the inevitable downturn in the tax 'take' means that jobs in the Civil Service must be badly hit in the coming decade.

Nevertheless, after all his wailing and gnashing of teeth, Jeremy Rifkin in *The End of Work* claims to have come up with an answer – work in the third sector: volunteerism. The unemployed volunteer will work for the good of the community, and it will all be paid for from value-added taxes and tax-deductible donations. Battalions of able-bodied unemployed will rush to care for the elderly, work on enviromental tasks, and in hospitals. Dream on, Jeremy!

Where the new jobs are

Where are new jobs being created today? *Business Week* calculated that in 1993 in the United States the entertainment and recreation industry created more than 200,000 jobs, that is 12 per cent of all new employment that year (Mandel, Landler and Grover, 14 March 1994). Furthermore the industry expects to create 500,000 more in the next decade. It is perhaps indicative of the uncertainty of our times that gambling is the fastest growing part of the entertainment and recreation sector. This does not bode well, for it all smacks of 'bread and circuses', the precursor to the decline and fall.

The jobs in this sector are low paid, and offer few or no prospects: cocktail waitresses, car parking attendants and valets, doormen. Inexorably, entertainment is increasing its share of US consumer spending. In 1993, Americans spent $340 billion on this sector, against $270 billion on primary and secondary education, both private and public. This should be compared to 1980 when the figures were roughly equal (Landler, 14 March 1994). This discrepancy is not because the cost of higher education is cheap: US parents are dismayed by skyrocketing tuition fees for their children, currently running at $120,000 plus for a four-year university course. Consequently, many social critics have become alarmed at what they see as a corresponding decline in personal savings. In 1980 Americans saved nearly 8 per cent of their disposable income; in 1993 this figure was down to 4 per cent.

Most of the new jobs created in the entertainment and service sector tend to pay low salaries. Many are part-time, and are open only to younger age groups. For many youngsters, their first taste of employment is behind the counter of McDonald's or Planet Hollywood, hardly the first rung on the ladder of career development. But worse, there are only so many 'service industry' Mac-jobs that a country can support, before inevitably it must enter a tailspin of decline. The town of the future simply cannot be a mixture of casinos and burger bars. If no one is working and hence earning, who will pay to be entertained? No community can survive 'by taking in its own washing'.

Furthermore, it would be a mistake to think of gambling and entertainment as being fixed in space. Soon many of the jobs created in towns like Las Vegas and Atlantic City will evaporate. For these towns will find they have serious competition from casinos in cyberspace. In fact the shrewdest casino owners, who have no loyalty to towns like Vegas, are already investigating electronic gambling. A number of casinos across the United States are electronically linked into a chain of immediately identifiable 'one-armed bandits' offering million-dollar jackpots. The first giant steps toward global gambling in cyberspace have already been taken, not only by casino owners, but also by countries that run weekly national lotteries. Prize draws are shown nationwide on terrestrial television channels. These programmes are then followed up by satellite channels broadcasting the results to ticket-holders who are spread across continents.

On 19 November 1994, and coming fairly late on to the scene, Britain launched its national lottery. It was an instant success. Camelot, the commercial company that won a seven-year contract to run the lottery, expected to reach a maximum annual turnover of around £4 billion within four years. But within weeks of the launch Britons were spending £160 million each week: twice the expected weekly maximum. Many critics of the lottery insist that prizes should be limited, that even more money should go to good causes. Some sermonizing critics talk about dividing the prize money into more (hence smaller) prizes. They are totally out of touch. As unemployment rises, enormous prizes are what will attract the punters: bigger prizes – more punters. If proof of this were needed, just look at the many small-prize charity lotteries now going out of business, or observe that in any 'rollover' week, following a draw when no one has won the £10 million plus jackpot, sales of tickets increase substantially. What is more, the poor spend vastly more of their disposable income on gambling than do the well off.

But what happens when the first lottery launches into cyberspace via interactive television, and becomes truly global, with astronomical prizes? The whole economic base of the lottery industry will change. Bigger prizes of the international lotteries will take money away from conventional betting outlets. It will exist outside national jurisdictions, the natural successor to the Irish Hospitals' sweepstake, which itself used radio (my first exposure to it was in my teens through Radio Luxemburg, a primitive form of cyberspace) to reach an international clientele. The Irish are still at it. In the first half of 1999, bookmakers in Ireland were allowed to charge a mere 5 per cent tax on off-course betting, whereas the tax is 9 per cent in Britain. A significant amount of British betting could be transferred to Ireland and could cost the British Exchequer as much as £75 million annually in lost revenue. Jobs in betting shops will disappear. William Hill, the British bookmakers, are worried that since 70 per cent of their turnover comes from just 14 per cent of their clients, these high-rollers may take their bets offshore. William Hill know what they are talking about, for their non-British clients can already bet with their Isle of Man office and pay a mere 0.3 per cent tax (Mackenzie, 6 January 1999).

Lotteries have become a major job creation scheme in the retail trade, but these jobs will go when tickets are bought from voice-operated automatic vendors. What happens when lottery tickets are purchased from the Net? Governments too will lose their cut. The prizes, costs and profit will scoop up 100 per cent between them. Gamblers of the underclass will unite in support of their lottery; this may be the only hope that the jobless have of achieving the good life. At that stage there can be no self-delusion. Society will have finally polarized into winners and losers.

But gambling is still just gambling. Cyberspace is merely the mechanism for the receipt of validated tickets and the announcement of winning numbers. The high-tech medium has only changed the scale of the operation;

gambling itself is still very much down to earth. The data contained in the tickets and winning numbers are the same as they always have been. They are the types of cypher that anyone can relate to, only now they are floating around cyberspace. The cyphers may travel in cyberspace, but their meaning hasn't changed for millennia. I am labouring the point to dispel some fanciful notions of the job creation potential of cyberspace or 'cypherspace' as I prefer to call it. Jobs revolve around a meaningful application of these cyphers, and that meaning does not exist in some mystical dimension, but rather within human society. A globally networked version of the British national lottery or of Las Vegas is a much more realistic scenario for popular use of cyberspace, and hence for job creation and destruction, than is surfing the Internet for vacuous data and fatuous information. There are already 50 online casinos run from Caribbean islands, free from restrictive regulations, where punters can gamble 24 hours a day, 7 days a week. A conservative estimate of their earnings is $200 million annually (*Economist*, 13 December 1997). Although this is small beer compared with the $600 billion people in the United States spend on gambling each year, the only way is up.

Cyberspace as one big electronic Las Vegas is a real possibility, because the payment structures are synchronized with the delivery channels, provided of course that the system is secure and that the punters trust the veracity of the organizers. However, other much-hyped areas such as electronic publishing, distance learning, or the electronic theme park, which are often portrayed as self-evident future applications in cyberspace, are far more problematical. Jobs in cyberspace depend on the application of cyphers in such a way that they add value to individuals and organizations. The commercial viability of a particular application depends on the ease with which payment for the delivered cyphers can be collected, and of course on that payment structure not being easily or excessively circumvented. The relative ease with which book material, software and games are copied means that piracy is endemic. In the case of the lottery, fraud is the only problem, and that is far more specific and easier to deal with. Paying to be in a database is much easier to police than paying for what is in a database.

As always, the seedier side of society takes commercial advantage of new technologies. 'Where there's muck, there's brass.' Because of general availability of VHS video technology, in 1996 people in the United States spent more than $8 billion on pornography (Sharkey, 22 November 1997), a sum larger than Hollywood's domestic box-office takings, and larger than the revenues from rock and country music combined. Thirty years ago, before every household had a video player, the sum was a mere $8 million: a thousandfold increase! Reputable video outlets, with an image to maintain, don't stock 'porno' material, and so this has created a niche market for 'Mom and Pop' shops, which now make a third of their income from such films. For them it makes the difference between bankruptcy and keeping open and serving the local community with normal retail goods. Pornography then is facilitating a social service, and it is all semi-legal, which means the state is taking a cut. But this is a transitional phase. There will be no such social benefits when the Internet is the preferred channel of delivery.

Such is the changing nature of employment that will trigger the end of the Industrial Age. The factory metaphor, a product of the old order, which was used to control production, has no place in the future. The natures of work, the worker and the workplace, which were a direct consequence of factory thinking, have changed. Some elements of these natures are mutating. Others are degenerating, and that degeneracy is all around. These are the **effect** of the break-up of the underlying order, **not the cause** of it. They are the consequence of old power structures become impotent in new economic conditions. Yet the old barbarians in our society believe that its social, political and economic institutions, large or small, are permanent, and that these institutions can impose control and hence dictate a continuing order.

One of today's universal truths goes like this: 'The masses are the market. If we don't pay the mass of workers and the unemployed, who will buy the goods? When goods go unsold, then the markets will collapse. Hence we must pay the workers and the unemployed at a reasonable level.' QED. This particular universal truth cannot possibly be universal. It could not even have been formulated 300 years ago, because it wouldn't have made sense. Within the social reality of those times the way we use the terms 'market' and 'work' today would have made no sense at all. No doubt champions of the universal truths from three centuries ago were disproving (and disapproving of) the first faltering steps toward the idea that workers should be paid well so as to maintain the market. This truth is merely the observation of a transitory **effect** that, with some self-deluding mental gymnastics is turned into the **cause** of that regularity.

Inverting cause and effect in this way shows a complete misunderstanding of the human condition. Control doesn't create order, quite the contrary. Order must be there first, and this order tolerates control. Order will have come about in the complexity of human actions, but not necessarily from human intent. Only by the concession of order does the consequent control impose structure and stability. All order is transitory regularity. Order allows controls to work, and then order fails. Consequently the certainty of control and structure collapses.

The collapse in the present stable nature of production and markets will be reflected in the breakdown of the mechanisms that fund the political stability of the Machine Age, taking with it all forms of governance developed in that age, as we will see in the next two chapters.

6

Whom do we work for? And what is work anyway?

As we enter the Information Age, we have to accept that the idea of the job, born with the Machine Age, is changing beyond all recognition. Companies have realized that they can no longer afford to carry a large inventory of 'people product' of varying value and quality. But it doesn't end there. Not only has the nature of work changed, so has the 'Nature of the Firm' (Coase, 1991). In the 1937 article of that name, Ronald Coase, the 1991 Nobel laureate for economics, asked the question: 'Why do firms [as we understand them] exist at all?' Why should entrepreneurs and workers choose to group together in a firm, rather than buy or sell services on the open market? Coase's conclusion, still just as valid today, is that the deciding factor is transaction costs, that is the costs incurred by buyers and sellers in the development of their commercial contracts. However, it must be added that Coase's original work did use the term 'transaction cost' in a far more non-specific way than it is used today. He claimed that companies, in fact all economic institutions, are formed when it is cheaper for such units to organize themselves in groups, rather than to buy and sell contracts from the marketplace. But, and it is a big but, firms will stop growing at that point where the goods and services they need can be purchased more cheaply on the open market.

The end of yesterday's firm

It is this latter statement that is dynamite for the Information Age, because it explains much of the turmoil described in this book. For now 'spot markets' are forming in cyberspace. Information technology, together with international travel and transport, have changed fundamentally the nature of transactions, hence the costs of transacting business, and hence the 'nature of the firm'. Even if we believe that other explicit costs, such as production, travel, research and development, and transition should be factored into the equation of the firm, new technology has altered these costs similarly, and so the consequences are still the same. Almost unnoticed, these forces have been pulling away at the very foundations of yesterday's firm. It has been happening for decades. Quietly, surreptitiously, the way we used to do business has been totally undermined. No one is immune to the pressures. The dominant monolithic firm, the juggernaut of the factory metaphor, which won the battles of natural selection during the Machine Age, is finding itself totally outmanoeuvred by the new organizational forms such as outsourcing and teleworking that are emerging in the Information Age. Worse, the familiar hierarchical company is facing meltdown.

The transnational company is a clear demonstration of how tomorrow's firm has decentralized and distributed itself around the globe: of how it has become the 'virtual enterprise' – project-based and networked around global information systems. Its control procedures are totally different, as are the internal and external costs it incurs. Is it even organized in the sense that we understand of firms today? Whatever the answers to these questions, the coefficients in Coase's equilibrium formulae will have to change. The structure of yesterday's company answered the question 'What is a viable company?' against the judgements of the transaction costs from the Machine Age. But the answers delivered in the Information Age will be radically different from those from the age of machines.

It is clear from Coase's theory that the large number of job losses reported across the Western world is not the result of some temporary downturn in the economic cycle, but is instead the result of structural change (a new order?). Telecommuting is the first step of workers leaving the cities for cyberspace. Telecommunications and the quick and safe international delivery of goods, not to mention the instantaneous 'distance no object' electronic delivery of 'information products', imply that the transaction costs of production in the global marketplace have become substantially lower. Arguably the costs have dropped to a point where now a billion new workers have entered the global job market.

The easy availability of this new pool of labour is sending shock waves through Western workforces. The costs of overcoming time and space no longer buffer the impact of this vast resource of cheap labour. Why should the world's unemployed and sub-employed all live in developing countries? The West must now bear its share. It is no good waiting for the upturn when new service work will be created. For fundamental changes in the natures of work and the firm are taking place. The changes are as profound as when agricultural workers left the land for the cities, and the whole fabric of society mutated.

Nation–states have to be part of the global economy in their own national interests, but as a consequence they are now incapable of fending off foreign incursions. The impending cancer of mass unemployment is likely soon to afflict every nation state. That having been said, it must also be recognized that some transaction costs are actually going up, as with the need to impose standards that satisfy widely differing markets. Also, the vastly increased requirement for security, in what are now a firm's highly decentralized and hence vulnerable business units, has had the effect of raising transaction costs. Whether the costs are going up or down, the nature of the firm must change.

The real power of Coase's work is that it is not just about firms, but rather all types of social groupings that exist in an economic environment arbitrated by costs. That is why I happily use the words 'firm', 'group' or 'institution' in their widest senses, to include any self-organizing social grouping: club, company, enterprise, community, country. I mean a particular society or the society at large. Peel away the layers and underneath an institution is just a community. Coase is clear that the nation–state too is an economic institution, a national firm that will also have to be judged against changing circumstances. So his theories not only describe the rise and fall of corporations, but also explain the economic well-being or otherwise of states. Implicit in the theory was a warning to governments in the form of a prediction, lately proved all too true, that the high transaction costs of centrally planned state economies, as in communist countries, must inevitably lead to collapse. For us in the West it should be a sobering thought that it is only a very short step to predicting the collapse of social democratic 'nanny states', who feel that they too must interfere in all aspects of every individual's life and every company's operations.

Why the company is dead

The description given above of Coase's highly sophisticated theory is obviously vastly oversimplified. I do this to place the theory into a wider context, and thereby to indicate some of its shortcomings, shortcomings that do not detract in any way from its importance as a first approximation to an explanation for why firms exist, why they thrive and why they die. Most importantly Coase shows why the idea of a company, at least in the form that we find so comfortable today, has passed its sell-by date. The concept of transaction costs is itself complicated by the fact that value is added to the company by the synergy of social interaction. However, social interaction isn't all beneficial. There is the downside of organizational costs that arise out of the increased complexity and the societal equivalents of friction, heat-loss and entropy. Differential economies of scale and scope, and other aspects of the cost of production must also be costed into the total. What is more, production costs are not the same between firms, or between countries, whatever the economists may say about their eventual convergence. These cost differentials too must be added into the economic equations that arbitrate on the size and the survival of institutions.

Douglass North, the economics Nobel laureate of 1993, argued that transaction costs can never be zero; there are always latent costs. There can never be 'perfect information' about markets, and the whole issue is complicated by biases introduced by institutions, and by cultural, religious and other social factors. The social dimension too needs to be understood, since the homeostatic self-reinforcing properties and risk aversion rituals of social networks are crucial to prosperity. The fact is that the firm does not exist solely in the one-dimensional universe of economic viability. Explanations must look beyond commercial, fiscal and monetary policies. That having been said, it is well to remember that competition is a harsh taskmaster, and any company or country that strays too far from the tough discipline of the economic dimension will be rapidly and severely punished.

Fundamental to Coase's theory is the idea that property rights rather than goods are being traded. What is at issue is how these rights, and the transaction of property rights, are costed and protected, and how conflicts over such resources can be resolved. North says that 'institutions structure human interaction so we know how to deal with each other. They define the way markets work, whether a technology is worthwhile developing. Understand that structure and we'll understand the constraints we impose on ourselves.' He too emphasizes the need to develop stable economic institutions, and stresses the importance of property rights, rules and laws, and a judicial system, so that individual entrepreneurs can be helped to help themselves.

Later in this chapter we will see another totally separate economic theory that reaches the self-same conclusions. Both theories agree that in the Information Age the continuous innovation of the knowledge worker is the key to success. But there are clever people everywhere, so why is prosperity so unevenly distributed between countries? Why, if two countries have the same economic endowment, technology and skills, do their productivities differ? The way institutions behave in different societies is what separates success from failure – how a society sets about ruling itself, the type of rules it makes and the way it treats the creators of wealth.

Even in the very superficial description given here, it is clear that Coase's theory does throw a clear light on the nature of institutions. However, he does have his critics, who claim that his point of breakdown for the firm is too rigid. Robert Puttnam (1994) and Douglass North (1990) have been prominent in arguing that market mechanisms in themselves cannot define the break point between cohesion and collapse. For each economic entity is an investment mix of social and financial capital, a weave of mutually agreed formal and informal contracts and rituals. Social as well as economic rewards come from collaboration and co-operation, and group members value them both. The balance sheet is not a simple question of financial profit and loss. As long as there are sufficient profits in the wider firm, and someone is willing to cross-subsidize and pay the difference for the sake of the institution, then excess transaction costs can be written off. But there must be sufficient profits to pay for it. And there's the rub. Inefficient companies and countries are rapidly using up their fat stocks of goodwill.

In the past, the reality was that some group members were happy to pay more (or receive less), just to be part of a group. However, the questions being asked today are 'How much more or less?' and 'For how much longer?' Yet there is a perceived value of being part of a firm, part of an institution. The consequent formalized trust and mutual interest that membership of a group implies, the very glue that holds a group together, actually have the effect of reducing internal costs. However, that trust cannot be created without a strong civic sense of society and the existence of clusters of social networks. When participants trust one another, costly checks and balances are not needed. Individual members are willing to lower their expectations (their price), all of which increases the efficient use of resources. Of course, the opposite is true for degenerate groupings. In Western societies for example, structural unemployment, particularly among uneducated young males who are being thrown on to the margins of society, is highly disruptive, and thus increases security and other costs. Society becomes less pleasant, less safe, and those who foot the bill feel less inclined to continue doing so.

Trust in a society is always very finely balanced, and it can so easily be upset. History offers numerous examples of governments destroying trust in the economic underpinnings of the state. Consider the many examples of medieval kings who 'clipped' the edges from their gold coinage. 'Whenever disorganization of the coinage had advanced so far that the presence of a stamp on a piece of metal was no longer any help in determining its actual content, commerce ceased entirely to rely on the official monetary system and created its own system of measuring precious metals' (von Mises, 1981).

Another fact of life is that formal and impersonal (bureaucratic) arrangements always involve greater transaction costs than the informal and personal. For informality is a statement of trust within a group; formality is a statement of control. The present craze of auditing everything that moves is in effect a statement of lack of trust, which must raise costs. The Western management culture does not help either; excessive management is not the answer. By imposing restrictions and controls, organizations are restricting and reducing their internal variety, the very variety necessary to cope with an ever-changing environment. The trick is to have an organization with enough internal trust so that it can be left to be self-organizing in face of external threats and opportunities.

Costs of downsizing

Institutions should be very careful when arbitrarily downsizing and delayering, for this too reduces variety, as some companies have found to their cost. Coase's theory does give us a pointer to right-sizing of a company, or even a society. A right-sized institution is one that minimizes the levels of latent internal and external costs, in both the short and long terms. Today's mania for increasing productivity levels, by performing major surgery on what is seen as costly social (and hence unproductive) layers, fails to take into account the importance of some of these layers in creativity and stable organic growth. The rash of outsourcing being undertaken by Western companies will certainly increase social costs. Rash cuts may have industrial and financial short-term benefits, but in the long run they undermine the morale of the knowledge worker who is essential for longer-term economic well-being. The problem then ripples out. The structural erosion of trust relationships in companies is wearing away civic trust in the wider society. The result of this disturbing feedback is a decline in social capital throughout many an economy, in both firm and wider society alike.

The economic performance of an institution depends on a balance between social capital and investment in both physical infrastructure and individual intellectual capital, considered against an ever-changing background of economic forces. This balance does not depend on some homogeneous labour force that acts as a source of physical power. Mark Casson (1998) argues that the mutuality of interests of the workforce, suppliers and financiers (or the citizens, or whatever collective noun is used for the institutional members) is just as important, as is their trust in the integrity of these relationships. This is particularly true with information goods, where assets lie in human talent that has the inconvenient habit of walking away from conditions it dislikes. Michael Porter (1998) goes further and claims that social clusters within networks of firms create the self-generating feedback of growth: 'hot-spots'. Neither natural nor human resources in themselves can explain the wealth of rich countries, but rather their internal arrangements, their institutions, their policies and their history.

Trust

In the to-date successful West, a lack of trust is endemic in commercial activities. It has been institutionalized in the legal system, a system that is expanding to a point where the transaction costs it imposes are pushing companies and countries to the edge. Peter Drucker has been warning the United States about this for decades. The problem has even entered their popular humour: 'What do you call a thousand lawyers at the bottom of the ocean? A good start!' Joining the swell are the auditing and financial services businesses that claim to deliver mechanistic instruments that mitigate the risk. But only talented individuals can deal with risk. The government itself adds to the costs with excessive regulation in the form of bureaucracies of enormous complexity and its so-called 'social contracts' such as welfare provision. The result is an ever-increasing burden on social capital in the wealthier sections of society. The consequential variability of transaction costs has now made the situation highly unstable.

In today's economic climate not all the institutions involved are necessarily beneficial to society, whatever their historical benefits. For example, cultures revolving around the inward-looking nuclear family tend to stand apart from society, fail to develop civic responsibility, and in general these tend to be less successful. Neither can rampant individualism be the answer in the long term. As always individuals must group together if they are to be effective economically.

The roots of social capital are a historical sense of civic trust. By implication any society without the historical underpinning for social capital will lose. Alien institutions cannot just be imposed on societies; they must fit with the indigenous culture. This is why so many development projects in the Third World fail so abysmally. There are always tensions that, if the culture doesn't have the mechanisms to dissipate the stress, will undermine everything. By the same token, an individual cannot expect just to fit in any-where. It requires host institutions to be welcoming – the individual must be wanted.

History matters; institutions matter – but not in any nostalgic sense. Puttnam and colleagues (1994) claim that societies with a long tradition of civic involvement, rich in social capital, with dense networks of social and financial institutions, are the ones that exploit opportunities best. He includes trades unions in this; however, this could be his sentimentality and his ideology talking. His theories may be valid in themselves, but the devil is in the detail. It is easy for ideological positions to slide in under the wire, and a perfectly valid theory can become polluted by wishful thinking. A tradition of civic involvement does not mean that institutions are set in concrete. With time the arbiters of success undergo change, and hence so do the nature and effectiveness of tradition. Stressing the merits of 'the group' is not to stress the merits of all of today's particular subgroups. Institutions in higher education are a case in point. No one would deny its essential place in the Information Age. However, I find myself forced to agree with the tidal wave of complaints from business indicating that the university as presently insti-tuted is just not 'delivering the goods'. Every group has a fixed reference point in time. For many, and I include the modern university in this, their sell-by date has well and truly passed.

The same can be said for the nation–state, which is no longer seen neces-sarily as a good thing. The cohesive forces that were once so attractive to citi-zens may well have degenerated to an arbitrary and counterproductive thuggery. Italy is a classic case. For around a century two different communi-ties have been tied together in one state, but they are now sliding inexorably apart. The north has a tradition of civic pride, often based around the city communities like Milan, Venice and Genoa, embryonic 'smart cities' that deliver a virtuous circle of success. This is evident in the dynamism of the small and medium-sized enterprises thriving there on trust and interco-operation in the application of new technology to business. Today in the north there is a groundswell of resentment against the 'parasitic south' (disparagingly called North Africa), an area with little sense of civic pride. Rather, the south has a culture steeped in an excess of trust, but an incestu-ous trust centred totally around the clan. This is a culture where business is often conducted on the basis of family ties at the expense of efficiency, a throwback culture of high transaction costs, corruption and greed. This cor-ruption has infected the north (or so they claim) to the detriment of its insti-tutions. Whether true or not, the rot has set in.

New institutions

New times require new groups, new institutions. The task of new institutions is to rebuild trust and social capital on a solid base. This means rejecting all calls for the imposition of social control and coercion. The Nobel academy oration for Douglass North recognized that he 'maintains that new institutions arise when groups in society see a possibility of availing themselves of profits that are impossible to realize under prevailing institutional conditions'. Many of today's institutions are not structured in a way that avail themselves of the profits from the new global economy. New barbarians are gathering, searching out new opportunities, preparing for meltdown. The new rootlessness of economic mercenaries in aggressive market economies, mercenaries who are looking out for welcoming institutions that are in tune with their own aspirations, has the power to destabilize the wealth of any unsupportive community. The new barbarians are all set to create new institutions and communities, or to recast old ones. Successful communities are those that are sociable, secure, attractive and welcoming to the mobile rich, and at the same time economically viable. However, very few of today's nation–states will be able to throw off the shackles of 20th-century populism and square this particular circle.

The economic forces that drive growth are the same as they ever were. Sixty years ago Joseph Schumpeter (1991) explained growth in terms of a rush of technological innovation unleashing competition between firms, thereby creating an upsurge in investment and new industries. Neo-classical economic theory would have us believe that the growth of an economy depends on the relationship between capital and labour, which can be explained mathematically by a so-called 'production function'. However, these two inputs have failed to explain satisfactorily the variations in output, and so economists have added a third parameter, technical progress. In his popular explanations of this situation, Patrick Minford describes two schools of thought on such progress (6 September 1993). The first sees technical progress as fairly stable, as was labour, leaving the investment and accumulation of capital as the means of controlling growth. The second, 'New Growth Theory', sees wide variations in technical progress, mirroring wide variations in human skills and knowledge. The joy of the latter theory is that it proposes 'increasing returns' – now winners can win even more. Not that it denies the law of 'diminishing returns', where income from increased production and sales rises more slowly than costs. Both phenomena coexist and are complementary. Diminishing returns may dominate a rational marketplace of stable products, but in the white heat of technological innovation such 'fundamental laws' throw little light on the irrational behaviour in an economy where the sky's the limit. In this new world, firms do not merely react to market signals and accept their judgements. New barbarians set their own prices; they broker and define their own value.

Paul Romer considers such technical progress as two separate issues: human capital (an educated and skilled workforce) and ideas (their ownership and development potential). The key to growth is the availability of knowledge workers who can profit from a hoard of old ideas and the abundance of new ones, thereby accelerating the acquisition of new knowledge workers and ideas. Suddenly physical labour and intellect are no longer treated under one heading. No longer are individuals seen as standardized units. Suddenly talent, entrepreneurship and innovation, the great dividers of humanity, are accepted as diviners of economic success. Such talents are in short supply, and hence are in great demand. Egalitarianism goes out the window in this 'dog eat dog' world. Growth is no longer dependent on physical capital and labour. The principal source of future wealth is the quality of technological knowledge available in a society together with the way that knowledge is growing. 'Endogenous growth' (growth from within) is the buzz phrase that even blind-sided politicians are now using.

The 'great man' reborn

Suddenly the populist ideologies of the 20th century are unravelling. Individualistic and elitist interpretations can again be spoken in public without embarrassment. The days are over when 'the lower species ("herd", "mass", "society") unlearns modesty and blows up its needs into cosmic and metaphysical values' (Nietzsche). These herd values have come down to earth with a bump. Now the 'Great Man' theory of history, discredited and defamed (but not disproved) for much of the 20th century by the ideologies of the self important 'common man', is being revisited. The 'new barbarian' is reborn. Tolstoy was a great man among the discreditors of the 'great man', saying that battles are won by corporals and sergeants, not generals. He may well have been right, but this doesn't disprove the theory. It only showed that his society had identified the wrong great men. Although that having been said, the idea that Ghengis Khan, Napoleon, Bolivar, Hitler, Churchill, Gandhi, Stalin, Kennedy, Chairman Mao, Mandela and so many other greats played secondary roles in history is a laughable proposition.

Implications of the 'great man' theory spill over into the world of business, and also economics. The economy can no longer be treated as a black box in which a production function sucks in inputs, chews them up in a complex series of throughputs, and then spits out its deterministic outputs. There is no mathematical silver bullet that will destroy economic evils. That silver-black box is far too linear a view, too independent of time. The output of an economy must feed back as inputs, and in certain special and very unpredictable cases, this explodes on to the scene as economic growth. It shouldn't be necessary to say that the actions of a few leading economic generals (the Bill Gateses and Rupert Murdochs of this world) can lead to a cumulative feedback sequence that has enormous growth implications. But neither should we forget the small-time innovators, the unknown sergeants of the economy (Bill Gates's rank just two decades ago). Their existence, as unknown inputs before the event, in time totally distorts the economy after the event. What event? The innovation!

Innovation is about leaders who are simply the best. The mediocre do not lead innovation. They follow it. Nor does capital investment by itself create growth. It is the innovators who create jobs and generate wealth. An arbitrary investment in training the workforce, or investment in an educational infrastructure and capital equipment, can all lead to waste like any other form of investment. Politicians need to realize that without an investment in knowledge workers countries will fall into a vicious circle of decline. Innovation does not happen simply because of scientific discovery and technological research. These deliver mere possibilities. Knowledge cannot be banked like capital or stored like a commodity, to be used anywhere. There are no plans for innovation, only the initiation of the process of discovery. Innovation requires an economic stimulus or catalyst. It happens when science and technology are applied as inventions in a dynamic self-generating economic hot-spot of innovation, investment and profit. Innovative firms cluster in hot-spots, the very concentration acting as a magnet for established innovators and a spur for new enterprise: witness the development of Silicon Valley, Singapore or Dubai.

Spectacular growth comes from these self-perpetuating hot-spots that thrive on their own energy. This energy drives a rapid, almost uncontrolled diffusion of technological techniques and knowledge. The hot-spot itself fuels the engine of endogenous growth by delivering innovation, but only within a network of trust relationships, where only invited talent is allowed to join in the institutional environment that both mobilizes the intellectually gifted, and promotes and finances entrepreneurial activity by delivering the right incentives. In hot-spots, companies will hire start-up companies, trusting in their own judgement of the staff in those new firms. Companies in 'cold-spots' look to trade with firms bearing an 'established 1800' label – hardly the environment for innovation. Suddenly we return to Douglass North's ideas and the importance of the right institutional structures and value systems. Issues of trade reform and intellectual property rights, of trust and judgement, and of cultural differences, all go to explain why some areas seem to have no problem in creating hot-spots, while others are doomed to failure.

It bears repeating: history matters; institutions matter – but not nostalgia toward the history of any particular institution. Historical inertia prescribes losers as well as winners in tomorrow's world. When it comes to our understanding of the winners and losers in the Information Age, and of the comparative advantages of certain cultures, analyses of institutional and historical trends in the economy are possibly as important as mathematical and economic theories, if not more so. However, the genealogy of a particular institution, and reverence for a list of past glories, count for little. What is important is how that history is expressed in the way society does business today.

If the history of a company, or a country, sends out the wrong signals, then it needs a new communal contract. New times need a new company – the virtual enterprise. New times need a new community – the 'smart city' perhaps, a reinvention of the medieval city–state? We shall see.

Part III

Assault on the status quo

7

Limits to taxation?

Let me tell you how it will be
There's one for you nineteen for me
Should 5 per cent appear too small
Be thankful I don't take it all
'Cos I'm the taxman. Yeah I'm the taxman.

(from *Taxman* by the Beatles)

At a time when their skills are in increasing demand by global companies, knowledge workers feel more and more undervalued and betrayed by their governments. The new elite is tired of being a target of envy. Their loyalty and their social capital are all but used up. Now that exile no longer holds any terrors, it was inevitable that predatory global networks would drive loyalty to the state into a steep decline among the swelling number of would-be 'economic mercenaries'. Loyalty to the 'self', and other lateral loyalties, will replace allegiance to the tribe. To the new barbarian knowledge worker, allegiance is no longer an accident of birth, but a contract, freely entered into as an individual on the basis of unashamed rational self-interest.

The new power struggle

Companies are becoming increasingly reliant on their symbolic-analysts, who are the creators and (they say) owners of intellectual equity. We are witnessing an intensifying power struggle between the new barbarian symbolic analysts and the owners of financial equity in companies clinging on to the past. This is likely to change fundamentally the very nature of capitalism itself. Ownership of the physical tools of production is no longer sufficient to drive growth in the Information Age. The means of production is now human talent and no longer capital investment, and that really terrifies stock markets. Withdrawing access to computers and telecommunications is just a momentary inconvenience to the knowledge worker. Equipment costs are quite low, and other employers will be lining up to hire the very best people, ready and willing to use the latest technology as bait.

The coming battle is likely to be at least as significant as that between landowners and industrialists in the early part of the 19th century, which was formative of today's capitalism. The turning point of that particular battle came in 1846 in Britain with the Repeal of the Corn Laws. The Corn Laws were import tariffs introduced in 1804 to protect British corn growers from cheap foreign imports. Industrialists and the middle classes had to pay higher wages so that their workers could afford to buy bread. They were in effect subsidizing the landowners. The turmoil caused by the repeal of the Corn Laws split the Tory Party of the day, and it took a generation to heal the wounds. Will today's political parties destroy themselves in their futile attempts at subsidizing the status quo (that is overpaying the service and production workers at the expense of the knowledge worker)?

Today it is the knowledge worker whose underpriced talent is subsidizing the capitalists, and whose taxes are supporting the non-productive masses. Will progressive income tax be seen as today's symbolic injustice that is equivalent to the Corn Laws? Income tax actually came along quite late in the day, and perhaps it too has passed its sell-by date. There was an income tax in the United States during the American Civil War. Another was imposed in 1894 but the Supreme Court declared it unconstitutional. It only became a permanent feature in 1913 with the ratification of the Sixteenth Amendment to the Constitution. Even then, prior to the Second World War, this tax was a minor contributor to the overall tax take. The British knowledge worker has been haunted by the tax since that black day, 3 December 1798, when Pitt the Younger introduced it to pay for the Napoleonic Wars. The tax was repealed in 1816, one year after the Battle of Waterloo, but in 1842 Sir Robert Peel brought the tax back as a temporary measure, and it has remained ever since. The Inland Revenue even had the gall to set up an exhibition so that their 'customers' could join them in celebrating two centuries of tax collection! Customers have a choice; taxpayers don't.

With the politicians sidelined, the real battle for the new order has already started, between the old barbarian owners of financial capital and the new barbarian knowledge workers. The old financial order – shareholders and pension funds – is bracing itself for the coming showdown with the owners of intellectual and talent capital. 'Investor power' forced Maurice Saatchi out of the advertising company he founded because of poor stock-market results. But that particular new barbarian left the original Saatchi & Saatchi to form a new company, taking with him a number of key symbolic-analysts and some major clients. The low share price consequently dropped even lower (Kane and Oldfield, 15 January 1995) – not at all what the power-crazed but increasingly powerless investors expected.

The star system

In this battle for the control of a company we may be seeing the way forward to a stable compromise between capital and highly skilled individuals. It is possible that the 'star system', so prevalent in the sport, entertainment and financial industries, will be the chosen viable model for paying employees. A few stars earn enormous sums of money, the middle is comfortably off, and a large rump of 'wannabes' work for low pay on a casual basis in the hope of making the big time. Andre Agassi was given a $200,000 appearance fee for the 1993 San Francisco ATP tournament, almost five times the prize money (Fran and Cook, 1995). Ronaldo was offered $180 million by Barcelona FC for an eight-year contract, to which Nike has added $75 million in sponsorship. Inter Milan then offered even more (Financial Times, 31 May 1997). Nike topped their Ronaldo deal with a $90 million sponsorship contract with golfer Tiger Woods (Nissé, 25 August 1999). The top 100 movie stars all earn more than $10 million per film: Leonardo DiCaprio asks $33 million per film, with the top women Jodie Foster and Julia Roberts trailing at numbers 40 and 41 respectively in the 1998 earnings list on a mere $24.5 million per film (Herald Sun, 7 July 1998). George Lucas and his company Lucasfilm received advance licensing fees of more than $3 billion from the marketing of Star Wars: The Phantom Menace before the film even opened (Hoover's Company Profiles, August 1999). The list goes on and on, and up and up.

In the United States, battles over salaries are ongoing between owners and the top players in baseball, American football, basketball and hockey.

However, when the disputes culminated in strikes by players, the outcome was not at all what either side expected. The sports sector gives us a strong indication of how evolutionary forces are at work across all business sectors. In baseball the owners tried to cap the salaries of top players, but after a strike and a court case the owners were forced to return to a free agency market. The strike had cost the sport an estimated $700 million overall loss in revenue. The poorer teams fell into severe financial difficulties and were forced to sell off their best players to remain solvent, entering a vicious circle where it is now impossible for them to attract and keep new top players. Short on talent, it is highly unlikely that they will ever again win the top prizes, thereby reducing even more their attraction and their income potential. Meanwhile a few rich teams have managed to ride out the storm and have entered a virtuous circle. These teams are now intent on picking up the best players at 'bargain basement' (but still enormous) prices, and so are even more likely to win the trophies. Consequently the rich teams will get richer, because better results deliver a greater share of TV coverage, and hence greater support, advertising, sponsorship, marketing spin-offs and ticket income. Soon only the few talent-rich, money-rich teams will be able to win premier competitions.

Ultimately the mutations caused in the chaos of feedback are stabilizing. The rich teams, and only they, will be able to pay the large salaries demanded by the best players. Rich teams will take the new barbarian position and realize that they should be happy to pay big salaries to the best players, because it creates a barrier to entry against the aspirations of poorer teams. It virtually guarantees the continued pre-eminence, at least in the medium term, of the 'big boys' in an increasingly polarized world.

A similar situation has arisen in Europe. As a result of the 'Bosman ruling', soccer clubs can no longer insist on a transfer fee when an out-of-contract professional player of a member state moves to another club (judgment of European Union Court of Justice on case C-415/93: Union Royale Belge des Sociétés de Football Association Asbl and Others v Jean-Marc Bosman and Others).

This ruling has changed fundamentally the movement of top soccer players between European clubs. Teams are now forced to sell on their top players to other rich clubs before the end of their contracts, to the fury of the fans, just so that they can recoup part of their investment outlay. The national league structure, typical across all of Europe for most of the 20th century, is now coming under enormous strain from the super-teams, which are looking toward an international super-league where their earning potential is substantially higher.

To stay on top, all companies, not just in entertainment and sport, will have to employ the best talent. They will have to pay for it, and they will have to look for it all over the globe. We have seen how investors in sports teams have already recognized this reality. They know they have no control over the situation. Over a 48-hour period in April 1995, as well-founded rumours were spreading that the soccer star Jürgen Klinsmann was to leave Tottenham Hotspur FC, the club's share price fell by around 5 per cent. The mere rumour of Michael Jordan coming out of retirement to rejoin the Chicago Bulls basketball team led to investors pouring money into the companies whose products Jordan endorses. Their market value increased by more than $1 billion (Mathur, Mathur and Rangan, 1 May 1997).

The music business too ($35 billion annually worldwide) is fighting the first skirmishes in this battle for power. The British pop singer George Michael took on the might of Sony in the High Court, accusing them of failing to market his work properly, and of giving him too small a share of royalties on his recordings. He lost the case and subsequently refused to release another record until he was freed from the 'professional slavery' of his contract. After three years of silence he started recording again when a combination of the Dreamworks and Virgin record companies paid off Sony with $40 million and agreed the very attractive royalty rate of 20 per cent for Michael, with a $10 million advance on two new albums (Lynn and Olins, 16 May 1995).

In May 1996 the German government was obliged to amend new tax laws under pressure from pop music fans, and because it was destroying the concert business in Germany (Kirschbaum, 23 May 1996). Michael Jackson among others cancelled plans to play in Germany; a general boycott by foreign artistes was on the cards. In January 1996 finance minister Theo Waigel had increased taxes on the gross takings from concerts from 15 per cent to 25 per cent, on top of other taxes – far higher than in other European countries. The compromise reached meant that foreign musicians have the alternative of offsetting their production costs by filing a German tax return. They are treated in the same way as German nationals from entertainment and sport who try to dodge taxes by setting up homes in Belgium or by channelling their earnings into overseas companies. Time will tell whether this limited climb-down will stop the threat. The example of the Rolling Stones refusing to play in Britain for tax reasons suggests that it won't.

Relatively few companies or countries have grasped the inevitability or the implications of the trend that knowledge workers no longer have to bend to the will of financial capital, or to pay for the schemes of politicians. One such scheme is the Common Agricultural Policy (CAP). Under the CAP, European taxpayers spend £4.5 billion annually subsidizing farmers to overproduce food that is then sold cheaply outside the EU, but not inside it (Purnell, 22 June 1998). In 1997 fresh fruit and vegetables from the glut, to a value of £213 million, were destroyed to prevent these same taxpayers buying the food they had already partly paid for in taxes, at lower market prices. So taxes are paid in order to create another tax! But of course the very same governments would make full use of the various forms of antitrust legislation to hit any company or individual who would dare to act in a similar way to manipulate markets.

Politicians really don't see the folly in their stance. In Britain in 1995, Cedric Brown, the then chief executive of British Gas, and senior executives from other large companies, were dragged in front of the House of Commons Select Committee on Employment, and had the indignity of having all their finances paraded in the name of 'the public good'. Jealous that Brown was earning 10 times their salary, they did not consider that perhaps Brown was worth 10 Members of Parliament (MPs)! They demanded that he justify his 'exorbitant' £475,000 plus perks. In July 1996 the same MPs voted themselves a 26 per cent pay rise (*Daily Mirror*, 12 July 1996). Brown was running a £13 billion company at a time when over half the FT-SE top 100 companies, many smaller than British Gas, were paying their senior directors annual salaries of more than half a million pounds (Marckus, 21 January 1995). Not for much longer will such men as Brown have to justify themselves to mere politicians. Such knowledge workers will finally be recognized as too important to the national economy and the corporate good.

Less tax for the elite?

What is more, the demands made by knowledge workers will be not only about high salaries. We are rapidly approaching a situation where, in order to attract the elite with their knowledge and money to enliven the economy, the elite group will be expected to pay less tax and not more! Examples are everywhere. Ireland already gives writers, artists and composers preferential tax deals on earnings from their creative work (Kelly, 6 August 1994). The great majority of governments are being forced to lower top tax rates in line with declining global levels. 'Top income tax rates fell an average of 16.5 per cent between 1975 and 1989'. 'The main producers and repositories of wealth – multinational companies – have increasingly been able to adjust their accounts and the prices of their internal international transactions so that their profits are declared in low tax countries, while they continue to operate in high tax ones' (Mulgan and Murray, 1993). US companies assembling computers in Scotland, where corporation tax was 33 per cent, had their sales and marketing arms in the Netherlands, where the tax was 3.5 per cent (D'Arcy, 20 November 1991). Not surprisingly they had transfer-pricing arrangements where products were sold to the Netherlands subsidiary at cost price! One survey found that more than a quarter of British-registered companies pay little or no corporation tax (Hugill, 9 April 1997). In the 1930s, US corporation tax made up a third of the tax take; now it makes up only 12 per cent. In the European Union the rate of tax on capital and self-employed labour fell from around 50 per cent in 1981 to 35 per cent in 1994, whereas the average tax on wages (including social-security contributions) rose from 35 per cent to 41 per cent (*Economist*, 31 May 1997). An Ernst & Young survey revealed that the British Inland Revenue was investigating nearly half of the multinational companies studied in their survey (Ivison, 28 November 1995).

Very soon companies will be negotiating preferential tax deals, not only for themselves but also for chosen elite employees. What can any government do when a quarter of the world's productive assets is controlled by 300 transnational companies? These companies have the muscle to impose crippling sanctions on any state trying to impose unreasonable taxes, not least by moving even more production to low-tax countries than they do at present. But there are still those unreconstructed socialists who wish to redistribute wealth via the tax system. As usual it won't be the rich who will be targeted for the money that politicians need for their profligate schemes, but the middle classes, who, having bought their homes with over taxed income are getting increasingly irritated when they find themselves living next door to 'barrow-boys' who paid for their property with untaxed cash. However, the number of taxpayers is shrinking. From one end, unemployment is hitting the middle classes too. The other end is getting smarter. They are leaving for cyberspace to 'the greatest tax haven of them all, Bermuda in the sky with diamonds' (William Rees-Mogg).

There are many politicians who would clearly like to tax the rich, but those with the most money keep their assets offshore (or off-planet), out of the taxman's reach. Only outdated politicians think they can 'pass a law against it'. In 1994 President Clinton proposed a tax on futures and options trading, ostensibly to dampen market volatility. Politicians always seem to find 'perfectly justifiable' reasons for setting taxes rather than being honest about grabbing the money. The Chicago Mercantile Exchange issued a public statement warning that such interference would lead to the business being moved overseas 'in a nanosecond'. On reflection Clinton dropped the plan (Brown and Morse, 1997).

A major growth market will be the security and servicing of the global information flows of the now-mobile rich: anywhere, anytime, anyhow. Government interference will drive this business abroad. One estimate claims that 60 per cent of the world's private banking is held in trust in offshore unsupervised tax havens (Mulgan and Murray, 1993). Through its secrecy laws and minimal regulation, George Town, capital of Grand Cayman (population 25,000), has become the fifth largest banking centre in the world, with more than 500 banks and nearly 30,000 registered companies; $600 billion pass through the island each year ('Dirty money', broadcast *BBC TV*, 20 September 1994). Even though the United States intimidated Grand Cayman into signing a Mutual Legal Assistance Treaty in 1986, the island only allowed investigation of accounts proved to be holding drug-related money. They were shrewd enough to protect their banking industry by excluding from the agreement searches by both the US Internal Revenue Service and the Securities and Exchange Commission looking for capital flight money (Maingot, 1995).

Meanwhile, with levels of unemployment rising and work becoming increasingly flexible (often a euphemism for casual or part time) among service and production workers, the disposable income for most of society will be drastically reduced. Substitution of part-time jobs for full-time is a factor causing a stagnation of household income around the globe. This means that unemployment figures, although statistically accurate, don't tell the true picture. Take the example of Australia, where someone who works one hour a week is technically employed. At the same time as the official figures claimed 820,000 unemployed, there were 1.3 million unemployed or underemployed people looking for full-time work (Santamaria, 15 November 1997).

Growing unemployment and new employment practices, such as downsizing, delayering, right-sizing and outsourcing, are polarizing the purchasing power of every business's traditional customer base, both corporate and individual. The rich get richer, and the poor get poorer. Figures from the Center on Budget and Policy Priorities show that despite the booming economy in the mid-1990s, the incomes of the poorest fifth of US families have fallen by 21 per cent since the late 1970s (*Economist*, 20 December 1997). Yet the incomes of the richest fifth have risen by 30 per cent in that time. The number of US dollar millionaires has increased tenfold in two decades (*IT Times*, 4 September 1997), and in Britain the number of sterling millionaires will top 200,000 as we enter the new millennium, double the 1996 number (Blackstock, 3 August 1997). The net worth of the world's 200 richest people is equal to the combined wealth of the poorest 41 per cent of the world's population: 2.25 billion people (Purnell, 13 July 1999). At the same time, the number of US children living in poverty jumped from 4.4 million to nearly 6 million over a 15-year period (Ellis, 10 July 1998). Meanwhile, in 1994, 26 per cent of British children (almost 3 million) were living on supplementary benefit or income support, compared with 7 per cent just 15 years earlier (Openheim, 27 September 1995).

'Can't pay, won't pay'

Consequently communities and companies will have to produce completely new products for totally new markets, requiring a complete rethink of their operational procedures and strategies, if they hope to survive and prosper in radically different operating environments. Every business will have to redefine totally the classification of its markets. For when Leona Helmsley said 'Only the little people pay taxes', she was unwittingly making a prediction. This new barbarian, the 'queen of mean' as the populist press disparagingly called her, was sent to jail for 20 months by a jury of 'little people' for non-payment of taxes. History will mark that (shameful!) judgment as the beginning of the end of the old order of taxation. Entrepreneurs who hire the best tax advisors and who can flee will be immune to taxation. In fact these wealth-generating job creators must be bribed to stay. In the decade to 1996 Rupert Murdoch is reported to have paid only £11.74 million in taxes on the £979.4 million profits of his News International group (Cohen, 3 December 1995). The end of progressive taxation is in sight. The only inelastic sector of the tax base is now the immobile low-paid worker.

Helmsley joins a long line of famous US 'tax dodgers' sent to prison. In the middle of the 19th century, an apocryphal story has Ralph Waldo Emerson visiting Henry David Thoreau in jail, where he had been imprisoned for non-payment of taxes. Emerson asked 'Why are you here?' to which Thoreau replied 'Why are you not here?' Thoreau saw himself not as a criminal but as a prisoner of conscience, a political prisoner, and was asking why all free men were not acting in the same way, defending the right of the individual against coercion by government. Thoreau again (1849): 'I heartily accept the motto "That government is best which governs least"; and I should like to see it acted out more rapidly and systematically carried out, it finally amounts to this, which I also believe, "That government is best which governs not at all".' Or as my mother used to say, 'There's no government like no government.'

Thoreau knew that 'the mass of men live lives of quiet desperation'. That is why organized anti-tax resistance has a long and bloody history in the United States, particularly among the rural poor. They 'can't pay and won't pay' (the slogan shouted by demonstrators during the poll tax riots in Britain in 1990). Federal agents have always acted heavy handly against anyone who refuses to pay federal taxes – particularly taxes related to tobacco and alcohol. Yet this is the country of the Boston Tea Party, which sparked off the American War of Independence. That war was started over a tax that was a mere three cents on the dollar (Fleming, 23 November 1997), a percentage half the size of today's local city taxes.

A little more than 200 years later, early in 1983, a North Dakota farmer, Gordon Kahl, who had previously been jailed for non-payment of tax, shot and killed two federal marshals trying to arrest him. Although in his sixties, he went on the run for several months. He had killed another marshal before the FBI laid siege to the Arkansas farmhouse in which he was hiding, set fire to it and finally shot him dead. Claims regarding state thuggery regularly emerge in the United States. A Senate hearing in September 1997 heard evidence from anonymous tax inspectors that the Internal Revenue Service (IRS) regularly bullies citizens into paying excessive tax. Of the $13.2 billion levied as penalties, more than 40 per cent was withdrawn on appeal. There have been claims that the state only picks on those without the wherewithal to fight back. The IRS focused particularly punitive action against a list of 'tax protesters'. They allegedly drove dozens of homeowners to suicide, but left big business well alone. Claims were made that the IRS targeted political enemies of government, a tactic perfected by the Kennedy administration. Paula Jones, who was suing President Clinton for sexual harassment, was audited for the first time less than a week after she rejected an out-of-court settlement in her case. The Heritage Foundation and the National Rifle Association were also subject to sudden inspection (Rhodes, 23 September 1997). How ironic that the true nature of taxation should surface in a senate hearing with whistle-blowers giving their anonymous testimony in distorted voices from behind large screens, just like 'informers' betraying former friends in organized crime.

Such events are going to happen more and more, as nowadays the power in global economic forces means that the tax burden is irrevocably moving on to the shoulders of the immobile – off income and on to expenditure. Tax on purchases is far more evenly spread around. Everyone, every schoolchild buying sweets in the corner store, is paying tax. Governments can no longer afford to clobber the rich. The rich are rediscovering the power to say no, but this has a disproportionate and detrimental effect on the poor, and goes counter to every notion of social justice that has been expressed over the past 200 years. However, in the new order of things, social justice is an anachronism.

More demands on the taxpayer

Inexorably, the demands made on tax revenue are set to increase, and substantially. They already cost around £40 billion per year in Britain. Democratic politicians are trapped 'between a rock and a hard place'. To get elected they have to promise to deliver top-quality education and medicine, and good pensions and welfare handouts, but the only people they can squeeze for the money are the ordinary electorate. There is only so much they can squeeze, and because of social, technological and demographic trends, the figures just don't add up: in 50 years it is expected that the number of British pensioners will have increased by over a half to around 14 million (Marsland, 6 March 1997).

The expense of running hospitals, because of the very high costs of pharmaceutical research and of state-of-the-art electronic medical hardware, is bound to go up. Good medicine and hygiene over the past half-century have meant that people are living longer. This means that not only will the total pension bill go up, but also the average number of times each person has an illness requiring hospitalization will increase. It has been estimated that, because of these demographic trends, Britain's National Health Service requires an annual increase in capital investment of around 2 per cent in real terms just to stand still. Today the care of the over 65s, 16 per cent of the population, accounts for nearly half the spending on healthcare; this percentage of pensioners is set to double by 2050 (*Economist*, 15 March 1997). The messages of anti-smoking campaigns, which claim smokers are expensive to society, are shown clearly to be false accounting. In actuarial terms, the ideal citizen is one who dies of a single illness like lung cancer, preferably quickly (in terms of cost to the state), around the age of retirement.

As jobs get scarcer, children will stay at school longer in an attempt to gain qualifications more attractive to employers. These qualifications will require increasingly more electronic (and expensive) support, and the costs will far outstrip the savings made by keeping these children out of the welfare queues. And there are more and more university students. Britain has increased the number of students attending university from a figure of 552,000 full-time equivalent students in 1989 to around 900,000 in 1996 (Authers, 20 March 1995). There are now around a total of 1.5 million full-time and part-time students in Britain (Smithers, 5 March 1995). All of this occurred with little or no extra (some would say a decrease in) support: the public funding per student in 1995 was less than three-quarters of that in 1989. The price can only be paid for by a drop in quality. The resentment will be tangible, when each student appears at the other end of a degree course with a certificate that guarantees them nothing, hardly worth the paper it's written on. What else can we expect when governments debase the currency of education?

With the new barbarians escaping taxation, the income tax levied on ordinary workers will not pay for all this extra expenditure. In the developed world today there are five workers to every pensioner. Early in the next century it will be four to one, and then three to one. Furthermore, these figures assume that there will be no calamitous collapse in employment levels.

Some politicians think they can solve the problem by raising the age of retirement, but this will not work because it will simply reduce the number of jobs for the young, and thereby transfer the unemployment and cause even more trouble. The British government is even considering forcing the self-employed to take out extra private pensions knowing that the state pension will not be sufficient (Hughes, 4 July 1998).

How will democratic governments tell those people who have paid state-pension contributions all their lives that when they retire there will be no pension for them, unless they have made private provision for themselves? In other words, citizens will not be able to afford the costs of their old age unless they have turned their backs on government promises. How will they tell people who have paid for a health service all their lives that there will be no long-term nursing? This is exactly the situation that Britain is facing now, where the population can expect the steady slicing away of their fully paid-up entitlements (soon to be called 'privileges'), and the value of their old age pensions will slowly fade away to nothing.

Even at the present time the pension does not suffice, and it has to be topped up for those identified as in dire need. State welfare benefits too are reserved only for those in need, which usually means those fully unpaid-up members of the 'dependency culture'. In other words the main people to gain will be those who have squandered their way through life. The hard-working and thrifty who have fallen on hard times will get nothing, but will have to use up their meagre savings to pay for themselves until their assets have fallen below £10,000. The only asset of many middle-income earners is the family home, which they hope their children will inherit. A vain hope. Increasingly this asset will be stripped away to support them through old age, and their heirs will be left with nothing but debt. A long illness will even mean the house being seized by the state to pay for hospitalization. But the more 'distressed gentlefolk' lose their homes, the fewer people there will be with the money to buy. This will lead to a greater supply of houses on the market, and consequently the value of domestic property will fall. Such is the contrariness of economic feedback.

Nowadays most younger people know they have to provide for themselves. They have no illusions about provisions from the state. But unlike their parents, they haven't paid all their life into a system that has failed them. In February 1997, the British government was intent on blocking the large number of schoolteachers who were taking 'early retirement on health grounds' because of the drain on funds. Government put a notional value on the money absorbed from the teachers' pension fund at £36 billion. It is suggested that if the amount taken off teachers in pension contributions had been invested by a competent fund manager that figure would have exceeded £110 billion (Carvel, 14 December 1996).

So who is going to pay for it all? Those who are working or buying. You can still find the smug who say they are happy to pay their taxes to maintain a stable society, and to help those less privileged than themselves. But what happens when the demands on government expenditure explode, and income tax has to be levied at 60, 80 or 110 per cent? What happens when value added tax, sales tax and state taxes have to be charged at 30, 50, 100 per cent or more? What happens when inflation, deflation and stagflation inevitably follow?

We are entering a vicious circle, and only a complete restructuring of government spending will stop the meltdown. Higher taxes mean less disposable income. Investment is restricted and growth limited. This reduces the number of jobs, and so reduces what is spent in the shops, endangering the official economy and pushing people into the black economy, which reduces legitimate jobs further. Less spending means cuts in VAT (sales tax) income, which necessitates a tax increase to cover the shortfall. In 1995, the British Chancellor Kenneth Clarke had to announce a 3 per cent drop in VAT revenue (*Times* editorial, 9 May 1996), some of which was an embryonic manifestation of this feedback. Only a return to growth in employment will stop the whole house of cards collapsing. Growth is the fundamental energy driving the pyramid-selling structures that underlie all government pension and welfare schemes. As we have seen, this growth is already difficult enough to achieve, let alone maintain.

Tax revolts

But you can't fool all of the people all of the time. The people in the middle are tired of picking up the tab. With tax bills escalating from the irresistible upward pressure of public spending, tax-revolts are inevitable. The days are over when only the poor, like Gordon Kahl, revolted against taxation. The middle classes are tired of seeing perfectly fair taxes such as the community charge (poll tax) in Britain being withdrawn because of revolts in the streets, while at the same time they are being bled dry by punitive taxation and the taking of all they had earned from a lifetime of work and diligence.

One option of revolt for the hard-working is to pay in cash for work done, at a discount, and to accept payment in cash, thereby avoiding taxes. Under present conditions it is no surprise that worldwide the black economy is booming, with a growth rate far outstripping growth in the official economy. Everybody is at it. According to research, undertaken by the Institute for Fiscal Studies on behalf of the British Inland Revenue, the true incomes of the self-employed are as much as one and a half times the amount they declare for tax (Smith, 13 March 1994). According to economist Friedrich Schneider of Linz University (*Economist*, 3 May 1997), the black economies (he calls them 'shadow economies') of Belgium, Italy and Spain account for more than 20 per cent of their gross domestic product (GDP). Even in Germany and France it is 14 per cent. In Russia the official and shadow economies are about equal. Wealthy countries basking in the penumbra should not be too complacent. Their shadow economies are growing three times faster than the official ones.

In Britain the Inland Revenue conservatively estimates a black economy of around £50 billion, which is more than 6 per cent of the GDP. This is a huge increase on estimates from previous decades. By the black economy they mean jobs ranging from earning pin money by 'moonlighting' to the megabucks gained from dealing in illegal narcotics. These figures are calculated from the particularly high volume of cash in circulation. It was expected that wide availability of credit cards would reduce demand for cash, but this has not turned out to be so. This discrepancy can only be explained in terms of the underground economy, an alternative economy whose wheels are oiled with untraceable cash. A report by accountants Deloitte & Touche asserts that the black economy in Britain actually accounts for 12 per cent of the GDP, a figure of around £100 billion. Others too come up with a similar figure, claiming that the Exchequer is losing £30 billion annually (Smith, 30 November 1997).

Every time taxes are increased, be they sales or service taxes, National Insurance contributions, corporation tax, excise duties or income tax, more and more people cross over the line into the black economy. With an increasing number in society becoming criminalized, the morality of tax evasion and avoidance takes on a different aspect. Tax started when kings charged a tribute for protecting traders who moved across their territory, in effect guaranteeing the traders that the kings themselves would not impede their progress. But what happens in cyberspace? Where is the territory? Who are the kings? What happens when there are several kings in any particular territory, each with vested interests, and none of them knowing what they are doing? Consider the case of the European Union where tax has to be paid only once, in the member country of manufacture (whatever that means – in the case of alcohol is this where it is brewed or bottled?). British excise duty on beer is seven times that in France. It is not surprising that the British, suffering such liquor taxes, take day-trips to France to stock up with beer and wines (a £7 bottle of wine in France costs £12 in Britain; a £22.50 bottle of Scotch whisky in France costs £32 in Scotland where it is distilled) (*Business Times Singapore*, 29 December 1992). Many of the warehouses in Calais, run by British entrepreneurs, transact their business in sterling. Customs estimate that the annual loss in revenue because of this cross-Channel trade is £1.5 billion and growing (Nuki and Rufford, 2 August 1997).

In this way not only do the day-trippers avoid all duty payable in Britain, quite legally thanks to the European single market set up on 1 January 1993, but they deprive British stores of trade, which in turn destroys jobs in the retail sector. Counting the legal day-tripper together with the bootleggers, some estimates put this trade at 4 per cent of the legitimate turnover of the British drinks industry (Vander Weyer, 27 May 1997). Consequently the taxes take from both income and profits will fall: just another example when raising tax can actually reduce revenue. It is only a short step from the day-trip with personal duty-free purchases to large convoys of vans importing huge quantities of contraband. Selling in car boot sales and garage sales, the low prices for tobacco and alcohol attract ready and eager customers.

In the summer of 1992, the Italian government led by prime minister Giuliano Amato introduced a 0.6 per cent 'one-off' tax on bank deposits. Rumours abounded of government insiders moving their money out before the bank snatch. Naturally Italians then became highly susceptible to every whisper. A rumour of another one-off bank robbery at the end of September 1992 led to a run on the banks, exacerbating the problem caused by Italy's suspension from the Exchange Rate Mechanism (ERM). New barbarian savers rushed to empty their bank accounts, and the capital flow from Italy into Switzerland and Austria was astronomical. An estimated 12 trillion lire ($9.6 billion) left in July, and double that in both August and September (Brady, 15 October 1992). During the lire crisis of 1992, Italy caused real damage to the French retail trade near the border. French citizens poured over the border into Italy to buy cars and all kinds of consumer goods, where they were 20 per cent cheaper than in France (Jones, Conradi and Lang, 1 June 1997).

The economic problems don't just go away; they have a habit of percolating around for years to come. In March 1993 the Northern League, then in opposition in Italy, advised its supporters to withdraw their money from current accounts as they expected another government tax on bank accounts as part of new austerity measures necessitated by an increasing budget deficit (Reuters News Service, 29 March 1993). During the first half of 1992, Italian investors bought more than 40 trillion lire of foreign assets, nearly double the total for the whole of 1991. All of this is happening against a background where the savings rate in Italy has fallen from 27 per cent in 1975, to 20.5 per cent in 1984 to 15.6 per cent in 1991 (Business Times Singapore, 29 December 1992). By rubbing their noses in it, new barbarians will ensure that governments finally learn that their actions have consequences outside their control.

Fair taxation?

No longer able to target the rich, how will government convince the immobile taxpayer to support the state without risking an all-out revolt? It can only be by resorting to those weasel words 'responsibility' and 'community'. Both left and right sides of the political spectrum have recognized that an arbitrary redistribution of the shrinking cake is no way to run a country. Wet right-wingers, centre-bound socialists, even reconfigured Marxists are having to reconsider the meaning of the word 'fair', as in 'fair taxation'. Geoff Mulgan and Robin Murray (1993) of Demos, the London-based left-lobe think-tank, struck a popular chord with politicians with their ideas on 'hypothecation'. Their idea is that there would be support (that is a popular commitment to pay) for a particular tax if a direct link is established between the tax and a particular area of expenditure. The theory is that voters would support a higher duty on alcohol and tobacco if the revenue was spent on hospitals, particularly if it was also linked to a lower rate of income tax.

Governments are thinking of shifting their targets for taxation from labour and capital to energy, resources and consumption: road tolls, higher sales taxes, a noise tax on vehicles, a pollution tax and a surcharge on energy prices. But soon the politicians will find themselves entering a grey area. Everyone would vote for 'motherhood and apple pie', hospitals and schools, but an energy tax is problematical as the British government found out when large numbers of pensioners objected to VAT on gas bills (Lambert, 1 December 1994). What about paying to support the homeless, alcoholics and drug abusers, single parents, the unemployed, convicted criminals, and all the other groups where the light of self-interest never shines? And will the new barbarians concur, even with hypothecated taxes? They have no social conscience for a society from which they feel alienated.

Do discredited politicians really believe that they can reconnect these barbarians as well as the ordinary taxpayer to the community? It seems they do... .

8

The end of liberal democracy?

Do politicians really believe that they can reconnect these barbarians as well as the ordinary taxpayer to the community? It seems they do. They really do believe that social or liberal democracy can deliver communities that will maintain the national status quo. The words of Dr Pangloss can be heard in the crumbling corridors of power: 'All is for the best, in the best of all possible worlds' (Voltaire). They actually believe that democracy is a stepping-stone to a global social utopia through the actions of men and women of good will – men and women who suppress their individuality to the will of the national collective. However, history has taught us that good will doesn't travel well, and certainly not far beyond national borders, except that is for trade.

A formula for mediocrity

Democratic politicians are part of the problem, rather than part of the solution. Modern democracy is basically a single platform – that of the virtue of tribal moralities: back to 'basic values'. New barbarians see no particular virtue in the 'common good'. They know that these uncertain times call for leadership, but not leadership that panders to the 'greatest good' and to egalitarian ideals, for that is a formula for mediocrity. To succeed, leadership must be strong in its striving, and ruthless. New barbarians assert that healthy systems expel all poisons from within. Nietzsche's words bear repeating: 'Nature is not immoral when it has no pity for the degenerate.'

The social and liberal democracy of the 20th century has become degenerate and it will be replaced by a more vigorous mode of governance.

Why is this happening now? And what is making it happen? The answer is quite simple: today's new technologies have unleashed unstoppable global economic forces that are empowering adolescent forms of a new barbarism. Sameness, democracy and equality, the *Zeitgeist* of the industrial age, have become error, and are finished. Democracy is power fixed in the tribe, whereas the new barbarians ignore tribal boundaries and tribal loyalties. The new barbarians are 'from the tribe, but not of the tribe'. They are the imaginative individuals and organizations that have become outsiders. They know that there are enormous opportunities for those who have the vigour and vitality to break free of the limitations of boundaries drawn from the past, and who have the vision to redraw their own borders and their own future.

Of course there are also plenty of old barbarians around as well, simply biding their time. The new millennium will finally bury the sentimental ideologies of the last century. The 200 years of 'social progress' instigated by the then-new barbarians of the French Revolution are slowly being rolled back. History isn't ending, but it could be going into reverse (Baudrillard, 1994). From the clarity of hindsight, the 20th century will be remembered for the false opposites of the political left and right, and as the century of the masses, where the individual was intimidated by the tribe, and trade was controlled by collective ideologies. However, the 20th century, the century of the masses, is over: it ended at the Berlin Wall in 1989. As far as global enterprises are concerned, social and liberal democracy is an artefact of the Machine Age, an ideology from a time when the masses were needed – but it will soon mutate into an irrelevance. Our new century will see the rebirth of individualism.

Some democrat extremists will try to swim against the tide. The excesses of a popular ideological thuggery beckon. The hell of a collectivist heaven will poll the opinions of the herd to reinstate capital punishment, to ban homosexuality and immigration, and to insist on a fair(?) distribution of wealth by taking from the few rich who remain. The rich are seen simply as the 'lucky ones' who have taken an above average share of property that actually belongs to 'the people'. History has taught the new barbarian that in such states only political leaders will have a lion's share. Today's barbarians won't let that happen without a fight.

The envious mode of thinking will be democracy's undoing. 'A democracy cannot exist as a permanent form of government. It can only exist until a majority of voters discover that they can vote themselves largesse out of the public treasury' (Alexander Tytler). In our time, that largesse is free welfare and medical payouts, and other social security safety nets. Plato was right in claiming that democracy always leads to despotism and tyranny. Our particular brand of democracy is creating a tyranny of and by the masses.

Rich cosmopolitan innovators want no part of a society that behaves in an old barbaric way. However, they won't confront it. They will just disappear. Without the enthusiastic input of their entrepreneurial spirit, the wealth of their ex-society will soon dissipate. The all-too-realistic prospect for many in society is a democracy that degenerates into being merely the means of governing the immobile and dependent service workers. No more 'one man (and more recently one woman), one vote'. The Boston Tea Party-goers insisted on 'no taxation without representation', but why not 'no representation without taxation', or even better 'the bigger the tax, the bigger the say'? In a society that pays by credit card, prior to each election we could each be given an audited personal statement of the total tax paid since the last vote. Then in the ballot box we vote for (credit that amount to) the party of our choice: the more tax we pay, the more votes we have. Companies too would vote with their corporation tax, and everyone with salaries paid for by the state would have no vote at all. It's still democracy, but not as we know it.

That citizens elect their slave masters makes their democracy (every form of democracy) slavery none the less. The vast majority of people will have no choice, other than to be slaves. However, the new barbarians are free, and they will profit from the products of this slavery. The seeds of slavery germinate in every collectivist philosophy, and technology is an effective fertilizer. Consider Sweden, and its apparently benign form of socialism. The Social Democrat government there has been held up as an exemplar of good management, being economically viable while socially aware. Now it emerges that, for 40 years from 1935, 60,000 Swedes were sterilized in a 'controlled breeding' programme: eugenics for the good of society. Mentally disabled people were fed with sugar-rich food in a study on tooth decay (*Daily Mail*, 11 September 1997), and 4,500 mental patients were forcibly lobotomized over a 20-year period (Jacobson, 12 April 1998). As if these stories weren't bad enough, they were closely followed by evidence of the Aryanization of Swedish companies chasing German business during the Second World War. In their eagerness to be *Judenfrei*, banks and legal firms knowingly sold details of the ethnic origins of their clients to Nazi sympathizers (Wavell, 30 November 1997). This is slavery, and all in the name of the 'common good'.

The majority of society, the service and production workers, the unemployed and the underclass, are a drain on a region's economic potential. In the Information Age, governments based on a universal franchise and chosen by this majority are governments elected by losers. The 'politics of envy' is suicide and the 'will of the people', voting for full employment, a minimum wage, and fair(?) taxation is merely the turkeys voting for Christmas. The big political question of the coming decades is how to find a socially acceptable means of dismantling democracy.

It is not surprising then that many voters are dissatisfied with representative liberal democracy in its present degenerate form. They have come to realize that their insignificant input into an inconsequential election every four or five years has little or no influence on the general scheme of things. 'The English people think themselves free; they much deceive themselves; they are free only during the election of members of parliament: once these are elected, the people are enslaved, they amount to nothing' (Jean-Jacques Rousseau). In the hope of revitalizing democracy, these voters are turning to new technology that enables frequent testing of their opinions. Some are questioning whether elected representatives are needed at all. If individual voters can ask questions and make their views known, perhaps the ancient Athenian form of democracy, that of direct (but now electronic) voting, will reappear? Then our present representative democracy will prove to be merely a failed 200-year experiment.

Alternatives

Novel and more effective alternatives are emerging (Martin, 1978). One vision of the future information society (Toffler, 1980) is that information technology will provide the foundation for vast networks of individuals. These communities will provide a countervailing force against any abuses by national authorities and commercial interests. Institutions (both governmental and private) would be closely monitored and held accountable for every infringement and failing. Citizen power would become the order of the day, and could portend the elimination of all authority, and the creation of 'electronic anarchies'.

A related scenario (Masuda, 1980) foresees the emergence of a fully participatory democracy. Information technology now makes it possible, quickly and cheaply, to allow a large majority of citizens to become involved in areas of decision-making that were traditionally the domain of an elected executive. Alvin and Heidi Toffler (1995) promote 'semi-direct democracy'. Here voters influence policy decisions by sending their opinions to politicians via new telecommunications technology. TV companies poll their viewers at every opportunity, over every topic, letting 'the people have their say'. CNN even has 'town meetings' as part of its programming: perhaps subconsciously its producers have realized that the local community will be the dominant political force in the near future. The Tofflers claim such public interaction will improve the political debate and save democracy. However, the novelty of 'teledemocracy' does fade. A series of ballots held in New York in 1976–77 and publicized on television first drew a 10 per cent response, but this soon declined to around 1 per cent (*Economist*, 17 June 1995). Are British citizens really interested in political debate? During the 1997 General Election campaign the BBC extended its 9 o'clock news bulletin by about 20 minutes to report on the election campaigns. Its normal viewing figures of 5.5 million dropped to less than 4 million (*Economist*, 3 May 1997).

Nevertheless, there is an upsurge of referenda and opinion polls. As technology becomes all pervasive, the difference between these two forms of public information-gathering will diminish. Since the start of the 1970s activists have concentrated on referenda, and the frequency of national referenda has roughly doubled (*Economist*, 17 June 1995). Politicians complain about having their opinions ignored, but only when the results support the views they do not want to hear. As for the polls themselves, although some are statistically legitimate, many others are what Bob Worcester, head of pollsters MORI and a colleague at London School of Economics, calls 'voodoo polls'. Newspaper readers or television viewers are encouraged to telephone in their opinions on some burning issue of the day. Unfortunately these polls are open to manipulation and abuse. There was an attempt to 'fix' the 1996 BBC Radio 4 'Personality of the Year' poll in favour of the Labour leader Tony Blair. An over-enthusiastic Labour Party member sent a 'broadcast fax' to thousands of potential sympathizers to drum up votes (Midgley and Sherman, 27 December 1996).

It takes very little effort to play these games. A laptop computer and a mobile phone can be configured as a fax machine. At any protest meeting activists type in the names and addresses of those attending, and personalized messages from every person present are instantaneously targeted at politicians. For a little extra cost, signatures can be digitized and included in the transmission. Once such personal data has been captured, it can be used over and over again (not necessarily with the person's consent).

Another problem is that the mass media are more interested in sound bites and extremist positions than in constructive examination and debate of policies. Rudeness and bickering makes for 'better' television. Whenever television transmits a live set-piece debate on a controversial issue, the so-called randomly selected audience often turns out to comprise two totally intransigent opposite groups. The will of the unorganized silent majority is nowhere to be heard: they can't be bothered to take part. Too often the forum turns into a bear-pit, a model exploited to advantage by Jerry Springer and his many imitators. A classic example was the television poll on the state of the monarchy in Britain, held in January 1997 (Shaefer, 9 January 1997), which degenerated into a farcical screaming match between ardent monarchists and republicans. Maybe the media have got the public mood right after all?

True, cable, telephone and the Internet will enable us to receive far more relevant and in-depth explanations of political issues, and it will provide more public information (propaganda) so that we can participate more intelligently and benignly in the political process. But will we participate? Only if we are committed citizens and of a sufficient educational level. Suddenly we are back with Rousseau and John Stuart Mill. Rousseau considered that direct democracy would only suit those states where people can meet and get to know one another. Mill was sure that education is a vital prerequisite to the right to vote. Will the Net raise the level of education and spread civic awareness widely among today's citizens? Or will access limit itself to a small self-selecting group? What happens when the novelty wears off? It remains to be seen whether we actually want to know.

The United States administration has placed more than 100,000 documents on the Internet (*Economist*, 17 June 1995). Unlike the paper medium, the cost is the same whether one or one million citizens access the data. Since there is public access to the Net in libraries and council offices, the claim is that it is available to almost all. It seems surprising that governments are more eager to put data on the Net than on paper. Or are they? Cynics say that a snowstorm of selected information from Washington (or Brussels, or Westminster) does not necessarily clarify the democratic situation. They ask who selects the material, why it is there and why there is so much. Most importantly, what is **not** on the Net?

The potential for misinformation and disinformation is enormous. But if the politicians think that by pouring out an information overload they can cling on to control, then they are deluding themselves. It may be cheap for governments to snow the people, but it is just as cheap for the organized individual to return the compliment. The old cosy relationship between lobbyists and politicians is surely coming off the rails. Through technology the legal profession, trade associations, corporations, quangos and think-tanks have all become democratized. 'Influence peddling was once the province of the privileged, it is now everyone's game' (Jonathan Rauch). Now all advocates can and must become lobbyists and mount campaigns. The American Association of Retired Persons can mobilize more than 30 million members to lobby their representatives; this is quite a force. In 1994 President Clinton proposed the funding of welfare reform by taxing casino profits. He was forced to back down (Martinez, 28 November 1995), not by the casino owners, but by an organized revolt of casino employees, waiters, construction workers and others in the communities dependent on gambling for their livelihood. How things have changed! In the not too distant past only political parties, trades unions and the press controlled the means of manipulating the voters. Now we can all do it.

Influence peddlers must now lobby the voters, not the politicians. Voters themselves see the chance to get at their representatives, thereby controlling them – when you are in a position to instruct your representatives they are no longer your masters. This is a time of new forms of manipulation. The new school of organized public opinion is now more powerful than the old approach of bribery and corruption and the 'old school tie'. Anyone holding a grudge can de-select Members of Parliament, as both Sir Nicholas Scott and Sir George Gardiner (Donegan and Smithers, 31 January 1997) have found to their cost. In the United States, Senator Larry Pressler paid the ultimate price for offending the environmental lobby (*Congress Daily*, 20 July 1998). Senators and members of Congress, who in private support 'a woman's right to choose' abortion, sit on the fence, wary of the fundamentalist lobby.

Gone are the days when an honest politician was 'one who, when bought, stayed bought'. The intrigue of smoky back rooms has been replaced by the mobilization of the masses to fax-blitz elected representatives, or carpet bomb them with mail (e-mail and 'snail mail'), sometimes even during the important debates. Politicians have nowhere to hide and are becoming paranoid with all these 'we're watching you' messages. Much of this mail may actually come from outside their constituencies, but they have no way of knowing. In addition there are advertisements, opinion polls, talk-radio spots and mass phone calls funnelled through toll-free numbers. The green lobby is at the forefront of this tactic. In the United States, the League of Conservation Voters is keeping scorecards on the environmental records of Congressmen, and has identified its 'dirty dozen' for special treatment. The old Marxist techniques for the control of politics have been reborn with new technology. However now in the United States, it is the right wing, conservative and religious organizations that are permanent features of 'talk radio' and burgeoning satellite and cable channels. National Empowerment Television reaches 11 million homes (*Economist*, 17 June 1995). The radical right's already large television exposure is set to become even larger.

The exposed politician, a 'rabbit caught in the headlights', has to 'please all of the people, all of the time', on every single issue, or face their wrath come re-election time. The populist majority is imposing its will on minorities and on politicians. Paradoxically Big Brother turns out to be the voice of the tyrannical masses – the exact opposite of the telescreens and truth ministries that George Orwell expected in *1984*. The moral majority use celebrities to back calls for support on single-issue campaigns, and widely disseminate blacklists of names of those who stand out against them. Politicians will be isolated, and are less likely to support broadly unpopular but economically and socially essential bills. No doubt anti-smoking authoritarians were behind Oregon's decision in a November 1996 vote to hike their cigarette tax by 30 cents a pack in order to pay for a state-run healthcare plan (*Investor's Business Daily*, 11 December 1996). That their action is likely to reduce the tax take is totally lost on them.

The power of interest groups

As political power shifts from politicians toward 'the people', interest groups find they have to mobilize the voters, rather than tame their representatives – a far more complex, difficult and expensive task. Come election time, voters find themselves targeted by special-interest lobbyists as well as by self-interested politicians. The variety and scale of the tactics required mean that only the media and advertising agencies can possibly gain in the war of attrition that is popular democracy. In Florida voters were to decide whether or not to impose a 1-cent-per-pound tax on sugar growers to help restore the Everglades. About $27 million was spent by both sides of the campaign. It has been estimated that around $200 million was spent in 1996 on all such campaigns in the United States, up from $140 million in 1994. In that year in Missouri, pro-gambling interests spent more than $10 million in winning a vote to legalize gambling in that state; the opposition spent a mere $100,000 (Chen, 2 November 1996). Organized labour raised more than $1.5 million to promote Proposition 210, the minimum wage initiative in California (Silverstein, 26 October 1996). The numbers get astronomical. In a democracy, like everywhere else, money talks.

The message is spreading that when a single-issue group gets involved and organizes itself, then even entrenched vested interests can be swept aside. Power to the people: true democracy at last! Well that's the theory anyway. Jonathan Rauch argues the contrary. Far from bringing about a new democratic age, allowing voters into the policy and decision-making process actually impedes good governance. These new forces will drive government to its knees by causing stalemates on every issue, and by forcing through economically insane proposals. He identifies a disease of government: *Demosclerosis* (1994). An explosion of lobbying by interest groups using the telephone and fax linked to a computerized database will, he says, swamp government.

Demosclerosis is already here. On 5 November 1996, voters in California approved (by 56 per cent to 44 per cent) Proposition 218, which ensured that all property-related assessments, fees and charges have to be approved (but more likely disapproved) by the vote of property owners. The proposition was designed to close loopholes in the 1978 Proposition 13 that opened the floodgates for tax revolts by drastically curtailing the ability of counties to raise revenues to cover their expenses. One loophole was that utility taxes for amenities, such as libraries and police protection, were in reality fees rather than property taxes, and so were not covered by the original proposition. No longer! These measures reflect a growing self-awareness among taxpayers that they are sitting ducks, targeted to pay for the excesses of high-spending politicians.

Following Proposition 218, there would have been an inevitable loss in revenue for, and a reduction in flexibility of, local authorities. Consequently at the end of 1996, Moody's lowered the ratings on the various bonds of the City of Los Angeles (*Reuters*, 13 December 1996). Not surprisingly the city council, which could lose tens of millions of dollars in revenue, voted to fight the new law in the courts (*Reuters*, 2 December 1996). As well as passing 218, Californians also rejected a proposal to impose a tax increase on high-income earners. Florida approved a measure requiring two-thirds of the participating voters to approve new taxes or fees, effectively capping tax increases. Similar measures were passed in Nevada and South Dakota (Taylor, 11 November 1996). In Oregon, Measure 46 required voter approval of tax increases, with those registered voters not voting to be counted as opposed. Voters in Nevada and Nebraska decided that any new tax or tax increase must be approved by a two-thirds majority of both houses of the state legislature.

However, the populist old barbarians are fighting back with crazy self-indulgent initiatives. There were new minimum-wage proposals in California, Oregon, Montana, Missouri and the municipality of Denver, even after the US Congress had already raised the federal minimum wage; sensibly the latter three failed. The proposals were the result of concerted action and funding by trades unions and liberal, religious and consumer groups, despite dire warnings that they would hurt small businesses and destroy jobs. Economists at California State University estimated almost 96,000 jobs would be lost. Consulting firm Spectrum Economics put likely job losses at 100,000, and an annual loss of $2 billion to the state's economy (Taylor, 30 October 1996). The Hoover Institution and Stanford University found that the Living Wage Initiative would cost California families $1.1 billion a year in higher prices (*Investors' Business Daily*, 24 October 1996), with low-income families paying a disproportionately higher share. Business faces an extra $1.7 billion in costs. For organizations that employ millions of people, and that pay billions of dollars in taxes, this is madness. The study went on to say that not only would the poor become worse off, but also that some rich families would actually gain.

Populism and politicians

No society can vote itself into an economic utopia. Politicians promising a wish-list of 'jam today and jam tomorrow' don't help. For example, at present it is very difficult, if not socially impossible, to cut nominal wage levels. In fact most expect annual increases. But inflation and recession are nature's ways of cutting real wages – hence the Keynesian proposal of reflation as a means of reducing unemployment. This may have worked in the bounded national economies of the 1930s, but not in today's globally integrated economy. The invisible hands of untamed economic forces are at play. Individuals, companies and countries can only steer within the limits allowed by the flow of self-organizing trends in the global economy. Going against the flow is futile. If a society doesn't earn its wages, then economic reality can be kept at bay only for a little while. Ultimately, by insisting that society can pay itself unreasonable salary levels, either inflation or recession will return, and jobs will simply disappear. Persisting in this folly can even give rise to 'stagflation': rising inflation, slow growth or recession and high unemployment.

John Maynard Keynes thought that the purpose of fiscal policy was to average out the surpluses and deficits over the recessions and recoveries of the business cycle: government as a modern-day Joseph (whose economic policies can be found in Chapters 42–45 of the book of Genesis) balancing the Pharaoh's seven lean years against the seven years of plenty. However, a long-term increase in budget deficits is a powerful curb on the public spending needed to attempt this balancing act. Recently in the United States the tax base has been almost completely monopolized by paying interest on the public debt. This not only restricted the US government's scope to counter downturns in the business cycle, but also limited its undertaking of 'entitlement' programmes aimed at gaining votes for the incumbent party, such as social security schemes, and prohibited spending on any new venture (not altogether a bad thing!).

Continual deficits lead to an excess of government, which will attempt to deny if not eliminate the business cycle by socializing the economy through rigid central planning. It is only a short step to unrealistic planning targets, false accounting and ultimately to the collapse rather than the elimination of the business cycle. The extreme case of this was Mao Zedong's 'Great Leap Forward', which claimed that revolutionary zeal would deliver national self-sufficiency. The result was the Cultural Revolution and 28 million deaths from starvation, while the Chinese government was keeping up the pretence of targets (*Reuters News Service*, 25 June 1998). North Korea is doing its best to exceed that figure.

Global companies have no interest in any type of populism, whether violently extreme like the Cultural Revolution, or deceptively bland like social and liberal democracy, unless it adversely affects their business, when they will simply defect the country. In the Information Age 'populism is bad for business'. A large population, particularly an uneducated and ageing population, is now a liability, and has become the major problem facing all Western governments. The masses will themselves put employment and economic well-being before the dubious privilege of electing powerless representatives. That is just as well since government regulation inhibits trade, a fact that many politicians refuse to understand. How ironic that Karl Marx anticipated politicians becoming ineffective, but for other reasons! And as George Orwell foresaw, a Saturday night lottery will soften the blow for the populace. What price democracy in the new order? The 29 adults populating the remote Atlantic islands of St Kilda were told that it would cost their local council around £5,000 to administer the 1997 British general election. They decided not to bother and save the money (*Economist*, 19 April 1997).

Inducements

Naturally, we all want social stability through economic well-being, and so every area will offer inducements to global companies because of the employment they bring. Because of the need to employ local labour, the major social problem for politicians in the coming decades is going to be how to attract employers to partner local companies, and how to keep them attracted. In 1997 the International Labour Organization calculated that there were nearly a billion unemployed or underemployed (sub-employed) people in the world (International Labour Office, Geneva, 1996/97), that is nearly a third of the entire global workforce, and they are by no means all living in the Third World. The Chinese government estimates that there are 200 million surplus rural labourers and vagrants roaming their country (Poole, 25 June 1998). Governments will have no choice other than to acquiesce to the will of global enterprises. Ford was given government subsidies to open an engine plant in South Wales (Hotten, 19 October 1995). BMW asked for a government subsidy of more than £150 million, or otherwise it would consider moving to Hungary. That same new barbarian car company in July 1998 threatened to buy its spare parts from overseas because the value of sterling was too high (Poulter, 8 July 1998).

Companies (and individuals) and not countries generate the wealth. New technology has released these organizations and knowledge workers from any geographical constraint, and they are roaming the world looking for free-thinking countries as partners. However, companies do not want to 'brain drain' large numbers of workers from one country to another, because this would only serve to undermine relationships with the government of any region likely to lose from such a haemorrhage. Global companies want to spread their operations across politically stable countries, and the loss to the tax base of high-earning knowledge workers will destabilize any country's taxation and regulation policies. That is in no one's interest. The very same technology that allows money to fly through international financial markets at a phenomenal speed and accuracy has enabled research and production facilities to be farmed out to regions whose governments support and encourage their presence. Corporate incomers will help the areas to build the necessary infrastructure, and they will happily move, provided the freedom and profits are there. Once in place they will identify the very best knowledge workers, and then these 'fast-track' individuals will be sent anywhere in the world as and when they are required by the company, but most workers will stay (and be taxed) at home. This is not to say that there won't be a brain drain. However, it will be the workers themselves, not the company, that will initiate the moves to optimize their personal ambitions, and there will be plenty of countries that will welcome the talented (but only the talented).

Because of the need to entice global companies for the investment and employment they bring, not only will state be pitted against state, but also area will compete against area, town against town, even suburb against suburb. Company and individual strategies must be structured to take advantage of such rivalry, and to cope with the inevitable market instability. Each state will permit entry to holders of 'UN-style' company passports, giving senior executives the equivalent of diplomatic status (and hence no income tax). Tax credits, tax holidays and other financial inducements and reduced regulation aimed at attracting employers will be the name of the game everywhere. In its drive to create a 25-kilometre Multimedia Super-corridor between Kuala Lumpur and its airport, the Malaysian government made the very shrewd decision of offering foreign companies a 10-year tax holiday. These companies are also to be allowed to employ unlimited numbers of foreign workers. They are already raiding the intellectual talents of India and eastern Europe in their drive to create a thriving information economy for Malaysia.

Different states in Europe have already embarked on 'regulatory arbitrage' to tempt financial sector companies away from their 'European partners' (sic). On the American continent, British Columbia, that charges C $350,000 for landed immigration status, is in conflict with Nova Scotia and other provinces that only charge C $250,000 (Drohan, 22 August 1990). Immigrants pay the lower price to enter Canada and then immediately move to Vancouver! It is inevitable that such trends will undermine local and national legislation and taxation policies.

Any area with independent aspirations will use economic weapons against its neighbours, and will distance itself from their legislative oppression. Not long ago residents of Staten Island voted to split from New York (Katz, 8 June 1995). One by one, Canadian provinces scrapped local taxes on tobacco, because Canadians were crossing the border into the United States to get cheaper cigarettes. As each province lowered its taxes, people crossed from neighbouring provinces to buy tobacco products. The result was a collapse of tax revenues from smokers in those provinces keeping taxes high (and it was a disaster for small tobacconist shops), whereas those with lower taxes earned more from increased spending than they lost in tax (Boadle, 8 February 1994). This exhibits a haunting parallel with the shopkeepers of Kent whose businesses have been hit by contraband from France and Belgium.

To make matters worse for Canada, a 1994 Toronto-produced television programme implied that British Columbia resents what it sees as its subsidy of the rest of the country. It hinted at independence for Cascadia (British Columbia with the US states of Washington and Oregon), which has a combined GDP of $250 billion and an economy almost the size of Australia's (*Economist*, 21 May 1994). It probably won't happen. British Columbia usually returns social democrat politicians – which drives business over the border into Alberta and knowledge workers into the United States. But is there a future for Canada? As Daniel Bell so eloquently put it, 'the nation–state is too small for the big things and too big for the small things' (1976).

The smart city

Some futurologists, such as Heineken (Naisbitt, 1994), expect that early in the next century the number of states in the United Nations will increase from the present number of 184 to more than a thousand. Perhaps the new self-consciousness in Lombardy and with it the rise of the Northern League in Italian politics, or the steady slide toward an independent Scotland, can be seen as part of a global trend. So how can an independent-minded state, area, town or suburb, and its indigenous businesses, succeed? It must develop a good understanding of changes in both its external and internal environments, over which it has little influence, but of which it can take advantage. The first priority is to attract wealth-bearing global organizations, and this necessitates being part of the information superhighway. If it does not, then that locality will lose out to the 'smart city' down the road.

But why a 'smart city'? 'The principal places in which strangers do business together are big commercial cities. The cosmopolitanism of these cities is no accident. It is an instance of functional necessity becoming a cultural trait. To make mundane, everyday deals with strangers and aliens, for no reason except that they're customers or suppliers, demands tolerance for people outside one's background and personal preferences and, often enough, even respect for them as well. Cosmopolitanism spills over into other fields, such as the arts, but its roots are commercial' (Jacobs, 1993). The inevitable consequence of global trade will be the rise of the new city–state at the hub of global electronic and transport networks. The non-democratic model of pre-1997 Hong Kong is an exemplar, even though the city itself didn't realize that it had defined the future until it was too late. Singapore under the enlightened leadership of Lee Kwan Yew is another. So is Malaysia in their creation of the Kuala Lumpur multimedia super corridor, provided the country doesn't erect barriers against global trade following the 1997 currency crisis. What European city will be the first to break ranks with the nation–state mentality holding back progress? A number of European cities can make the leap. Liechtenstein has already started. What about Monaco? And let us not forget Venice, Genoa and Milan. Perhaps they will all rediscover former glories. The spirit of the medieval city is still alive and well in Italy. It is only a matter of time before Lisbon jumps: it has the singular example of attracting the Gulbenkian wealth earlier this century. In the United States cities like New York, Chicago and Seattle are likely candidates for semi-independence.

The Corporation of the City of London too, has enormous potential, and could be revitalized. An independent cosmopolitan city–state of London as a tiger economy makes real economic sense; however, the dead hand of Westminster, the 'mother of parliaments', will make it far more difficult. As a wise man once said: 'A desperate disease requires a dangerous remedy.' Come back Guy Fawkes; all is forgiven. (Guy Fawkes was executed in 1606 for his part in the gunpowder plot to blow up parliament.) If the House of Commons really wanted to help London, then it should move to Birmingham.

London is the capital city of an empire in terminal decline. It is therefore highly cosmopolitan, as was Rome at the end of its empire. It is this very cosmopolitan nature that makes it an ideal focal point for global business, provided that it sets itself up as a smart city–state. By similar reasoning Moscow and Berlin have enormous potential. When Washington's coercion of the US entrepreneurial elite eventually implodes, New York too will be ideally placed for revitalization. The city leaders there would do well to observe the behaviour of London, Berlin and Moscow in the coming years.

Part IV

Transition

9

An age of rage

The Machine Age may be fading into memory, but its legacy of degeneracy is all too plain to see. Its profligate waste of the products of science and technology pollute the planet. Its weapons of mass destruction, many in the hands of unstable old barbarian megalomaniacs, have brought humanity to the edge of oblivion. And what of humanity itself? Now there is the real problem. The major lesson for the Information Age is that success comes from 'quality not quantity'; and the Machine Age has left us with the exact opposite.

A new order

The redistribution of wealth that has occurred slowly over the last century and resulted in today's notions of social justice and fairness, allowing the degenerate to prosper, is now being reversed, and rapidly. 'The bourgeoisie during its rule of scarcely one [now two] hundred years, has created more massive and more colossal productive forces than have all preceding generations together' (Karl Marx). Because the masses were needed in that production process, the bourgeoisie was forced to share the wealth around, and this eventually led to the present dependency culture. But in the Information Age, who are the new bourgeoisie, now that production takes place inside a human head rather than in a factory of machines? And what are their attitudes to the masses now they no longer need them?

Societies are stratifying. New elites are appearing. Something inevitably self-selecting is happening. In his book *The Bell Curve* (Herrnstein and Murray, 1994), libertarian Charles Murray predicts that society will polarize, as the rich or intelligent will choose breeding partners only from within their own social group, and the masses likewise. The future is about inequality, and at the very bottom of the heap, Western societies are already witnessing the emergence of a rapidly expanding underclass. 'All that is solid melts into the air, all that is holy is profaned, and man is at last compelled to face with sober senses his real conditions of life and his relations with his kind' (Karl Marx). The streets of London are again littered with beggars; critics of 19th-century conditions, like Charles Dickens, and yes Karl Marx, would feel quite at home in today's capital city.

In the transition to inequality we can expect massive civil unrest and disorder. Those with nothing have nothing to lose. But now even those with something to lose see themselves losing it unless they take action. The 'soon-to-have-nots' will riot: such was the worldwide Carnival Against Capitalism on 19 June 1999. In the winter of 1995, workers and students took to the streets against the French government (Duval Smith, 20 November 1995) in defence of their cradle-to-grave health and welfare systems. But at the same time as the protests over unemployment in Paris, market manipulators, the 'gnomes of London' as the French government called them, were raking in the profits of speculation (Smithy, 8 October 1995).

The lights are going out for wide sectors of society, and for whole categories of employment. We are entering a new Dark Age: an age of hopelessness, an age of resentment, an age of rage. Newspapers are full of reports about road rage and air rage. We will see a focus for that rage among the unemployed: 'victim violence' or 'redundancy rage'. Newly redundant workers attack senior management and ex-colleagues in the workplace, on the street and in their homes. It has become so common that Americans even talk about 'going postal', referring to an incident in 1986 when a postal worker ran amok killing 15 of his colleagues after he had been 'let go'. In 1989 a highly depressed Joseph Wesbecker shot 20 ex-colleagues at the Standard Gravure works (Cornwell, 1996). The question of whether or not he was under the influence of Prozac, or alchohol, or narcotics, or good old-fashioned hate is irrelevant; there are many out there who think it is open season on the employed and their employers.

Some of the rage will be targeted inwards. In the United States more people commit suicide than are murdered, by a factor of three to two (Sapsted, 22 October 1998). According to the Samaritans (Hawkes, 22 May 1993) in Britain there is a successful suicide every two hours, and one is attempted every two minutes. In the young, suicide has reached epidemic proportions. Suicide accounts for 19 per cent of deaths in the 15–24-year age group (Boseley,

25 June 1998), with one attempt every 30 minutes. Suicides straddle all social strata. The highest number is among the professional class and the second highest is among unskilled workers. Being unemployed, living alone and boredom are also strongly correlated to suicide. The sad cases of Cheshire teenager Calum Burnet (Dalrymple, 26 August 1994), who spelt out the word 'bored' in stones on the trackside before lying in front of a train, and of 31-year-old Paul Rix (Kirkbride, 22 September 1993), who killed himself in despair because he couldn't find work, are likely to become increasingly common events worldwide.

Stress and high expectations also seem to be factors, as of course is the availability of the means of killing oneself. In July 1993 an illustrated *Complete Manual of Suicide* by Wataru Tsurumi (McCarthy, 14 October 1994) was published in Japan and promptly sold over half a million copies. It cold-bloodedly described methods ranging from hanging to jumping from tall buildings, and even weird ones such as freezing oneself, self-immolation and driving into quicksand. Diagrams showed for example how to judge the timing for jumping under a train, and where to find ideal suicide spots. Some critics of Tsurumi's book claim that it has increased the annual number of more than 20,000 suicides in Japan; however, there is no clear evidence to that fact. The critics are mixing up cause and effect; the book has been successful because more people are contemplating suicide, not the reverse. The suicidal can now find even more information like this over the Net. In America, Derek Humphry, founder of the Hemlock Society and author of the best-selling suicide manual *Final Exit* can be contacted by e mail (Ergo@efn.org).

As far as the majority are concerned, the blame is placed fairly and squarely on 'the system'. Dissent is fermenting across all Western societies. In their pent-up anger, normally law-abiding citizens are joining the culture of protest. They may not know what they want, but they know they don't like the world the way it is, or the way it is going. Previously they would have donated money to 'good causes', and in very extreme cases they would have demonstrated in a polite way about mainstream issues to do with the environment or animal and human rights. They want to stop seal culling, the fur trade, whaling, exports of live calves, child labour, toxic waste, genetically modified foods, nuclear power and nuclear weapons.

However, now a new phenomenon is appearing, where well-heeled nimbys (not in my back yard) take to the streets to object violently to everything from the felling of trees to the blight of motorway construction on their property values. Governments are out of touch with this new phenomenon, as is obvious from their propaganda approach to road building. They believe that the argument that good roads are essential for national economic competitiveness is self-evident, and that it is a simple matter of employing public relations consultants in order to get the message across. Governments fail to see the fury engendered by their use of an individual's own taxes to push through a scheme that will cause huge financial loss to that same person.

Alienation from government and resentment of their waste of 'our money' are commonplace, and many citizens now see government as the enemy. People who a decade ago would never have dreamt of demonstrating now take on government and its cronies, and win. With the spectre of unemployment looming, the vulnerable in society increasingly attack what they consider economic exploitation and 'unfairness'. Whole sections of society that previously felt their future secure, can see it slipping away. Soaring unemployment levels among white collar workers make them furious that they are now losing their 'jobs for life'. A middle-class rage is bringing the well educated and articulate into the clutch of experienced agitators, anarchists and criminals, who then use middle-class fury to camouflage their attacks to overthrow authority.

The snowball is rolling, and demonstrators call for an end to unemployment and homelessness. They think they can achieve this by making a nuisance of themselves to the authorities. Protests have become social events. There will be a free pop concert attached to the 'demo'; protesters even take their children along as a family day out. The problem is that a few, but now increasingly more, drift from protest to civil disobedience and finally to outright violence. They become more active, lying down in front of traffic or harassing government ministers, and they end up as zealots with a grudge against the oppressing capitalist state.

Moral indignation and a sense of injustice make them aggressively certain of their rightness. They focus on a single issue, untainted by the squalid pragmatism of representative politics. There is a chain of logic that implies that because they have no self-interest then they must be right, and whatever they do for their cause is right. This leaves the authorities with the dilemma of deciding where genuine, legitimate (whatever that means?) protest ends, and deliberate and potentially violent provocation begins.

New warfare

Increasingly, the growing band of the disgruntled losers attack the capitalist enemy where it hurts most, in their computer and telecommunications infrastructure. They will hit the Net and via the Net. They know no company can survive in the global economy without the integrity of its information systems intact. Information warfare will become commonplace, not only between states, but also between individuals, pressure groups, companies and the state. Criminals also know this, and they will take advantage of the chaos. Since the days of Meyer Lansky, organized crime has been an avid user and abuser of international telecommunications. Who knows, perhaps posterity will acclaim Lansky, the New York gangster, as the midwife of the global information economy through his money-laundering exploits.

There are already anarchists on the Net; electronic copies of bomb-making manuals such as *The Anarchist's Cookbook* can be downloaded, and detailed recipes are sent via private e-mail. They communicate via electronic bulletin boards, with their files booby-trapped with viruses that attack the computers of those whose attention they do not welcome. They are spreading sedition by circulating information on how to infiltrate various 'class enemy' organizations, particularly the police, government departments and transnational companies. They are targeting schoolchildren by advising them on how to disrupt, 'trash' and even burn down their schools, and far worse, by supplying data on drugs, explanations of how to manufacture incendiary devices, bombs and chemical weapons, and how to sabotage telecommunications networks. Of course such instructions have been available in books and military texts long before there was an Internet. What is different is that now access is easy, and more importantly it can be anonymous. Dangerous malcontents who were previously isolated are now finding one another on the Net, and governments have no way of policing it. Grudge terror, whether the grudge is real or imagined, is now an all-too-frequent reality. Theodore Kaczynski, the unabomber (Varadarajan, 25 June 1998), and the attacks on Barclays Bank and Sainsbury's supermarket (Eaglesham, 8 April 1999) by the Mardi Gras bomber, sexagenarian Edgar Pearce, are just the beginning.

British anarchists aim mainly at economic targets, using e mail to organize shoplifting 'weekend breaks' for their European counterparts to join in the looting of shops (Levy and Burrell, 5 March 1995). They plan to rob banks, break into credit-card systems and attack transnational firms. It is all too easy to dismiss this anarchic phenomenon as the fantasizing of social inadequates. The fact is that information is being supplied to them by hard-core terrorists, groups that are known to have killed. Some of the Walter Mittys out there will become serious sociopaths. There are some haunting parallels in the actions of the Aum Shinrikyo cult, and its founder leader Shoko Asahara, found guilty of the sarin nerve-gas terror attack on the Tokyo subway system during the rush-hour of 20 March 1995, after which 12 people died and 5,500 were hospitalized (Kwan, 4 June 1995).

The police authorities are becoming increasingly concerned at the skill base in these groups and the resources available to them. Agitators now have the ability to communicate with one another, and they can find the means to do real damage. Governments no longer have the monopoly of chemical and biological weapons, or heavy artillery, not even nuclear weapons. Terrorism is now the province of increasingly smaller groups, who can nonetheless do terminal damage to the state. Meanwhile, the present liberal legal system seems totally inadequate in coping with this open aggression. All of this is happening at a time when the vast majority of the population in the West has very little to complain about. But what happens when the level of unemployment becomes a social disaster, and in their fury and resentment large numbers of well-educated (soon-to-be-ex-)middle-class recruits enter the fray on the side of anarchy?

The anarchists justify their violence as the only way to overthrow the state. It shows just how out of touch they are. They don't need to use the Net to overthrow the state. The Net is doing that all on its own without their help. The anarchists are correct that a class struggle will precipitate the demise of the nation–state as we know it. But it won't be the masses who inherit the earth. It will be the old and new barbarians who will fight it out and claim their birthright. Neither of these sides will be nearly as understanding of the anachronistic anarchists as are the present liberals running modern Western democratic governments. The 'Age of Aquarius' is here, but only for the elite barbarians.

Government is the enemy

Where is all this leading? If we want to see the future we need look no further than the siege mentality both among poor rural communities (the 'trailer trash') and among the urban rich in the United States. The rich 'circle their wagons' inside fortified estates. To all intents and purposes they are living inside castles but with electronic walls and drawbridges. They will be further protected by special devices that deter unwelcome visitors, such as weapons that immobilize any car cruising uninvited around their area. Elsewhere whole poor communities unite against a common background of crushing poverty and debt, and their inability to pay interest on bank loans or excessive tax demands. Entire rural economies, farmers, suppliers and consequently local businesses collapse in a domino effect as one cycle of bad debts, bankruptcy and repossession follows another. They lash out against Big Government, and yearn for the mythical time earlier this century when the State capital, not Washington, held the power. They want justice to be their justice, with local laws enforced by a local posse. The politicians of the European Union, who are using local community differences to weaken the component nation–states and thereby increase their own power and influence, should heed this lesson, or they too could find themselves the butt of resentment for those regions that lose out – just like in the United States.

Increasingly the rural poor in the United States are being joined by their poverty-stricken urban counterparts. They see themselves pitted against the anonymous but all-pervasive might of the federal bureaucracy. And it is not just the poor. The National Rifle Association fielded their president-to-be, actor Charlton Heston, to speak out against government interference: 'The first act of a dictatorship is to disarm the people' (Campbell, 14 December 1997). To them government has become an end in itself, looking after its own interests, growing like a slime-mould at the expense of the common folk. They perceive poor blue-collar ex-workers as the real United States, and they seek to apportion blame. They see their government in a gigantic international conspiracy with the United Nations, Japan, a few European countries (now that communists are no longer a threat), and of course 'the global financial markets dominated by Jews'.

On the disparate cultural and political fringes, strange bedfellows huddle together in a perverted nationalism: racists, xenophobes, militarists, protectionists, mystical Christian fundamentalists. A resentful cross-section of blue-collar America is forming into militias, heavily armed paramilitary organizations, to defend the Second Amendment of the American Constitution that gave the people the right 'to keep and bear arms'. Far-right militants are exploiting a deep mistrust of Washington and calling fellow citizens to learn about guerrilla warfare techniques and the use of state-of-the-art light and heavy weaponry. 'Only in America'. No! A racist militia has been formed in Australia. The Australian Freedom Scouts have several thousand armed members organized in 90 cells, sworn in and ready to wage guerrilla warfare in defence of their country from a supposed imminent invasion by the Indonesian Army (Ham, 19 July 1998).

Some estimates put the number of organized militias in the United States at around a hundred, with up to 50,000 members (Cornwell, 22 April 1995), although others claim that the Michigan militia alone is 12,000 strong (Hoffman, 1 July 1995). Militias are to be found right across the United States, and not only in the old Western frontier states. Many are just gun clubs whose anti-gun-control members fantasize war games in relative safety. But some are more sinister. Ku Klux Klansmen, neo-Nazis and other varieties of racist believe they must destroy the government before it destroys them. Much of this militia mentality and the white supremacist movements stem from an inadequacy of a sector of society that is losing its position in the pecking order to a perceived government-inspired invasion of immigrants.

It was hideously inevitable when, on 19 April 1995, a huge car bomb tore apart the Alfred P Murrah federal building in Oklahoma City that housed the hated Bureau of Alcohol, Tobacco and Firearms (ATF), killing 168 men, women and children, and seriously injuring many more (Wilkinson, 6 August 1999). Anyone surfing the Internet looking for information on the far-right and the militias will know that this kind of violent direct action has long been on the cards. Militia extremists have been openly calling for direct paramilitary action against the authorities for some time.

In response to the general threat, but in particular to this bombing and that of New York's World Trade Center on 26 February 1993 in which six people died (Cornwell, 6 September 1996), President Clinton asked the FBI to set up a new Domestic Counter-Terrorism Center, giving the Bureau far-reaching new powers (*Economist*, 29 April 1995). But the far right blame what they see as the already excessive powers of the FBI and ATF for the trouble. Ratcheting up state power can only lead to a further alienation and escalation of violence. The far right claim that there is a growing trend by government to launch witch-hunts against them, and to criminalize, or label insane ('loony libertarians'), the dissent that wells up out of frustration. In 1996, a group of 'Freemen of Montana' held out in an 81-day standoff in their Justus Township against the arrayed might of the FBI (*Economist*, 22 June 1996). They know that 'federal scumbags' are already trying to penetrate or entrap their groups.

They point to the case of Randall Weaver, portrayed by US marshals (with no proof) as a member of the Christian Identity Movement, with links to the Aryan Nations white supremacist group. In 1991 he was arrested for selling two sawn-off (by a mere quarter inch) shotguns to undercover FBI agents, but skipped bail with his family and a friend, Kevin Harris. In August 1992, they were located in a remote cabin at Ruby Ridge in northern Idaho. A series of gunfights in a six-day siege left three people dead: a deputy marshal, Weaver's wife Vicki and his 14-year-old son Samuel. 'Randy' Weaver and Harris were wounded. More than 400 heavily armed FBI agents took part in the misconceived siege, backed up with armoured personnel carriers, helicopters and a bulldozer. The government action was a chapter of accidents. It only ended when US war hero, James 'Bo' Gritz intervened and brought out the survivors, including Weaver's three daughters (Toczek, 21 April 1995). What did all this achieve? Weaver and his friend were found not guilty of the murder of the deputy. The jury decided they acted in self-defence. However, Weaver was convicted of failing to appear in court and of violation of bail conditions, but was found not guilty of the main charge of selling illegal weapons because of entrapment. The Justice Department later paid Weaver $3.1 million in compensation for the death of his wife (Eddy, 10 August 1997).

The far right point at government tyranny and the FBI using 'bullying tactics' against alternative lifestyles. In particular they cite 28 February 1993 and the shambolic raid by agents of the ATF on the Mount Carmel compound of the Branch Davidian sect in Waco, Texas, culminating in an attack with tanks and tear gas on 19 April (Davies, 20 April 1993). The leader of the sect, David Koresh, died among 80 other men, women and children in the conflagration that followed.

Although this was an attack on a multiracial sect, perversely it became a rallying symbol for white supremacists. However the fears of such people have a habit of becoming self-fulfilling. Governments must respond to the actions of all unruly citizens. For example President Clinton's pragmatism over the Domestic Counter-Terrorism Center has provided a perfect illustration of what the far right most dislikes: the inexorable extension of the powers of the federal government. All this rage in society leaves governments on the horns of a dilemma. In a successful society, economic reality and political reality must be synchronized. When out of synchronization, politics can claim short-term victories but economic power always wins in the long run. Therefore politicians must make up their minds about whose side they are on: those who vote them into power, or those who pay the bills. For most of the latter half of the 20th century the masses had power, so these two groups were more or less the same. Democracy was synchronized with economic forces. But in the Information Age, governments must support the rich. The rage of the dispossessed, and of everyone else for that matter, has only just begun. Look to the future; it is already happening in the United States of America.

10

Corrupting the old order

With the deskilling of work, with inevitable unemployment, with so much rage in the air, why do communication and computer technologies engender so much optimism in our society? Do we really think they will make the lives of the majority better? Do we really believe that technology is a 'democratizing force'? Or that the Internet is a technological peasants' charter? Will it create open government? Will it expand popular education by delivering cheap ready access to the very best teachers? Will it allow many more of the population to earn their living via electronic commerce? As the communications revolution brings about *The Death of Distance* (Cairncross, 1997) will it usher in an era of global peace? I doubt it very much. I see the Internet creating consumers rather than producers; I see uncontrolled communication and arbitrary connection creating a world simmering with petty jealousies, resentments and imagined slights. I'm with Oscar Wilde: 'The basis of optimism is… sheer terror.' Much of today's optimism is just displacement activity, an evasion of the fact that large sections of our society have become deskilled, disenfranchised and dispossessed by the technology. Worse, our societal and commercial institutions, so firmly grounded in the Industrial Age, will not be able to cope in the Information Age, and will implode under pressure from an alternative economy, a large part of which could be criminal.

Buyer beware

Society's terrified optimism is aggravated by its self-delusion that technology, particularly computer technology, will always somehow provide a solution. It just has to! But as Pablo Picasso so shrewdly observed: 'Computers are useless, they can only give you answers.' More often than not, these answers are irrelevant, or just plain wrong, or they solve the wrong problems, only to create new and even worse problems. Just consider the rat's nest of would-be answers congesting the Internet. We don't know who exactly are launching these answers into cyberspace. What is the legitimacy of the authors of Web sites? Just what is their claim on knowledge? Can we trust them? Are we just stumbling into governments' subtle propaganda, companies' marketing hyperbole, the scams of confidence tricksters, the ramblings of lunatics, or worse the filth of perverts? How can we check? Do we check them out anyway? And why should they trust us?

Most of today's trading regulations are based on the assumption that society's policing institutions can close down rogue traders, because buyer and seller live within the same legal jurisdiction. Unfortunately this is no longer the case with electronic commerce; the Internet bypasses these regulations in so many ways. On the Internet you can claim to be anyone. Illegitimate electronic shop-fronts and false customer identities are proliferating. Who would have thought that the respectable-sounding European Union Bank, the world's first offshore bank on the Internet, was in fact being run from Antigua by Russian-born 'entrepreneurs', who vanished in August 1997 taking $10 million with them (Nelson, 30 November 1997). *Caveat emptor*, buyer beware, now more than ever before. The question of trust, and lack of it, is what will ultimately colour our perceptions of the Net. Where is the corroborating evidence of a sale if it is made electronically? Unless we get our act together, the Net won't be giving us a nice warm rosy glow, but the gloom of grey and black. We simply do not have the trust-inspiring institutional structures that can cope with commerce in cyberspace, in the same way that high street buyers and sellers in general trust one another. The unpalatable fact is that the naive way in which we are stumbling along the Net is a gift for operators in the black economy and for shady elements in the grey markets.

These shadowy gangs don't even have to invent new operational procedures for the new electronic world. The model for recycling grey goods is already out there: simply export the particular good from jurisdiction A, where it would have to be scrapped, to jurisdiction B, that has different rules. Give the product new packaging, and re-import to A. There is a thriving grey market in meat from supermarket shelves that has passed its sell-by date. Britain does not allow the irradiation of meat, a process that kills off bacteria but that does not destroy other toxins. Such grey meat is exported from Britain to countries with no such regulations, where it is 'nuked' and re-imported to Britain quite legally. Of course much of this grey market is perfectly legitimate; the shady operators are simply piggybacking on practices developed by discount shops and supermarkets. In fact in its purest form the grey market is a form of arbitrage highly beneficial to consumers, where shops can manipulate the inconsistent pricing practices of many 'designer label' companies, as for example importing goods from the United States where prices are much cheaper than in the European Union. However, when highly organized criminal gangs counterfeit or repackage grey goods they don't even bother to export. Old goods, bankrupt and damaged stock are repackaged and sold as new. No wonder governments are trying to place grey markets under some semblance of control, but because most are legitimate, the legislators will have to tread a very fine line between the rights of designer companies and those of supermarkets insisting on finding the lowest-priced goods for their customers (Cope, 17 July 1998).

Criminal counterfeiting has become a real problem, particularly in the alcohol and food businesses. In 1981 contaminated industrial oil sold as cooking oil claimed more than 30,000 Spanish victims, including 435 directly attributable deaths (Ober, 2 October 1997). Automobile (van der Zee, 2 July 1998) and aeroplane (Clark, 13 July 1996) spares are being counterfeited on a large scale. Who knows how many fatal crashes have been caused by such faulty parts? The legitimate business calculates that counterfeit parts account for up to 10 per cent of the market (van der Zee, 2 July 1998). Do we only buy counterfeit goods when we are duped? Is it only anti-social individuals on the fringes of society who buy knowingly from this alternative marketplace? Would decent people buy goods that are barred by the authorities? Of course they would! They already do. Death-trap spare parts are not the only goods available from this shady world. Pornography and other proscribed material are a huge global business, and are already major applications on the Net.

Globalizing new communication technologies make it easy to sidestep national constraints on banned materials; they have for decades. Consider two books that were banned in Britain: *Spycatcher* by Peter Wright, the ex-MI5 employee who spilt the beans on his ex-colleagues, or *The Housekeeper's Story* by Wendy Berry, who dished the dirt on Prince Charles and Princess Diana. Britons telephoned or faxed friends in Australia and the United States where these books were available, and box-loads of pre-ordered copies arrived in the mail or were flown in with friends. In these latter cases the recipients were in touch with real friends. However, over the Net new 'friends' with something to sell will be contacting you. They will find you. As supermarkets and other trading groups develop 'profiles' on all their customers, criminals will enter these databases and list likely targets for their goods. They will appear very plausible, and they will find ready markets.

Take for example the purchase of pharmaceutical products that in most developed countries can only be obtained on prescription or are completely banned. Despite government restrictions, every impotent British male can get his supply of Viagra, the little blue pill that supersedes ground rhinoceros horn, via adverts appearing on Internet. Then there are the counterfeit medicines and chemical products that have always been available on the black market: Glaxo's Zantac is probably the best-known example to have been copied by criminals. It will be Christmas and birthdays all rolled into one for hypochondriacs, and an enormous opportunity for the quacks of alternative medicine and every sort of snake-oil salesman. How do you guarantee that your correspondents on the Net are who they say they are? Are they misrepresenting themselves? Is the doctor really a doctor? Even if the qualifications you see are valid in jurisdiction A, are they recognized in B? Don't delude yourself into thinking that national checks and balances will guarantee peace of mind. There have been many examples of self-deluding basket cases masquerading as doctors. Some have actually been employed in hospitals and have got away with the deception for years. 'Dr' Muhammed Saeed of Bradford escaped detection for 30 years before pharmacists started to query his bizarre prescriptions (Wilkinson, 18 June 1992). We should be very worried, because it is so much easier pretending to be qualified over the Net.

Now with easy access to suppliers via the Net, chemicals and drugs (some highly dangerous) can be sent through the mail from countries with more lax laws concerning these products, or they can be pre-purchased and collected during a vacation: the Net will tell you where to go to find 'the goods'. It is bad enough if the drugs are genuine, but what if they are counterfeit or have passed their sell-by date and re-entered via the grey market? All the well-meaning regulations put in place by the government and medical profession to protect the public will be blown apart. There are many customers out there queuing up for these services. Consider a case that is illegal under European Union regulations. Recently veterinary surgeons were barred from prescribing drugs, originally designed for humans, to pets, even though prior to the ban it was common practice. What happened? In Britain pet-owners pretend to suffer from a wide range of ailments so that doctors prescribe them the drugs their pets need, thereby annually costing the National Health Service huge sums of money. On the Net they no longer need any subterfuge.

The limits of government

Governments are not in control. They can't just indignantly 'pass a law against it'. The Canadian tobacco wars are a classic example of a state's inability to maintain taxes in a global economy. At one time Canadians were paying C $36 in tax on each C $47 carton of cigarettes (*Financial Post*, 6 November 1992). The native Americans of the 'Six Nations', whose lands straddled the Canadian–US border, developed a thriving business by importing cigarettes from the low-tax United States for resale in Canada. Half a million native Americans are exempt from income taxes if they live on reserves. They do not pay customs duties, excise, gasoline, alcohol and tobacco taxes. The Mohawks had been smuggling contraband across the border for the previous 200 years, so they were all set to profit from the windfall that a government hike in taxes had blown their way. Larry Miller and other organized smugglers moved in. Miller used his links with the tribe on the Akwesasne reserve to move huge numbers of cigarettes back across the border between New York State and the Canadian provinces of Quebec and Ontario (reported in a TV programme 'The Fifth Estate', *CBC*, 4 August 1999). A ludicrous situation developed where 80 per cent (95 per cent of certain brands such as Export A) of Canadian-made cigarettes exported to the United States were smuggled back, to be sold at a fraction of the taxed varieties (*Financial Post*, 9 April 1992).

Things got so bad that an export tax of C $8 per carton was levied on exported cigarettes, which simply devastated the indigenous cigarette industry and delivered a bonanza to US cigarette factories. Canadian factories laid off workers and threatened to move across the border. The tax was dropped after only eight weeks (*Reuters News Service*, 13 July 1993). The retail trade in cigarettes fell off so badly that traders in Quebec eventually began openly flouting the law by selling contraband tobacco from their stores (Boadle, 8 February 1994). One by one, the provinces caved in and lowered taxes. During the turmoil the premier of Ontario insisted that he would not lower taxes, furious that taxpayers, tired of being milked dry, dared to go into neighbouring provinces and buy cigarettes where cartons were nearly C $20 cheaper (*Financial Post*, 11 February 1994). He eventually folded, forced to follow the lead of Quebec. In Alberta the tax on cigarettes was costing citizens C $14 more per carton. The politicians there were so incensed at the pressure they were getting from the inter-provincial movement of tobacco that they made it illegal to possess more than five cartons of cigarettes from another province. They levied fines of up to C $1,000 and a 30-day jail sentence for a first offence, and a C $5,000 fine and six months in jail for a second offence (Geddes, 6 May 1994). The politicians' indignation concerning their right to 'rip off' the taxpayer beggars belief.

It is not just Canada. Wherever we look, from Thailand to Kyrgyzstan, Brazil to Slovakia, tax hikes lead to smuggling. Criminal groups are using Andorra, the low-tax principality in the Pyrenees, to re-import British cigarettes into Britain and Ireland. Figures from two British manufacturers showed that their combined exports to Andorra rose from 6.65 million packets in 1995 to 60.55 million in 1997 (Webster, 15 March 1998). South Africa is also feeling the pinch with tobacco smuggling. The Rembrandt Group finds it impossible to compete with cigarettes from eastern Europe because they were lumbered with high raw material costs. Also, they had not mechanized their procedures, in order to keep up employment levels for the good of the local community (*Reuters*, 26 July 1994). But that community did not see the self-interest in buying from its own. They bought the cheaper cigarettes. Companies must compete on price or die.

After Canadian taxes on cigarettes were reduced, smuggling became unprofitable. However, the smugglers turned their attention to booze, and the Canadian drinks industry was badly hit. In 1990 the 'mounties' seized C $199,725 worth of smuggled liquor, but in 1993 this had risen to C $12.1 million (Francis, 13 December 1994). It was estimated that half the booze drunk in Quebec and a third in Ontario was smuggled, hardly surprising when taxes made up about 43 per cent of the cost of liquor in the United States while in Canada it was 83 per cent. Cigarette smuggling mostly involved Canadian-made cigarettes, which were exported and then smuggled back into Canada. With alcohol, it was mostly US-made spirits being smuggled. Since the mid-1980s Canada's indigenous brewing industry has lost 6,000 jobs and closed 18 plants, largely due to smuggling (*The Grocer*, 28 January 1995).

The lesson has not been learnt yet. Canadian politicians have started raising tax levels again (Leger, 10 May 1998). And not only in Canada. On 1 May 1994, the state of Michigan increased tobacco taxes from 25 cents to 75 cents per pack. This led to a 30 per cent drop in legal sales, thereby pushing a number of small convenience stores to the point of bankruptcy (Kaplan, 15 December 1995). They also faced a surge in the number of break-ins. On 1 December 1994, Arizona raised taxes by 40 cents a pack. Sales dropped by more than 40 per cent, and grew by 33 per cent in native American reservations and by 8 per cent on military bases where no tax is collected (*PR Newswire*, 25 May 1995).

For years politicians have slapped heavy 'sin taxes' on alcohol and tobacco consumption. It enabled cash-ravenous governments to carry out tax theft on the population, all the while masquerading as health and welfare policies. In Britain tobacco accounts for 3.5 per cent of all taxes and 25 per cent of excise duties, totalling more than £10 billion annually (Turner, 22 June 1997). But the day of reckoning has arrived. The sinners are now really sinning, by conspiring with criminal elements, and buying contraband tobacco and alcohol. People may not see it as immoral to trade with organized crime if tax levels have been set too high. With the government adding goods and services tax (GST) to make costs even higher, a spontaneous but unorganized tax revolt in Canada has resulted in a thriving underground economy. Suddenly the law of diminishing returns is hitting government, as the more they hike taxes, the lower the revenue they receive.

As a direct consequence of this farce, the anti-smoking health-cost argument has been shown to be a sham. One researcher from George Mason University puts the potential cost of a total prohibition on US-tobacco products at $300 billion (*PR Newswire*, 11 October 1994). The prevalent anti-cigarette propaganda, that hospitalization of smokers costs the health services more than that of non-smokers, is simply not true. Smokers die younger and relatively quickly, usually before they have claimed the pension they have paid for all their working lives. The exorbitant taxes on tobacco actually subsidize the state. Non-smokers on the other hand go on and on to senility, clocking up time in hospital beds, all the while claiming pensions and other benefits. We have already noted that, to the state, ideal citizens are those who die on the day they are about to retire.

The fact is, whenever the state introduces penal taxation levels or bans 'anti-social vices', violent crime increases, as alcohol and tobacco addicts cannot afford their habits. Smuggling soars: an estimated 235 billion cigarettes are smuggled each year (*Reuters News Service*, 27 August 1997). Organized crime moves in; terrorist organizations have a steady source of funding. The trade simply moves underground and 'criminalizes' large sections of the population. This was true of Prohibition in the United States; it is true of the worldwide underground narco-culture. It has always been true. Even at the height of the Napoleonic Wars, trade in brandy and other contraband goods thrived between England and France. Smugglers have never let a silly thing like a war between countries get in the way of their trade. Smuggling is certainly a fact of life in today's China, which has an extremely high tax on cigarettes. China, which now accounts for nearly a third of the world's smokers, is proving a huge and highly profitable market for smugglers. BAT Industries supplied vast quantities of its 555 brand of cigarettes (Chairman Mao's favourite smoke) to a Hong Kong-based company called Giant Island. To BAT's embarrassment Giant Island proved to have links with triad gangs, who smuggled the cigarettes into mainland China (shown on 'Inside Story: Smoke Rings', *BBC1 TV*, 20 August 1997). The smugglers, who are often in league with corrupt members of the People's Liberation Army, are costing China's government around £7.5 billion in lost annual tax revenues (Sheridan, 2 August 1998).

Governments with excessive taxes and excise duties always create the demand for smuggled goods, and precipitate new criminal schemes. Examples of rapacious governments inspiring criminal schemes are legion. In the 1980s the Colombian government introduced penal import taxes on foreign cars. But drug dealers have an enormous appetite for Ferraris and Lamborghinis. US senator John Kerry (1997) tells the story of Gabriel Taboada, a Colombian drug dealer, who set up a scheme where he bribed foreign diplomats, who were exempt from duty, to bring in the cars.

Nothing is new, except for the scale of the problem, and the ease with which international criminals and their customers can communicate. Whole sections of the population can become criminalized as exasperated taxpayers conspire with smugglers against the taxman. In 1996 26 Russian tax collectors were murdered in the course of duty; 74 were injured, 6 kidnapped and 41 had their houses burnt down (*Economist*, 31 May 1997). Tax officials are no longer merely disliked. They are a target. For many people, their society has become a criminal society. Crime is seen as work: the black economy is good! After all it oils the wheels; it creates incentives that set people to work. Surely that is far better than them staying abed every morning? Now the population is 'back to work'. This work wouldn't exist if it were legal, because it would be taxed and that would make it overpriced. The work ethic is alive and well, and it is criminal.

Black economies

According to Britain's Department of Social Security (Smith, 30 November 1997), the poorest 10 per cent (decile) of the population (calculated by income) spend more than those in the group above them (the second decile), and about the same as the third decile. This apparently illogical detail can only be explained by the fact that they are all 'at it': the black economy that is. Transparency International, a not-for-profit organization based in Berlin, which campaigns against 'corruption', has developed a corruption index of countries (Wolf, 16 September 1997). It is a scale from 0 (most corrupt) to 10 (least corrupt). Scandinavian countries do extremely well, with Denmark coming out top with 9.94. Nigeria trails with 1.76. Other examples are Germany (8.23), Britain (8.22), USA (7.61), France (6.66), Japan (6.57). Belgium comes half-way down the list (5.25), below Spain (5.9) and Greece (5.35) and just above Italy (5.03). This tells us something about the effect the European Union bureaucracy is having on honest Belgians. Poor Mother Russia (2.27) is down the bottom alongside Colombia (2.05), and far below the Czech Republic (5.2) and other ex-communist countries.

However, it is not just the losers in society that get involved with criminals. International businessmen often enter into shady deals, deluding themselves that they are too clever to be cheated. The lucky ones live to regret it. Gulf Oil laundered $4 million to cover payoffs to Korean and Bolivian politicians. Lockheed moved $25.5 million for Italian politicians (Kerry, 1997). Greed is the natural human condition. The Central Bank of Nigeria regularly warns businessmen by placing advertisements in the newspapers and magazines of 36 countries about the '419' scam: an advance fee fraud named after statute 419 of the Nigerian penal code. The fraud starts with a letter or fax offering to move large sums of money into the bank account of the recipient: the 'mark'. According to the scam, the money is being moved out of Nigeria to evade taxation or other forms of seizure by the authorities. Once out of the country the funds are to be shared between the correspondents. Of course an up-front payment is required from the mark: after all there are initial expenses in facilitating the funds transfer! The Nigerian fraudster may even ask for, and be given, access to the bank accounts of really gullible marks. Once this advance fee has been paid, the fraudster abruptly disappears, often having also raided the bank account. Too many people fall for this obvious sting. The Central Bank of Nigeria is routinely in receipt of pathetic letters from those duped in this way, who are attempting to recover their money. Some 'suckers' have even resorted to the law, despite the fact that in answering the original letter the marks were conspiring to defraud the Nigerian government. Two such US dupes, named Sorth and Tei, separately sued the Nigerian Bank in a Missouri court; however, the judge threw out the complaint. The documents submitted in evidence by the plaintiffs were fake, and they had never met any genuine officials of the bank.

Meanwhile phoney banks are appearing everywhere, many with names deliberately chosen to resemble reputable firms: Morgan Guarantee, Prudential Bank and Express Bank are just three examples, some thankfully now defunct. However, even real banks can be run by some very shady characters. BCCI, the Bank of Credit and Commerce International, the $23 billion financial institution that was finally brought down in July 1991 under a mass of fraudulent deals, was known to the CIA as the 'Bank of Crooks and Criminals International'. The BCCI story is fertile ground for conspiracy theorists who see a web of intrigue and a cover-up of the more politically sensitive aspects of the bank's relationships with some very senior politicians from both sides of the Atlantic (Sebastian, 3 November 1996). Why is it, they ask, that so many of the perpetrators of the BCCI fraud walked away with little more than having their wrists slapped? They may well ask!

Many phoney banks can be bought off the peg. The leading light of these scams is the Dominion of Melchizedek, 'a tax-free ecclesiastical sovereignty with territorial claims in the mid-Pacific and elsewhere' (Gartland, 18 July

1993). Melchizedek does exist: no less an authority than the Bank of England says so. It is sited on Malpelo, an uninhabited and mostly underwater island 200 miles off the coast of Colombia. Apparently it is also the uncharted Karitane Island of the Polynesian Te Parata group, south of the Cook Islands and north-east of New Zealand (Lawson, 23 July 1996). No matter that you can't find it on a map. It has commercial offices in Washington DC and Vancouver, and callers can leave a message on the answer-phone.

The man behind Melchizedek is a Mark Logan Pedley, alias Mark Wellington, alias Branch Vinedresser, who has a record of financial fraud as long as your arm. In 1986 a court in Boston gave him an eight-year prison sentence for his part in a Mexican peso conversion scheme that swindled investors out of an estimated $6 million. He is quite a joker. Using another alias, Harvey Penguini, he has registered companies based in Antarctica! Austrian Gerhard Bacher, aged 22, self-appointed crown prince of the Dominion of Melchizedek, aka SHK Prince Gerald-Dennis Sayn-Wittgenstein-Hohenstein (*South China Morning Post*, 20 May 1995), was charged in a Hong Kong court for 'procuring an entry in the records of banks by deception'. Bacher first opened an account at Citibank's Hong Kong branch with a cheque for $318,980 drawn on a Melchizedek bank, Asia-Pacific. Then there was Leon Excalibur Hooten, the so-called ex-president of Melchizedek, who ran several companies backed by millions of dollars in bonds issued by the imaginary dominion (Mintz, 14 October 1996). He was being investigated by Texas authorities, but he died of a heart attack in Scottsdale, Arizona, before being convicted. His wife Karen, who was suing him for divorce at the time, was not convinced. She pointed to the case of another Melchizedek luminary, David Pedley, a convicted fraudster, who is thought to have faked his own death in a Mexican jail in the mid-1980s (Gilard, 24 September 1995).

As the underclass increases, such incidents can only get worse. There will be an explosion in the black economy, in essence an alternative economy. Involvement in organized crime will be the only option open to those who are surplus to requirements in the legitimate economy. With so many people dependent on crime for their livelihood, real world crime will find its equivalent form in cyberspace: computer and telecommunication variants of protection rackets, blackmail, murder, kidnapping, smuggling, counterfeiting, fraud, threatening behaviour, vandalism ('fax graffiti' and computer viruses) and pornography will inevitably appear. Kidnappers are accessing the electronic financial records of their potential victims to calculate the optimum size of their ransom demand. As communication technologies get even more sophisticated, how can any national jurisdiction cope with the criminal scenario where a citizen of country A plans a crime while in country B, against citizens of country C, who are living in country D, using criminals selected from country E, paying for it from a bank account in country F?

Such reprobates cannot be considered as anything other than criminals, but the distance between the legitimate and criminal acquisition of wealth is not that great, and it can vary. The law, which differentiates between the two sides, is all about power in society, and is only tenuously related to any form of natural justice. Inevitably the state will decree that any behaviour that undermines state revenues is criminal. Tax avoidance is merely tax evasion that the state hasn't made illegal yet. But new technology is introducing whole new ways of avoiding tax, particularly since in virtual enterprises it is difficult to identify exactly where profits are being made. Governments do not have the resources to deal with this, so they will have to come up with clever plans that redefine the citizens' relationship to their tax liability. Previously tax authorities would have to prove people guilty of tax evasion. Now it will be up to us to prove our innocence. The presumption of guilt is likely to be retroactive on taxes that haven't even been invented yet. Soon perfectly legitimate trade will be criminalized. Soon whole sectors of society will be criminalized, just so the state can stay in control.

The virtual enterprise

The organization of the future, the virtual enterprise, is changing the power structures in society and the consequential transaction costs. The virtual enterprise will itself be affected. As we have seen, its size will be optimized around the new transaction costs: the biggest transaction cost being the security of the firm's information systems. Why security? Willie Sutton, the infamous US bank robber, had the answer. When asked 'Why do you rob banks?', he answered 'Because that's where the money is.' Information systems are where the money is, because that's where the business is. The information system is the firm; nothing else is permanent among what is an agglomeration of transitory projects. If the integrity of that system is corrupted, either by illegitimate criminals or the legitimate kind (governments), then the organization is finished. Its viable constituent projects will break apart and network with other systems, other virtual enterprises. Hence security **is** the organization of the future: its only permanent element!

Great care must be taken with the security of computer hardware, documents and disks. Ex-employees with in-depth knowledge of a company's systems are obvious targets for the attention of criminals and anarchists. A new type of scavenger is abroad, one who scours the garbage heaps of discarded people and IT material for the slightest scrap of information tradable to opportunistic white-collar criminals. These are not middle-class amateur opportunists, and their crimes are not victimless. We are all their victims. Organized crime is infiltrating legitimate business. Any company that holds data files on the world's rich can expect attacks. Guaranteeing the security of this data is an essential added value to the products they are delivering.

It is clear that 21st-century criminals are not street hoodlums (Moore, 1994). They will be well educated and sophisticated, wielding state-of-the-art technology and weaponry far more advanced than that available to most law-enforcement agencies. And attacks will come, not from a lone bandit, but from the most ruthless form of organized crime. British academic Barry Rider (1993) estimated that in 1990 the yakuza made a profit of £5.56 billion, eight times that of Toyota. Scandal-hit Nomura Securities had to reach down two layers of management to find Junichi Ujiie, with an untarnished reputation, following disclosures of payments made by the company to gangsters (Economist, 26 April 1997). Ninety-eight per cent of companies listed on the Japanese stock market make large payments to organized crime for 'research' and other services. We in the West can't be too smug, because these dealings don't look much different from campaign donations to political parties.

However, self-organizing processes, intrinsic in criminal behaviour, will conspire with governments to ensure that the explosion in the numbers of second-class citizens will not lead to social breakdown. In 1996 hundreds of gangsters paraded through the suburbs of Cape Town complaining about the vigilante violence aimed at them (International Herald Tribune, 19 August 1996). Criminals want anarchy as little as the middle-class citizen. Instead a brutal and brutalizing morality will appear among the criminal fraternity to maintain sufficient social order among the dispossessed. Criminals are parasites, and as such they need healthy ordered societies to prey on.

The cost of laundering money has risen to 25 per cent, from about 5 per cent in the 1980s (Courtenay, 1 October 1996); it is now almost cheaper to pay taxes. In fact the two economies will exist side by side in an uneasy symbiotic truce, with legitimate businesses calling on criminal elements from time to time to come down heavily on troublesome individuals, in ways that would be unthinkable within the official legal system. Very strange symbiotic behaviours can be observed. Chinese politicians hire Hong Kong triad members to guard them when travelling abroad (Kerry, 1997). One group of Russian gangsters visiting London brought along a government minister just to fetch the coffee! Governments will tolerate and happily co-exist with criminals. And why not? The very involvement of criminal gangs in money laundering has the effect of frightening away many small businesses from trying their arm at capital flight schemes. Whom can you trust when you move your money around: Martin Frankel, who disappeared from his Connecticut home taking $3 billion in the world's biggest insurance swindle (Usborne, 29

November 1999); or the next BCCI perhaps? Almost by accident the criminal fraternity is doing government a favour. Governments have never been able to stop the high-rollers, but the sheer scale of the huge numbers of small players evading tax would cause far greater damage to government finances. The official police forces can't cope since 'the $2 trillion that zips each day through the world's banking system makes it almost impossible to trace ill-gotten gains' (Kerry, 1997).With increasing criminal activity, it is no good looking to the police to help. As the nation–state collapses, because of the lack of government resources the main role for state police, perhaps the only role, will be the maintenance of civil order. However, because of the lack of revenue, other police duties, such as solving crime, which today we take for granted, will increasingly be outsourced by short-sighted politicians to private agencies (Tendler, 17 July 1998).

Thankfully criminals can only go so far with their violence: most have middle-class aspirations. That was how Pablo Escobar, head of the Medellín cocaine cartel, came to be gunned down by Colombian police. He was cornered only because of a tip-off from both his cartel and the Cali cartel, for whom his psychopathic behaviour had become an embarrassment (Kerry, 1997). The Cali cartel even has a political strategy to this end: the creation of narco-democracies. They don't buy everyone in the government of a democratic country, because that defeats the object: for then the government is tainted. They buy just the necessary key positions. The government's legitimacy is maintained, while their influence is total (Kerry,1997). They aim to be a government within a government.

Whatever happens, it is clear that new barbarians are going to need a totally new attitude toward crime and criminals in our corruptible and increasingly corrupted society.

11

Attitudes toward crime

Large sectors of Western society are being criminalized, to a greater or lesser extent. Yet our law officers (police and tax collectors), when they talk about organized crime, tend to see it in terms of right against wrong, sanity against insanity, good against evil. They fail to see that society's situation is actually *Beyond Good and Evil* (Nietzsche, 1968). For law officers are not saints on the side of the angels. Many of the 'criminals' they castigate are neither insane nor evil. 'Criminals' simply hold a different, and to middle-class eyes, an old-barbaric set of social values. They are a throwback to more vigorous and brutal primeval times – which is what really terrifies modern Western sensibilities.

Definitions of crime

Perhaps many criminals are really sociopathic rather than psychopathic? Perhaps in our terror we are mixing up cause and effect again? Is sociopathic behaviour criminal, or does crime merely provide an outlet for sociopaths? Is sociopathic behaviour the norm when society is breaking down? And just what is 'crime' anyway? How can law officers be so certain of their simplistic definitions of 'crime', and of their classification and demonization of criminals, particularly in respect of economic crime? Treated as media copy meant for popular consumption, moral posing may have a practical purpose, particularly when it is that time of year when the police must beg for extra resources from their government paymasters. However, if society's guardians seriously want to come to grips with their predicament, then they must not let themselves be deluded by their own propaganda. As practitioners, they are working in a world of relative social morality, not of absolute moral values. They must choose between amorality and the hypocrisy of a false moral position. Naive morality, in which a crime is a crime is a crime, has no place in the pragmatic policing of complex societies in the Information Age. This is particularly the case when some (many?) of their political masters are themselves tainted by sleaze and corruption.

To many, law enforcement is itself seen as ideological thuggery, aimed at protecting those privileged in the status quo. It is a thinly disguised attempt to turn every citizen into the ideal, docile, domesticated herd-animal. The perverse reality is that the overwhelming majority of the human herd, including perhaps most people from the United States and Europe, disagree totally with smug self-assured middle-class morality. For many people, the nation–state is itself as much a criminal organization as the Mafia – and not only the governments of banana republics and totalitarian regimes. A substantial number of US citizens see Washington's political class as conspirators, and they think of government as the enemy. This strand in US thinking, which has been there from the very beginning of its existence, now often appears as the sub-text in numerous Hollywood movies. Consequently it is being exported throughout the world.

Citizens everywhere, from all social strata, are losing faith in the integrity of the nation–state. They see a degenerate political class in an unseemly rush to satisfy vested interests, at a time when the state itself is becoming increasingly powerless. From their side of this unholy bargain, the leaders of the nation–state demand ownership of its citizens, body and soul. This is state-inspired slavery of its citizens. What is it but slavery when citizens are disposable, and leaders value individual freedoms far less than their own interests – or as they say, national interests? What is it but slavery, when leaders insist on the right to force young men (and now increasingly women) into military uniforms and demand that they kill and be killed for the good of the state? Over the past 200 years states have killed hundreds of millions of innocents – in comparison, the number of killings perpetrated by state-classified 'criminals' pales into insignificance.

Furthermore, what sort of morality helps create an illegal and hence a highly profitable market in narcotics by banning them? Then it chases the killers involved in the very drug crime it created, while it scorns the far greater number of deaths resulting from the legal alcohol and tobacco rackets – rackets that, incidentally, swell the tax-pockets of the state. The stance on narcotics smacks of hypocrisy. 'The international trade in narcotics is partly instrumental in keeping Western banks afloat... parts of the

Western banking system could be said to have become truly drug dependent.' A half-trillion dollars of drug profits mingles with 'the pool of hot [legitimate] investment capital upon which the US increasingly depends... The dollar profits from drugs trafficking are now repaying the dollar-denominated loans made by US banks to Third World debtors' (Rowan Bosworth-Davies, a former British fraud squad officer). Money laundering legislation to seize drug profits is merely the taxing of the narcotics business by the back door (Atkinson, 5 November 1997). This is hardly surprising since global money laundering is estimated at $500 billion annually (Kerry, 1997) and the US Justice Department already seizes (taxes) $500 million from criminals each year.

What is it but slavery when, despite the rhetoric, the state acts as if there is no such thing as private property? The state must combat illegitimate organized economic crime because every state must maintain that the state, and only the state, may steal from the citizen – they call it taxation. For taxation is just state-controlled extortion – obtaining money with menaces. All taxation is theft – and even the mafia doesn't charge 60 per cent for its protection rackets. There is a very thin line between legitimizing and criminalizing the acquisition of wealth. It is only societal ritual, not right, that distinguishes between the two sides. When the anarchist Pierre-Joseph Proudhon announced that 'property is theft', he was calling for revolution against the state and the bourgeoisie. But since the time of Pericles an extension of this motto, 'all individual property is theft from the state' (in his case the ancient city-state of Athens), has been used to justify larceny by the state, any state, no matter what its political colour, no matter what its form of governance. (Pericles made his now infamous funeral oration for the Athenian fallen in the Peloponnesian War at the end of the first year of campaigning, 431 BC. In saying that there is no higher honour than to die for the (city–)state, he was in fact praising the state rather than the heroes and their families.) Is it any surprise that governments dislike acts of philanthropy by the likes of Bill Gates (who is worth $50 billion) and Warren Buffett ($30 billion) (August, 8 July 1998)? Apart from monopolizing theft, governments also claim the sole right to beneficence. Extravagant donations to good causes by the super-rich are a reminder to us 'little people' that although governments may push us around, there are individuals who can stand up against state intimidation.

Is the reason that the US government classified 'strong cryptography' algorithms as munitions so that it could ban their export, as they claim in order to combat crime, or was it to undermine the notion of privacy of the individual? The US National Security Agency (NSA) insists that it must be able to snoop on all telecommunication messages. In Britain, in fact in most states, agents of national security think the same way. But if it is possible for the NSA and their ilk to pry, then so can others. Even if an agency is 'trustworthy', are all the agents of that agency? Not surprisingly international bankers are insisting on a level of security far in excess of that enabled by the present data encryption standard. Businesses were convinced that the NSA and other national security agencies had access to a master key to that standard. Consequently, and despite NSA objections, banks are developing their own cryptographic industry standard for the transfer of financial data. Naturally the international clients of these banks do not take kindly to US extraterritoriality.

Encryption software is readily available all over the world. It is used by cellular telephone services to ensure privacy and security, and by cable television to authenticate access to programmes. Yet US citizens are not allowed to sell or even give away cryptographic software without first obtaining a munitions(!) export licence. The US government threatened to prosecute Phil Zimmermann, over his PGP (pretty good privacy) program, after a friend allegedly put it on the Net (*Economist*, 6 May 1995). It comes as no surprise that the state wants to stop such freedom. States are ruthless in their harrying of individual privacy. Prisoners serving jail sentences for many economic crimes are in reality political prisoners. Each sentence is merely an assertion of state power – one person's economic criminal is another's freedom fighter. For many economic crimes, such as tax evasion, counterfeiting and monopoly, are attacks against the expression of state power. Financial losses to business from other economic crimes such as fraud are in reality a tiny fraction of those from state-inspired theft. There is nothing new under the sun. Since the time when money was invented, the powers that be have been manipulating money for their own advantage: the debasement of coinage is the history of coinage. State-inspired inflation is as old as paper money: from ancient Babylon, to 14th-century China, to the 'great debasement' of Henry VIII, to the Weimar Republic inflation, right up to the present day.

In the past, businesses themselves were sometimes willing, sometimes unwilling, partners in this state conspiracy. But now businesses can see a way out, as telecommunication technology has made them more international, as money is no longer the monopoly of the state and as loyalty to the state becomes irrelevant. However, governments will not give up that easily, and will set out to criminalize perfectly legitimate trade under the expanding label of economic crime. We can see this in US, and now increasingly European Union, extraterritoriality, with embargoes, sanctions and attempts to bully small sovereign states like Switzerland, the Channel Islands and Grand Cayman into disclosing information about private offshore bank accounts. US law-officers have the power to freeze US-based assets of any company that is merely suspected of acting against 'the interests of the United States'. This vague phrase is open to a wide range of interpretations, and there must be a lingering suspicion that actions may be launched against a company on behalf of competitors with ulterior motives. Some international business-people are considering limiting their exposure. They are rightly apprehensive, for if they are unwittingly involved with the guilty, at best their assets will be tied up while they prove their innocence, and their businesses will suffer; at worst there is the very real possibility of confiscation.

Like many citizens, international businesses too are now coming to see each nation–state as just another organized crime syndicate, but one involved in legitimate as opposed to illegitimate crime. This legitimacy does not stem from any unassailable moral position, as the state would claim, but from unadulterated raw power: the domination of the individual by the collective. National governments profess a superior morality, while at the same time turning a blind eye to crime if it is in the greater interest of their geopolitical strategic goals.

It is the claim of morality that deludes 'incorruptible' police officers and tax collectors as to the rightness of their legitimate brutality against the individual citizen. The fact is that, to maintain its power, the state cannot allow its citizens to be free. Fighters for individual freedom must be designated 'criminals' by the state, simply because their actions threaten the state, or rather the privileged position of the leaders of the state. Citizens are there for the good of the state ('for the good of the people'). 'The good citizen' is lauded, but not rewarded. No matter where we go in the world, we can see variations on the theme of the Soviet Union's state art or propaganda, glorifying the honest tractor-driver toiling in the fields. To protect the carefully constructed heroic image, the enforcers of state power are given the right to invade the privacy of its citizens.

What law enforcement officers call bribery and corruption is merely a change of allegiance of the individual citizen. Are those who have accepted bribes simply putting money and self-interest before nationalism? Who is to say that the disloyal are wrong? For their allegiance is merely moving from one power-based ideology, the state ideology of nationalism, to another: internationalism, an ideology whose passport is hard cash but whose political structures have yet to emerge. 'By nationalism I mean first of all the habit of assuming that human beings can be classified like insects and that whole blocks of millions or tens of millions of people can be confidently labelled "good" or "bad". But secondly – and this is much more important – I mean the habit of identifying oneself with a single nation or unit, placing it beyond good or evil and recognizing no other duty than that of advancing its interest' (George Orwell).

Passports for sale

National governments have already been caught cynically using their 'nationality' for fundraising. The Tongan police minister visited Hong Kong prior to the transfer of sovereignty to China in order to sell 7,000 passports (Schloss, 19 August 1996) to nervous residents for up to $20,000 each. Belize sold their passports and citizenship at $50,000 per family (*International Money Marketing*, 15 March 1996). The Dominican Republic sold citizenship for $17,900 and Panama for $19,900 (Kerry, 1997). Peru, Benin, Sierra Leone, the Marshall Islands (*South China Morning Post*, 26 July 1993), they're all at it. But it doesn't apply only to Third World governments. We have already seen how Canada does it, and how Ireland puts the employment of its citizens before the tax interests of other governments.

Other advanced countries have developed more euphemistic labels for their under-the-counter methods of attracting in the global rich. A so-called 'business migration scheme' attracted Hong Kong businessmen and women to Australia at A $500,000 each, and yet half the migrants failed to set up successful businesses (Green, 22 February 1992). That scheme ended because of worries about organized crime abusing the system, only to be replaced by another attracting businesses with an annual turnover of A $50 million, with certain conditions on language ability and business experience. Australian immigration minister Gerry Hand said it 'was not about buying a passport'. What else is giving passports to rich foreigners, while keeping out the poor? Prior to unification, the East German interior ministry gave 52 Hong Kong Chinese citizenship on 'humanitarian grounds', because they were willing to invest billions in the country (Murray, 1990). These examples are the tip of the iceberg. The simple fact is that the legal trade in passports for the rich is a multi-billion dollar industry.

When criminals see the games that governments play, they too want to get in on the action. There is a huge trade in stolen passports, some taken from citizens and others from government offices. Pre-1997 Hong Kong saw a flood of phoney passports for sale, from as far afield as the Dominican Republic and Lesotho. Quite often, genuine government officials are involved in the corruption. An Irish embassy official in London sold bogus Irish passports to Middle-Eastern nationals for between £8,000 and £15,000 each. A corrupt Scots civil servant, who delivered British passports to Chinese gangsters, took £5,000 as his cut for each one sold on the black market at £18,000 a time (*Sunday Mail*, 29 October 1995). Then there are the countries whose governments are indistinguishable from gangsters. Associates of General Manuel Noriega issued tens of thousands of Panamanian passports via Cuban intermediaries to Hong Kong residents and mainland Chinese.

The whole scam is said to have netted more than £200 million (Davies, 5 February 1990).

The only difference between government gangs and criminal gangs is that governments are self-interestedly attracting the rich entrepreneur. They are only too ready to offer genuine passports to the type of economic migrant that every other country also wants to attract, and that no country wants to lose. However, most governments have to do the dirty deed in an underhand way, so as to avoid protests by their own citizens. The criminals, on the other hand, are taking money off poor migrants in their attempts at bypassing immigration barriers, not only in selling phoney passports but also in smuggling them into rich countries. As countries increasingly think in terms of right-sizing because of changing economic conditions, then both types of trade can be expected to increase substantially. It is not surprising that US senator John Kerry claims that the criminal 'trade in people' is bigger than the trade in illegal narcotics (1997).

The other side of the coin, of a state stealing rich citizens and their wealth from other states, is each state stopping its own rich from escaping. Inevitably, state edicts will criminalize those international economic transactions that undermine state power, and will demonize any leader of global business who grows too independent. For the state must be seen to flex its muscles and bring these free spirits back into line, or it will lose credibility. When business was national, businesspeople had no choice other than to comply with state institutions, and so their threat to the state was limited. But now that trade has become international, and money has become electronic information and increasingly denationalized, businesspeople who are increasingly mobile have a choice. We can expect a vast increase in state propaganda that the state has the right, or even the duty, to use violence against stateless, and hence 'criminal', global corporations.

Even business transactions that are not 'criminal' will be interfered with under the guise of policing 'real criminals'. Such is the high-profile chasing of money laundering. But is it moral indignation, or does the state simply want to steal (that is tax) the money? Or does the state worry that a rapidly expanding international black economy will ultimately destroy its ability to tax, and thereby destroy the concepts of 'nation–state' and 'national currency'? Nation–states worldwide have always insisted on regulating (that is interfering with) trade. Businesspeople may have been sensible in the past to conspire in such political acts, when politicians were honourable, but no longer. Now politics is a profession, and today's so-called democratic countries cannot expect leadership from those entering it when the only entry qualification is a willingness to kiss babies, and then to kiss backsides.

Organized crime

Organized crime knows this. When it wants something done, it doesn't talk to politicians, it buys them. Business too has learnt the lesson, only it is called 'lobbying'. With degenerate politicians at the helm, the wreck of the nation-state is inevitable. Could it happen here? Giuliano Amato is still whispering in our ears: 'Corruption is the greatest where it is found out.' Even cynical voters prefer their politicians to be honest crooks rather than hypocrites. Jacques Medecin, ex-mayor of Nice jailed in France for corruption after four years on the run in South America, is still very popular among certain segments of the town's population (Bell, 2 August 1994). Marion Barry, ex-mayor of Washington jailed for six months on charges of cocaine possession, is still a hero of the black underclass in the city, and having found religion was re-elected as mayor in January 1995 (Gurdon, 2 January 1998). If it's not the politicians at it, then it's their families. Raul Salinas de Gortari, brother of Carlos Salinas, ex-president of Mexico, transferred tens of millions of dollars to tax shelters in Britain, Switzerland and the Caribbean (*Private Banker International*, December 1996).

In much of the world the population at large has been betrayed by its politicians, and so it looks to secret societies, organized crime or warlords for protection and security. What is freemasonry, or the trades union movement, but self-interested brotherhoods that look after their own? The mafia is seen by many as a protector of the masses against the excesses of the state: this was after all the *raison d'être* of the Sicilian mafia, Russian mafiyas, Japanese yakuza and Chinese triads. And their 'businesses' of drug peddling, extortion, fraud, gambling and prostitution are merely tax collection in the alternative economy.

The state spreads the lie that organized crime will lead to anarchy and social collapse, but nothing could be further from the truth. Organized crime has, if anything, a sharper sense of 'community' and 'citizenship', only one that just happens to be different from today's dominant liberal–democratic interpretation of these words. When a mafia family runs a neighbourhood, little old ladies don't get mugged on the street. Their justice is an old barbarian morality based on honour, tribute and retribution. This is finding increasing respect and a ready allegiance among those disillusioned by widespread degeneracy in the body politic. The criminals are widening their horizons. Gangsters are beginning to see themselves as the new sovereigns. The yakuza were quicker and far more effective in delivering food and blankets for the population after the Kobe earthquake of January 1995 than were the Japanese government (Guest, 16 March 1995).

It is easy to blame social degeneracy upon politicians; however, their behaviour is an effect of the decline and fall of the nation–state, rather than its cause. The nation–state is a product of Machine Age thinking, the all-conquering factory model of society. The masses were needed for both the mill and the military. They had to be organized, and there was power to be found in that organization – but no longer. In the Information Age, quality production, not mass production, is needed. That production itself needs far fewer and far better qualified people. Furthermore today's warfare is the warfare of smart weapons. Consequently the 20th century, the century of the masses, is over. Degenerate political systems based on manipulating the power of the masses are over too. Those masses, now unemployed, soon to be dispossessed and disenfranchised, will revolt.

In order to hang on to power, fearful political leaders must suppress any unrest amongst troublesome sectors of their property (sorry, citizens). But they must do this within the rules of state morality, for otherwise they will be found out. A classic example of this is to be found in the behaviour of some US states toward adult black males. Politicians in 14 US states feel morally justified in insisting that anyone who is sent to prison should lose the right to vote for life. The upshot is that 13 per cent of the country's adult black population is disenfranchised. In seven states the proportion is one in four, and in Alabama and Florida the figure is one in three (O'Brien and Brown, 25 October 1998). In the past such hypocrisy could be hidden behind state control of communication, but with emergence of global telecommunications any brutality will be transmitted around the country, and around the world, in seconds. It bears repeating: the big political question of the coming decades is how to find a socially acceptable means of dismantling democracy. For government based on a universal franchise is government elected by losers. Even with strong political leadership, maintaining this control will be an extremely difficult task, but the West, with its cast of parliamentary degenerates, hasn't a hope.

With the collapse of the nation–state as a cohesive system just around the corner, organized crime is standing in the shadows as the government-in-waiting. Crime syndicates do after all gross $15 trillion annually (Coyle, 12 July 1999). The head of the Cali drugs cartel, Gilberto Rodriguez Orejuela, testified before a US Senate committee that the narcotics business is not just about money, it is a form of guerrilla assault on the body politic of the United States (Kerry, 1997). Criminals already run a large number of countries around the world. When organized crime comes to power it invents its own morality, and it will legitimize its freedom to act brutally in the suppression of any civil unrest. Today's legitimate business will have no difficulty doing deals with these 'no-longer criminals'; it may even prove more profitable than dealing with the bureaucracies of modern democratic government.

We do not need any more moralizing about economic crime. We are not discussing questions of right and wrong, but of the relationship of policing to the winners and losers in a power struggle. We must forget the Hollywood myth of the men in white hats fighting for truth, justice and the American way. This is not 'good guys' against 'bad guys', but bad against worse – and it is not at all clear which is which. People parading around the streets in balaclava helmets waving machine pistols are now more likely to be the police; they have to protect their anonymity. Even in the law courts they now have to be unidentifiable. So who is in control here? Meanwhile witnesses are intimidated, and many choose to go to jail rather than risk the retaliation of criminals: such is justice.

Each individual is left to decide between the lesser of two (or more) evils. By denying the lie of absolute morality, all we see before us is the expression of power: everything else is pure sentimentality. The only questions facing everyone are: 'Whose side are we on? And why?'

Part V

Recognizing the new order

12

New rituals for old

O wad some Pow'r the giftie gie us
To see oursels as others see us!
It wad frae mony a blunder free us,
An' foolish notion.

(from *To a louse* by Robert Burns)

By now it will be clear that I have a somewhat peculiar notion of the workings (or otherwise) of modern Western society... but is it a foolish notion? Am I what the Jesuits so dismissively call a 'contrarian'? Or could there be something in what I am saying about our society ignoring the signs of decay? If I am right, then we will all have to look at ourselves from other perspectives if we are to have any hope of coping with the enormous societal upheaval closing in on us. Will we find a new approach? Or will we blunder into the future with a mixture of ignorance and indifference, in a permanent state of doubtful certainty?

The purposes of ritual

Why is it that we so often fail to see the absurdity of our position? Why do we delude ourselves that everything is so eminently sensible? The problem is society itself. For society is self-organizing and optimized to fit our observation of the recent past. Society operates in this arena via rituals. Ritualized behaviour blinds us to everything 'outside the loop'. Every time a country's anthem is sung, national flag waved or state honours awarded, patron saints and national holidays celebrated, Thanksgiving meals eaten, there is ritual. With every World Series or Olympic Games there is ritual. When a couple gets married, a freemason straps on an apron, when we place a cross on a ballot paper, every time a President makes a State of the Union address, when Oscar is presented, there is ritual. Every time we pass the port to the left, read newspapers, watch television, and in a million and one other subtle ways we are obeying the all-so-sincere nonsense that is the aboriginal rituals of institution, society and nation.

Such rituals are the fundamental believable lies that make 'us' what 'we' are. They enable us to interact with a world as bizarre as ours. We have no choice other than to impose constraints on our actions. However, we should recognize, but very rarely do, that all these constraints are self-imposed and society-imposed. There is no true and false, no good and evil, no morality except as social construction and ritualized delusion. 'There are no moral phenomena at all, only a moral interpretation of phenomena' (Nietzsche). It is ritual that maintains the pretence of truth. Truth is error become orthodoxy, via promotion through ritual. Untruth on the other hand is everything that is unacceptable, unpalatable. Goodness and morality are made intellectual and absolute, rather than visceral and conditional. We conveniently overlook the fact that 'the victory of the moral ideal is achieved by the same "immoral" means as every other victory: force, lies, slander, injustice' (Nietzsche).

Every society's underlying order, its certainties and truths, its sense of self-righteousness and goodness, and its 'formal tautologies' are flawed. Such ritualized invocations deliver the security of a false familiarity. Ritual is bound up with the persuasive version of the world as represented in and by society. Ritual is persuasive because it is self-validating; it suspends judgement. It does not uncover truths; rather it institutes and imposes them. If we are to have any hope in dealing with our future imperfect then we must overcome the past. We will have to come to grips with the nature of our rituals, deny them, and then move on.

Ritual is the conditioning of society by society with the repeated application of 'formulae' – ceremony and repetitive behaviour. Ritual is a society as magician, whose sleight of hand makes 'us' look in the wrong place, so that 'we', the members don't see what we don't want to see in the darker corners of our society. Neither do we see how the trick is done. 'Good' members of society believe that only by conforming to ritualized behaviour, by mouthing the creed of socio-political correctness and righteousness, can their society balance the *Purity and Danger* (Douglas, 1984), can its members recognize one other, and live with themselves and apart from others. Ritual is a pretence that we can cope with problems all around us; it is the magic wand that keeps everything ordered and tidy and banishes the 'evil spirits' to limbo.

Ritual creates a boundary around ourselves and all those that are like us: an 'imagined community' (Anderson, 1983). It is a voluntary cage, with invisible yet identifiable bars, that separates 'us' from 'them'. It is where everything that is different is dangerous. By imposing repetition and similarity on the world, ritual produces a state of well-being in the general community, a confidence in the way that we interpret our world, an effect whereby we are even unaware that there are problems – we just don't see them. The mutual reaffirmation of what is ordinary creates both the very experience of a society, and the feeling of cultural and personal identity bestowed through it. Because of this shared but unspoken accord, members of a community use self-evident and implicit assumptions. We reinforce that membership whenever we socialize with our fellows within the guidelines laid down by ritual, thereby reaffirming membership. In being 'one of us', we are blinded to the oddities and failings of our own society. Those outside our community will be seen as different, as a danger. And from **their** strange ritual position, we are just as peculiar.

Thus ritual not only identifies group members to one other, but also it may identify them to outsiders. As ritual behaviour becomes second nature, individuals are often unaware that they are subconsciously transmitting social signals that can draw them into danger whenever they move outside the sphere of influence of their particular society. Ordering a kosher meal on the flight of an airline whose computer system has been compromised will automatically identify a Jewish passenger to anti-Semitic terrorists. The same can be said for any social pattern that uniquely indicates a particular national, ethnic, religious or cultural group, be it a car numberplate, a surname, or a Dallas Cowboys jacket. Conversely, inside their society's territory, ritual creates a sense of security. It is the moral role of ritual that draws attention toward society's current understanding, and away from the alternative alien understandings of other communities. It separates the wanted (the 'good') from the unwanted (the 'evil'), the 'ordinary' from the 'extraordinary', the acceptable from the unacceptable, proper behaviour from improper, 'us' from 'them'. It is a homeostatic force that engenders trust, based on a sense of sameness and togetherness within the social grouping. Rituals keep a society stable by ignoring instabilities.

By complying with ritual, everyone, even the mediocre, can feel valued and self-important, and this in turn leads to the society becoming ever more self-important. The greater the mediocrity the greater the need for ritual, hence the plethora of semi-secret societies that overdose on ritual. And yet every society needs bulk, a herd of willing pack animals to support and celebrate the (not necessarily talented) leadership. Ritual is encouraged, because by forging identity and conformity, it generates and reinforces authority.

Maturity of ritual brings with it the embodiment of authority, despite its original practical purpose having been forgotten. Thus 'we', the good members of society conspire with the guardians of ritual, the 'priesthood'. In our secular national societies, politicians are the priests. God help us! We too don't want to spoil a comfortable and secure illusion. The priests of this morality derive their power from their (apparent) ability to get into contact with the world beyond the ordinary, the foreign world, and not be endangered by flickers of disbelief. They know that most dangers will dissipate through negative feedback in a coherent and cohesive society, and so they can harness the extraordinary for the affirmation of the community.

Through ritual, society is safe from contradiction. By focusing a paralysing criticism, society can deny unmanageable contradictions. Then it only has to deal with the manageable ones, where the danger can be isolated and rendered safe. In this way a society can combat 'social pollution': those actions, unknowns, behaviours, uncertainties and 'evil spirits' that contradict or are antagonistic to the society's accepted view of the world, the accepted morality. This morality, its statement of purity, is perceived to give members power to cope in a world of uncertainty made certain by ritual. For purity is a society's defence against the dangers of the unclean – and the uncertainty we feel today about our unsettled future is nothing but unclean.

In our 'scientific society' there is a very strong aversion to claims of even a remote similarity between 'us' (and how we do what we do today) and 'them' (and the role of rituals in primitive societies). However, it is not we who have advanced, just our technology. It may seem a very long way from primitive ritual to the technological sophistication of cyberspace, but it is closer than we think. For there is only ever a limited repertoire of human responses, a limited set of roles. The categorical methods of 'modern' society are mere variations on a theme – technological fetishism – old ideas, but in new forms. Modern rituals appear sophisticated to an adept member of society simply because they deal with the issues identified as important by that society. But this is just the reinforcing echo of that society's set of values; in our case it is the myth of modernity. We must reject the claim of superiority for our 'advanced scientifically enlightened' society over 'primitive' societies, for this is just arrogant self-esteem and ritual pasturing, and our chavinist understanding of the word 'primitive'!

Members of primitive societies don't expect their rain-dances to produce rain. They do not believe in some form of 'sympathetic magic' that can instigate a causal chain of events that ultimately delivers the contents of a wish list. The leaders of primitive societies no more focus on any instrumental efficacy in their rituals than we should in ours. Only in degenerate applications of ritual are the instruments themselves assumed to hold the efficacy. Rain-dances do not precipitate rain, but they help the not-so-primitive society cope with the lack of rain. Only the pious and simple-minded believe in the potency-in-themselves of ritual instruments. Yet there are many in our society who really do believe in the instrumental efficacy of the modern, particularly the ritual application of science. This is merely rain-dancing with pseudo-science.

We categorize rituals as 'primitive' simply because our understanding of another and to us bizarre society posits that society as primitive in relation to our own. The version of the world that persuades us is compared to that which persuades an alien society. That society appears strange or even hostile to us, because our way of approaching worldly phenomena, of distinguishing them as 'ordinary' or 'extraordinary' sensations, as safe or dangerous, reflects our cultural patterns and not theirs. How can we categorize and measure the degree of sophistication in alien cultures when not only do we have different yardsticks, but we are living in totally different universes, where there are no common categories of discrimination? They, of course, see our 'civilization', with its conspicuous consumption and the sophistry of computerized number fetishism, as equally weird.

It would be wrong to conclude that all rituals are primitive and absurd. They are just limited and of temporary usefulness. Rituals need not be bad, as long as they are effective and have not become degenerate. They create a collective and selective amnesia, so that influences that could disrupt the cohesion and coherence of the societal groupings, those embarrassing acts and facts, are conveniently forgotten or ignored. Instead a favourable history is fabricated, along with the pretence of a homogeneous society. There is real efficacy of ritual, but it is not instrumental. The primary role of rituals is their influence, which gives coherence and identity to a community. Because of ritual, social complexity is lessened, society is self-organizing, control becomes easier, trust is the norm and hence operational costs are lowered, making the survival of the society more likely. Beneficial rituals are used to direct routine behaviour and to reconcile society to the problems it must face.

Rituals enable a society to cope with phenomena that would appear dangerous when seen without guidance, yet which become meaningful, coherent and thus manageable or ignorable by means of the enactment of ritual. They are the way a society imposes its communal will on the environment. Without the intervention of rituals, difficult situations produce responses ranging from fear to avoidance. By reconciling phenomena with a society's values and beliefs, a society's existence is conserved and reinforced. For this reason, it is paramount that faith in their efficacy is preserved, because otherwise they cannot exert their function. Hence it is problematic to try and persuade a community that its behaviour is ritualistic. Rituals are essential to communal life as the communication devices for 'proper' discrimination, and hence 'proper' understanding – providing of course that they actually do convince. But 'what convinces is not necessarily true – it is merely convincing' (Nietzsche); it is mere 'fabricated reason and its reasonableness' (Heidegger). Ritual is pattern; it is repeatable, and hence safe (as long as it works!). In separating the ordinary from the extra-ordinary we recreate the order in our circumstances. The circumstances of what is ordinary change all the time. Ultimately, however, there are alien dangers 'out there', and they won't go away. If they are not confronted, 'tamed', made ordinary, then society is in danger. Unfortunately ritual will have often blinded us to such unavoidable danger. This self-reinforcing blindness means that we remember the security of yesterday, rather than seeing the dangers of tomorrow.

Standing entangled in this web of history, individuals derive their unique identities from being individuals, yet they recognize their individuality only in contrast to their fellows. They strive for individuality and personality, and yet they are drawn to their fellows and seek out the common ground on which to build friendship and society, knowing that collective unity is tyranny of and toward the individual. Indeed, the driving force behind all societal developments is individuals in their struggle with themselves, their communities and their experiences of the world.

The complexity in this mutual and chaotic feedback between individual, society and external world affords an insight into the role of rituals in our society. We individuals accept membership by agreeing to a version as a 'proper' understanding of the world. The ordered relationships that constitute the essence of a society are, thus, internalized to such a degree that we fail to recognize that we **think** with such pre-figured relationships, rather than **about** them. Indeed, doing the latter would require individuals to go against the strongest habits that they have acquired throughout their societal existence. If they were to abandon their version of the world, they would leave the sphere of the ordinary and move into the realm where the ordinary and the extraordinary are not separated by contours of meaning.

We are preconditioned to understand a situation in a particular way, the 'proper' understanding of which is embedded in the discrimination of what is ordinary and what is extra-ordinary. However, such understanding gives rise to anomalies, and any given culture will inevitably confront events that seem to defy its assumptions. It cannot totally ignore the anomalies without the risk of forfeiting confidence in the community. Thus, when anomalies arise, an element of persuasion is needed in order to encourage the reaffirmation of a particular version of the world. If, however, rituals are employed with disregard of the challenges the anomalies pose for the community, and instead are carried out in staunch defence of their validity, then disbelief and disassociation will be the result among sectors of that community.

facing degeneracy

Thus it is that members of today's society know something is radically wrong. At the same time we are unable to recognize just what the real problems are. We make the fundamental mistake of seeing the problems around us as the cause of the break-up of the underlying order, rather than its effect. These problems are the consequences of old power structures now become impotent – a classic symptom of social collapse. Our sloppy application of societal rituals no longer drives away doubt. The shabby nature of our present socio-economic and political existence is laid bare. Our society has entered a state of anomy. We are without viable norms and standards, and yet we still claim to maintain these rituals of old. The normal homeostatic processes of a vigorous power structure are gone. That power base can no longer purify itself. We are confronting a rapidly approaching degeneracy, and so it should come as no surprise that we are losing confidence in the meaning of our social norms.

There is no intrinsic power in ritual, in societal truth. Power has to be there first. Ritual is a mere reflection of this power. Morality is in essence 'the prejudices of the powerful'. In this prejudice, cause and effect have been inverted. Ritual is very good at creating this delusion, these 'regimes of truth' (Foucault). For ritual makes the effect, the morality, the prejudice, seem fundamental – a cause, and therefore right, in tune with the world order that delivers power to the society. This is why, to the many used to the old barbarian ritual chants telling of the virtue of universal suffrage, liberal democracy feels right, powerful and like the 'End of History'. This is why I am disconcerted by my conviction that the big political question of the coming decades is how to find a socially acceptable means of dismantling democracy. Surely only a lunatic would question the morality of democracy? But yesterday's lunacy may be tomorrow's sanity. Power moves on. Each society is a world of ritualized intent, but it exists in a world of consequences. It is not good enough to be complacent toward any questioning of cherished beliefs. To be successful in this unknown and unknowable future, understanding must be disconnected from the prevalent authority, whose legitimacy is ritualistically anchored in its now-defunct ideological stance. There is a crying need for a reassessment of the governance of societies, and of the problems associated with the expansion of democracy as an integral part of all political and economic organizations. In the context of punctuated equilibrium, rituals are likely to blinker observation against the unfolding changes either side of the punctuation mark. Ritual must be adaptable if it is to cope with the changes that are inevitable in the perpetual feedback of existence. Once power and ritual part company, then ritual fails to convince, and societies are laid wide open to ridicule.

New rituals for new times

When rituals no longer reassure, then society is prey to both new and old barbarians. Modern-day moralizers can bleat all they like that this is unfair: such natural forces have no conscience. Enter the new barbarians with new, far more vigorous, for more virile rituals, ready to take on the brave new world. Enter the old barbarians with fundamental and pure versions of old rituals that are far more convincing for those terrified by the present conditions. The old barbarians have been reborn, ready for conflict, insisting that the present leaders have failed the ritual, and that a more fundamental form of ritual will work. People who are frightened by uncertainty find this message very appealing. It promises a return to the security of the tribe.

The two barbarian groups have totally different attitudes toward dissent. New barbarians relish questioning. Their rituals derive from a rational analysis of present conditions. The new rituals solve today's problems, but possibly in ways that sentimentalists find objectionable. The old barbarians insist on total obedience, for their cynical position plays on a societal belief in the instrumental efficacy of their now-old rituals. They themselves often don't believe the nonsense, but by manipulating a large enough group in society that do, they can take power. They cannot, however, permit questioning of their position, knowing that solutions from the past will ultimately fail to deal with tomorrow's problems. But they, unlike the status quo, can at least put off the evil day of total collapse. With the old barbarians, ritual continues unchallenged in a vicious circle of the blind leading the blind. The application of ritual misleads the community into the pleasant tunnel-vision of belief in a 'one and only way'. Eventually, however, threats will arise that ritual is incapable dealing with, and the society becomes decadent and degenerate. 'To let oneself be determined by one's environment is decadent' (Nietzsche); being unable to impose one's will on the environment is degenerate.

The imposition of ritual must inevitably give rise to anomalies, because a truly chaotic world cannot permanently conform to the imposed logic of a ritualized schema. An individual who perceives the absurdity in ritual and then fails to reconcile it, ceases to be 'one of us' and becomes an 'other'. Such individuals put themselves at peril, because they are denying their communal roots by discriminating differently and inferring different conclusions. Their soon-to-be-previous community will immediately spell out the dangers of rebellion. They will be left in no doubt that ritual not only separates 'us' from 'them', but also that its other role is to insist there is no separation between 'us' and 'me', that each individual can only exist as 'one of us'. To re-enter society they must accept without question the lies their society tells them, and rejoin the current madness in a schizophrenic self-denial of the absurdity.

Society's hostility, disregard or fear of their deviant (and defiant) behaviour will be made clear to them by the old barbarians who are reawakening in society. They will be ridiculed and told that their actions are futile. Ideologues will threaten the miscreants with expulsion or ostracism, unless they undertake the required atonement rituals. The thugs actually believe that exclusion from their society is seen as the ultimate communal punishment, which it is to anyone who shares that community's version of the world. Yet, when enlightened individuals have broken their ritual links to that community, their new understanding of the world will render these dangers harmless, although none the less painful. The deviants, having seen the absurdity in these proclamations, will find such punishment an irrelevant matter of past membership. However, rejection by their fellows will be very much harder to endure, particularly when the thugs feel obliged to use violence against old friends in order to 'save their souls'.

Within this scenario individuals can play various roles. In fright and anger they can cling to their community's version of the world. These unquestioning intellectual geldings, neutered of their individuality, will be identified by the priests of the society and used to promote the rituals. These not-so competent members of the community may even promote themselves as 'pious commentators', echoing their community's version of the world in an attempt to assert their own personal ambition, all the while denying their doubt. They may claim to 'prove' the truth of their position, not realizing that their logic is blindly grounded in a now-defunct ritual.

Societies are correct in realizing that a very real danger comes from the doubting individual with the strength and sobriety to break ranks. Such renegades deliberately venture out from the community into the world of the extra-ordinary, to be touched by the dangers associated with it. They question the ritual, and find themselves in conflict with their society's persuasive version of the world. In their new interpretation of the world, they can harness the extraordinary for their own ends. New barbarians achieve this through alien behaviour and innovative rituals, so that what was extraordinary and dangerous to their society is for them remade to advantage. Hence, they are a threat, because even without the shield of old rituals they are unharmed by contact with the extraordinary. They possess powers, and are therefore feared by the pious commentators who are no match for them.

Yet these are the innovators, the entrepreneurs, the generators of change (not necessarily successful change) and the makers of the future. Perversely these are the possible saviours of society, necessary for its long-term well-being when the status quo fails, as it inevitably must. Ritual gives only a stable veneer of understanding, which covers the more chaotic whole that is the human condition. Every veneer is transitory, even that of the new barbarians; it is well to remember that even the old barbarians were once new barbarians! In time, as stability disintegrates, the ill-fated authority that backed it is compromised, and loses credibility. Uncertainty, as always, precedes the transition to a new order – to new ritualized controls and new societies.

When the status quo was firmly in place, we simply did not see the nonsense in its ritual. But as that order collapses, ritual becomes silly or even horrific. The solid ground, on which society was grounded, shifts. As the basis of its power disintegrates, ritual no longer holds the society together. Rather, it becomes divisive. 'Smart' authorities will jump to new paradigms developed by their new barbarians, but this means leaving a hapless community of belief behind. The not-so-smart authorities surrender to the bigotry of the old barbarian. Their ruthless enforcement of old rituals may arrest dissent within society for a little while longer, but they can never defend against the impartial brutality of economic reality.

In times of profound uncertainty, the extraordinary cannot be ignored nor even tolerated. The very fact that we perceive ourselves to be facing profound uncertainty is just another way of saying that we don't know who we are any more. Our rituals, and hence our social institutions, have degenerated and no longer work. For it has occurred to us that something out-of-the-ordinary has challenged us. Increasingly the belief in the society's version of the world is shaken, even among the committed.

However, the old order will not give up that easily. Criticism of ritual often collapses when rebuffed with the insistence that the ritual was not applied correctly. Perversely this response, basically a statement of power in the past, actually reinforces the acceptance of the ritual. Advocates of a formal ritual, the old barbarian junkies who are addicted to it, remain faithful to the 'one true way', come what may. They remain convinced despite all the evidence to the contrary. Then an excess of ritual is launched in society, an excess of 'intimidation and glorification' (Roland Barthes). This leads to far less tolerance, but perversely to greater awareness of the extraordinary – and the positive feedback loop is closed. There is a narrow threshold between negative and positive feedback (between purity and danger) that depends on a society's ability to enforce its will on external influences, and not to be coerced by environmental factors. That threshold is breached by excessive ritualistic behaviour. For then the imperceptible acts of intimidation, that is authority, become apparent, and the community's trust is lost.

Today the future is seen as a social pollutant, and it can no longer be ignored. In our society 'change is no longer thought of as achievement, as opportunity, as progress, but as an object of fear' (E H Carr). In this future, unavoidable problems will arise, and yet members of the society will refuse to admit the existence of serious social pollution. Change is essential if society is to survive and prosper in the future. We have reached that point where ritual has become degenerate, pure ideology mindless chanting, that is futile against the inevitability of social breakdown. For 'the froward retention of custom is as turbulent a thing as an innovation' (Francis Bacon). Then as the rituals fail to deliver safety, ultimately the society will lose faith in itself. For a point will come when it knows something is radically wrong, but because of ritual it is blinded and unable to recognize just what the problem is.

The friction between the contrived ritual and the societal or institutional context is often an incentive to embroider even more 'sophisticated' rituals. It is then that society enters the theatre of the absurd. The priests no longer fend off danger. Pious commentators are promoted beyond their competence. These pathetic yet self-important intellectual pygamies do not have the wit to ignore the minor distortions in the flux around them. They are terrified by their own inadequacy, doubtfully confident in their rituals; they feel driven to act. All is danger to them because the pious can only interpret via ritual (through bureaucracy). 'Interpret' may be too charitable a word. Perhaps they can only act by rote of ritual. Unfortunately, ritual does not deliver a sufficient vocabulary to explain the complexity of the dynamic situation.

Unresolved tensions are often best left unresolved, ignored, forgotten. Most minor problems, when ignored, would simply go away. However, minor or major problems are indistinguishable to ritual. Ritual acts ensure that the minor problems soon become major. The pious quickly get out of their depth. Rituals are overused because of a widespread lack of faith and trust in society. Overwhelmed, the pious resort to vacant and repetitive chanting of the rules, and to gratuitous acts of societal self-abuse and self-mutilation. The rain dance becomes frantic and hysterical. Ritual degenerates into displacement activity, and things rapidly get out of hand. The very ritual actions that are supposed to purify society make the situation even worse, highlighting even more the incompetence of the pious. They become even more insistent in the efficacy of their ritual sacrifices. Then the remaining competent priests, those who can see the nonsense in it all, are also sucked in. However, because of the restrictions placed on them by ritual, they too are forced by circumstance to take on the mantle of incompetence. In the spotlight of intense ritual, even they have no freedom of action.

Frantically, ritual initiates a positive feedback that drives the society back into chaos. The greater the external threat, the greater the insistence and dependence on ritual categorization. The extraordinary must be denied, and yet denial is impossible. Every problem is blamed on outsiders: the Jews in the Weimar Republic, the Asians in Idi Amin's Uganda, the ethnic Chinese in Indonesia during the 1998 riots. The greater the threat, the greater the scale of the sacrifice required. And as the fear increases, ritual explodes.

Authority still sanctions the failing rituals, and vice versa. However, such rituals no longer protect the wider society. They have been 'hijacked' as protection by frightened authorities, who are themselves under threat. The intended outcome of ritual application now correlates totally with the vested interests of authority. Overuse of rituals makes adepts even more certain of the rightness of their position, simply because it appears everywhere. The original benign authority, even if it wanted to, will find it very difficult to change, let alone replace, these rituals, as defence mechanisms will develop around them within the community. Ultimately the worldly-wise priests lose control; the pious commentators 'become virtuous from indignation' (Nietzsche) and take control. A rabid fundamentalism is let loose, from which there can be no indifference. Ritual becomes pedantic formalism, the now not-so-subtle instrument of domination, repression, 'unfreedom' and servitude. 'Domination is transfigured into administration' (Herbert Marcuse). The application of ritual becomes obsessive, compulsive, neurotic.

In this state there can be no peaceful coexistence with the extraordinary, with the different. The old barbarians will have recaptured the immoral 'moral high ground'. Ethnic, religious, political and capitalistic philosophies of difference come to the fore. Those who think that liberal democracy is secure in Europe must ask themselves why the old barbarism of national socialism is again at large. In the elections on 26 April 1998, the xenophobic Deutsche Volksunion claimed one in every eight voters in Saxony-Anhalt, one in four under 25 years old (Gimson, 28 April 1998). The far-right Freedom Party tied for second place in Austria's 1999 general election with 26.91 per cent of the vote (Reuters, 1999). On the Cote d'Azur with its wide extremes of wealth and poverty, Jean-Marie Le Pen and his racist National Front party have substantial support – in one department they gained nearly 30 per cent of the vote by playing on fears of unemployment, immigration and crime (Henning, 9 May 1998). The communists, under various guises, are re-emerging as a major political force to the east of the Berlin Wall. The fact is that the lure of the old barbarian, promising social stability and control, is too much to resist for the many who feel totally insecure in our uncertain world. Hence the rise of One Nation politics, not just in Europe but across the world, as in Australia or with the racist militias in the United States.

The control freaks react with self-righteous and extreme violence against anyone who dosen't do as they are told, as the starving of North Korea and the dead of Cambodia's killing fields know to their cost. Such profligate application of rituals responds to uncertainty with yet more ritual, forming rigid and inadequate structures that in turn lead to inert, deadening conformity and repression. Chanting such mantras, institutions incline toward bureaucratic procedures that ride roughshod over the subtle nuances of social context, and become completely unsympathetic to the very societies they are supposed to support. Individuals and sub-societies are brutalized by this insensitive application of ritual. Such excesses are not easily shrugged off because so many personal and organizational destinies are tied closely to them. But rituals must finally be challenged, not least by problems that they themselves have created.

The rise of old barbarians must be recognized and taken as a wake up call for new barbarians, if they are to defend the rights of the individual and with it the Enlightenment. (This intellectual movement of 17th and 18th-century Europe and North America celebrated reason as the means of understanding, and thereby bettering, the human condition. Fundamentally secular in outlook, its subversive message was feared by all whose power was based on received authority (ritual by another name). Its enduring legacy (to date) is the acceptance of an individual's liberty and personal freedom of expression and thought as essential to a civilized society.) Now that the communal efficacy of ritual is seen to have expired, individual members of the community must cease to draw their identity as members from such failing rituals, and form new communities based on alternative 'proper' understandings of the world. New barbarians must be ready when the rain-dance fails to deliver rain.

These rebels must recognize their servile position, but in the ant-hill of human ritual no individual thought is allowed. But what happens when the human ants discover they are ants? . 'All liberation depends on the consciousness of servitude' (Herbert Marcuse). 'Give me Liberty to know, to utter and to argue freely according to my conscience, above all other liberties' (Milton). The liberated new barbarians must come to approach the world in a different way. Consequently, they must challenge the communal efficacy of rituals and any attempt to stress the instrumental efficacy of rituals will appear to them 'primitive' and absurd.

Designers of grand schemes optimistically believe that, by mere intention, they can confine the consequences of their actions to the achievement of a wish-list of their original goals. They fail to see evolving circumstances that are not what was originally intended, but everything that acrues to their action – what it has become, what it will become, and not what it was intended to be. In more reasonable times the stabilizing feedback of ritual has the beneficial effect of creating a stable society. However, facing uncertainty is a matter of accepting that the unimaginable can and will happen, and being prepared to deal with it on the level of personal choice, and not being constrained by the uncritical usage of debased ritual.

A radical re-orientation is needed if enlightened individuals are to overcome the widespread cynical opportunism of old barbarian rabble-rousers who are promoting themselves in the political domain, preying as they do on the societal environment racked with doubt and uncertainty. Only an unsentimental understanding of what is sensible for the individual can lead to emancipation. Any approach to societal change based on a belief in the efficacy of failing rituals will open the door to the old barbarians.

| 13 |

Altruism: who cares?

> Things fall apart; the centre cannot hold;
> Mere anarchy is loosed upon the world,
> The blood-dimmed tide is loosed, and everywhere
> The ceremony of innocence is drowned;
> The best lack all conviction, while the worst
> Are full of passionate intensity.
>
> (from *The Second Coming* by W B Yeats)

Rituals fail. As things fall apart, it is not just the new barbarians who are full of passion. The old barbarians are there also. Religious fundamentalists, God botherers routed for two centuries by their old enemy science, can again ply their shoddy trade in souls now that science has lost faith in itself. Xenophobic nationalists, an embarrassment just a decade ago, form the rallying ground for the unskilled masses who are the losers to new technology. The 'robber barons' of capitalism like Andrew Carnegie and Henry Clay Frick will once again, but with more subtlety this time, 'hire one half of the working class to kill the other' (Frick). 'The worshipful capitalists will never want for fresh exploitable flesh and blood, and will let the dead bury their dead' (Karl Marx). Meanwhile, reconstituted Marxists and cynical socialists confront the coming anarchy with a camouflaged version of their old dogma of central planning.

Blissfully, unaware that their ceremony of innocence is drowning, the soft-left social and liberal democrats are re-categorizing themselves as communitarians or some other label linked to a trendy 'ism'. They are rallying around a call to 'basic values' and the common good, unknowingly opening the door to the old barbarians. Surprisingly, from the other side of the false left–right divide, they are being joined by wet conservatives, who are under the delusion that the old barbarities of socialism and communism are dead. Thinking the old enemy gone, they haven't the slightest idea what to do, and so they stick their heads in the sand of a desert named 'back to basics'. They are all scrabbling for the security of middle ground, just at the very moment when the centre cannot hold. They are all jumping on to the bandwagon just as the band is getting off.

The call for community

Today's rallying cry from the wagon is 'community', along with other abracadabra words like 'family' and 'duty'. Communitarianism promotes the cause in which 'individual rights and social responsibilities are balanced' and, in particular, where people should develop (or, as they would have it, redevelop) a sense of mutual responsibility. 'We must call for new communities, more pluralistic in form. People can and should be a member of several communities, at work, in the family and in the neighbourhood' (Etzioni, 1994). They don't actually want new communities, but rather reinvented old ones. Communitarians want to restore civic virtues, where people live up to their responsibilities and do not merely concentrate on their entitlements. They want to shore up the moral foundations of society, but in doing so they are papering over the cracks that are evident in a widespread fear of the future. They want to save their mythical society from extinction.

However, civic regeneration cannot be ignited simply from the rosy glow of a misremembered golden age; it requires dealing with the world as it is and as it will be. Communitarians blame the collapse of our social values on the emphasis on unlimited personal freedom so prevalent in the West. They point out that those societies to have gone furthest in fostering deregulation now have the most anxious and insecure populations. Approaching the new millennium, fear and insecurity are the predominant moods. Unemployment, rising crime, irresponsible and anti-social behaviour, high illegitimacy rates and disintegrating families, a decline in support for authority, corruption in public life and the inability to create a sense of mutual trust in society are typical.

Communitarians say that we are hopelessly mired in moral relativism, and then they make an appeal for common values. The word 'relativism' merits a particularly virulent sneer. They really must believe there is an absolute morality: theirs – the sign of true old barbarians. They won't see that morality is just codified prejudice, because then they would have to give an honest answer to the question of which prejudice is to be the chosen one. There is really no point in arguing about the most appropriate prejudice. That is best left to natural selection, because it is natural selection that will ultimately arbitrate between winners and losers.

The reason why we in the West are so mired in moral relativism is that the common values and rituals of the status quo no longer glue our society together. Many in our society are experimenting with alternatives; and new communication technologies make it so very much easier to find out about other communities, other moralities, and then to compare and contrast their relative merits. With this new-found knowledge, individuals are pulling away from their old communities and pulling apart their old moralities. Communitarians point at the virtues of self-help and self-reliance, which were strong in Western societies before the huge expansion of the state. People, they say, should act for themselves rather than wait for governments to solve problems. They praise neighbourhoods pauperized by their lack of resources, and exhausted by crime, that have been brought back from the brink by community action (Atkinson, 1995). Yet, however resourceful, these neighbourhoods are still on the brink. What is more, theirs is not reactionary communitarian action. It is the radical solidarity of a community set apart, vainly trying to secure resources from a political system that despises them and an economic system that has abandoned them.

These are Charles Murray's 'undeserving poor' (Herrnstein and Murray, 1994), categorized not by poverty, but by anti-social behaviour: by unkempt homes, by ill-educated children, by feral adolescents, increasingly (and most relevant according to Murray) by women seeing no shame in bearing illegitimate babies and by the unwillingness of the fathers to hold down jobs and support these families. He argues that lax welfare policies will create a permanent and destabilizing underclass of unemployables and criminals. Punitive measures are the only solution to counteract this 'parenting deficit' inside society. Bringing up a child should not be undertaken by those who are not financially, intellectually and emotionally equipped for it.

Communitarians welcome the social stigma that coerces women into having abortions, or turning to the state or church to have their babies adopted. A cultural universal is called forth: a single woman with a small child is not a viable economic unit. The logical conclusion is that 'respectable' married women will soon find their hard-won freedoms sacrificed on the altar of the morally indignant state espousing the creed of *Kinder, Küche, Kirche* (the female virtues of children, the kitchen and the church) – although not many *Kirchen* will support abortions (just yet!). What communitarians don't say is that there are plenty examples of moralizing communitarians who controlled their communities by ritualized social engineering – socialist states such as Hitler's Germany, Nicolae Ceausescu's Romania, Kim Il-sung's North Korea, Fidel Castro's Cuba and every president's Soviet Union from Lenin and Stalin onwards. They all start by oppressing anyone who is different, for the common good, and end up by oppressing everyone else for the same reason: government and its law officials become an occupying force.

Of course a healthy society is one where individual rights are in harmony with civic responsibilities, where there is a balance between independence and interdependence.

But how do we achieve this Nirvana? Governments can't just create these ideal communities by an act of parliament. There has to be an underlying will in society, either already freely existing there, or put there by force. Such communitarian civilizing of society can only work without coercion if everyone in the community sees the reward in conforming. The problem is that all governments tend to prefer the stick and forcing their morality down people's throats, rather than handing out carrots: responsibilities will come before entitlements. Sanctions will be applied to anyone who doesn't conform. Authoritarians will impose consensus. People will be intimidated into conforming.

Western politicians actually expect the unemployed to volunteer to work on half-baked and (most importantly) cheap government schemes with the promise of jobs in the future, because 'work experience' is good for them. The fact is that those who volunteer to do good works in the community are usually the employed, rather than the unemployed who by definition have far more free time. These government schemes don't give the unemployed a stake in the system, and all the while those without work are blaming 'the system' for not recognizing their invisible or non-existent talents. They are alienated as second-class citizens with non-jobs. They want no part of it, because they see themselves becoming cheap labour. If the failing individual sees no self-interest in a scheme then such community service is delusion on the part of government, and the devil will find work for these idle hands in the black economy, and worse.

If successful individuals come to believe that they too are being exploited, then they also will opt out. It is not just the dependency culture that is eating away at community; an independency culture is also growing among those who feel they are being milked to pay the price of dependency among the degenerate community. A community only functions well when there is a synergy to the actions of its members. If some pay and others take giving nothing in return, then there is a problem. Hence new barbarians are looking for new communities based around economic well-being for themselves, their families and friends.

To many, unfortunately, the notion of 'community' implies defunct tyrannical institutions, which claim historical authority and demand allegiance, but which have lost legitimacy within society. Such tyranny divides rather than unites. There is far more to the notion of community than where we have lived and what we live for. There is far more than duty and responsibility. A successful community needs a radical element that will help it evolve and adapt to external pressures. This doesn't mean going back unquestioningly to old values and old communities. It may mean accepting new values that are unacceptable to the authorities of the past.

To succeed, caring communities need people of good will, but there are far too many people of ill will out there. Just look at the most cohesive communities in the status quo, for example the Serbs, highly cohesive in their drive for ethnic cleansing. Look no further than the United Kingdom for two of the most cohesive communities in Europe, namely the Catholics and Protestants of Northern Ireland. Bigotry, not virtue, and the ritual revisiting of past rights and wrongs bind them together, and keep them apart. What basic values do we find in these communities? Far from maintaining the status quo, they are tearing away at its very fabric. Around the world there is a mean-spirited old barbarism in many communities based around perverted forms of religious and ethnic fundamentalism. This demonizes national government and its interference, such as with the perpetrators of the Oklahoma bombing, the burned-out Branch Davidian sect in Texas, or the subway-poisoning Aum Shinrikyo cult in Japan.

Definitions

So what is community? The words 'community' and 'communication' come from the same root. Change the meaning of 'communication', and you change the meaning of 'community'. Few can doubt that telecommunication has brought about the 'death of distance', and that communication is freed from the constraints of geography. Maps no longer correlate with political control. Now 'causes' can bring together people across national boundaries as new communities. New communities mean new rituals. The knowledge workers in cyberspace are recognizing that they have become a cyber-community. Will these new communities keep on supporting the public good of yesterday's public? It is very unlikely! The 'information poor' are remote from these new communities. Not being 'one of us', everyone from the information poor will be confined to the margins. Consequently the political leaders of the 'great unwashed' will be a threat to their freedom of communication. The 'information rich' have seen how politicians use the moralities of masses in society as an excuse to censor the free flow of information of the Net: they cite the case of Felix Somm (see Chapter 1).

'The public good be damned, I will have no part of it... Man is an end in himself, not to the means to the ends of others... man's life, his freedom, his happiness are his by inalienable right.' So says John Galt, the hero in Ayn Rand's book *Atlas Shrugged* (1957). (Ayn Rand (1905–82) was born Alisa Rosenbaum in St Petersburg, Russia. In 1926 she escaped to the USA from the Soviet communism she loathed, taking her new surname from the Remington-Rand typewriter.) In her novel, 'men of mind' band together in a pleasant community and vanish off into a never-never-land lying beneath a golden dollar sign. (At her funeral Rand was buried under a carpet of flowers in the shape of a giant dollar sign.)

Although her message was set in the Railway Age, and at the height of the iron and steel industry, an update for the Information Age has serious ramifications for today's knowledge workers. For what Rand is saying is that in the past the tribe dominated and exile was a terrifying prospect – but no longer. She was predicting that many entrepreneurs would begin to object to the barrage of taxation and regulation, and the scorn of their fellows, which is their lot.

Despite being rejected by the intellectual (mostly leftish) elite in her adopted United States, Rand's books have had an enormous influence on US youth. The Library of Congress pronounced *Atlas Shrugged* the second most influential book on US life (after the Bible), consciously and unconsciously affecting the thinking of the business leaders in the United States, particularly in the information technology and media industries. In Rand's ideology, the individual creator of wealth is at the centre of every healthy economy, and should be cheered, not jeered as in so many Western societies.

Rand's 'objectivist Ethics holds that **human** good does not require human sacrifices and cannot be achieved by the sacrifices of anyone to anyone'. In the old ethics, taxation is tribute, and it is moral to pay. However, to Rand, imposed taxation is theft and it is moral to resist the injustice. She asserts that 'the **rational** interests of men do not clash – that there is no conflict of interests among men who do not desire the unearned, who do not make sacrifices nor accept them, who deal with one another as **traders**, giving value for value. The principle of **trade** is the only rational ethical principle for all human relationships, personal and social, private and public, spiritual and material. It is the principle of **justice**' (Rand, 1964).

She is not saying that these individuals are alone and isolated, quite the opposite. 'Men can derive enormous benefits from dealing with one another. A social environment is most conducive to their successful survival – **but only on certain conditions**.' A social existence delivers knowledge and trade. Trade allows for a division of labour that enables individuals to specialize and perfect their skills, thereby enhancing their wealth through trade.

The good of the pack no longer constrains elite knowledge workers. Now at last they are heeding Rand's words and questioning their pre-programmed allegiance to those elected top dogs of the nation–state. They have become renegades, looking for fellow-travellers, often with the intention of setting up alternative collectives, not based on ethnic or religious differences, but on the shared values of self-interest. The pack of old barbarians, celebrating mediocrity at the expense of real talent, won't give up on its property that easily. The 'politics of envy' and 'the redistribution of wealth' still pervade much of today's thinking, reinventing many discredited socialist ideals.

Everywhere it is virtuous to stop the 'excessive' salaries of the 'fat cats', because they are held to be bad for society. Yet 'every government interference in the economy consists of giving an unearned benefit, extorted by force…'. Knowledge workers cannot be paid too much for their creativity. This wealth earned in a global arena must be to the advantage of those in the local community without those arts, but who is able to deliver plain and simple quality service in a pleasant working environment. Any social morality that institutionalizes envy ultimately reduces the business elite to a 'mediocracy', and destroys any chance of wealth creation in that society. Such are the consequences of socialist and oppressive government ('socialist' and 'oppressive' being synonyms to the wealth creator). Knowledge workers will either run away, or just not bother, joining the dependency culture instead, leaving it to the nonexistent somebody else to generate the wealth. It leads to disorder and chaos. In the thermodynamic theory of economic hot-spots, socialism is entropy.

Altruism

Ayn Rand (1984) calls the moral backing for the thuggery of the collective 'altruism' :

> The basic principle of altruism is that man has no right to exist for his own sake, that service to others is the only justification of his existence, and that self-sacrifice is his highest moral duty, virtue and value.
>
> Do not confuse altruism with kindness, good will or respect for the rights of others. These are not primaries, but consequences that, in fact, altruism makes impossible. The irreducible primary of altruism, the basic absolute, is **self-sacrifice** – which means self-immolation, self-abnegation, self-denial, self-destruction – which means: the **self** as a standard of evil, the **selfless** as a standard of the good.
>
> Do not hide behind such superficialities as whether you should or should not give a dime to a beggar. That is not the issue. The issue is whether you **do** or do **not** have the right to exist **without** giving him that

dime. The issue is whether you must keep buying your life, dime by dime, from any beggar who might choose to approach you. The issue is whether the need of others is the first mortgage on your life and the moral purpose of your existence. The issue is whether man is to be regarded as a sacrificial animal. Any man of self-esteem will answer: '**No**'. Altruism says: '**Yes**.'

She goes on to ask:

> Is man a sovereign individual who owns his person, his mind, his life, his work and its products – or is he the property of the tribe (the state, the society, the collective) that may dispose of him in any way it pleases, that may dictate his convictions, prescribe the course of his life, control his work and expropriate his products? Does a man have the **right** to exist for his own sake – or is he born in bondage, as an indentured servant who must keep buying his life by serving the tribe but can never acquire it free and clear? This is the first question to answer. The rest is consequences and practical implementations. The basic issue is only: Is man free? In mankind's history, capitalism is the only system that answers: Yes. Capitalism is a social system based on the recognition of individual rights, including property rights, in which all property is privately owned.
>
> (Rand, 1967)

In Rand's polemics there are echoes of Friedrich Hayek and his warnings about *The Road to Serfdom* (1944):

> The beliefs of the great majority on what was right and proper were allowed to bar the way of the individual innovator. Only since industrial freedom opened the path to the free use of new knowledge, only since everything could be tried – if somebody could be found to back it at his own risk – and, it should be added, as often as not from outside the authorities officially entrusted with the cultivation of learning, has science made the great strides which in the last hundred and fifty years have changed the face of the world.
>
> The principle that the end justifies the means is in individualist ethics regarded as the denial of all morals. In collectivist ethics it becomes necessarily the supreme rule; there is literally nothing that the consistent collectivist must not be prepared to do if it serves 'the good of the whole', because 'the good of the whole' is to him the only criterion of what ought to be done.
>
> (Hayek, 1944)

Communication technologies have really complicated matters by introducing dissatisfied members of a society to alternative world-views. The malcontents now have a choice: a world of choice. No longer isolated among the moralists of their society, and hence compliant, the disillusioned, the immoral and the amoral can find fellow travellers over the Net – new communities with new illusions. Who knows what good is any more? The genie of moral relativism is out of the bottle, although many in society will see it as moral choice. The old barbarian moralizers are furious with the failure of their rituals to maintain social cohesion.

The many alien choices and behaviours available are not new in our society. Maybe it has always been thus, but in the past the confines of borders have kept the influx to a minimum by holding society firmly under control. Added to this, a hefty dose of hypocrisy kept the morality intact. There have always been abortion, euthanasia, corruption, chauvinism and sexual harassment, only previously we just didn't bother to see them, because our rituals made them invisible or ignorable. It is not that there has been a vast increase in the scale of immorality and amorality to date. Rather, with new technology, we can see the alternatives and the hypocrisy more clearly. But the scale of the problem is set to explode because it is easier for us to act on our immoral and amoral urges. Increasingly we have the choice of making amoral decisions ('immoral' to the moral) and so our societal rituals are failing. If the old barbarian bigots try to stop it then the amoral can escape, physically or electronically, outside their jurisdiction.

Once the imposition of a morality on a society fails, or the hypocrisy of pretending to impose some morality fails, then that society is no longer homogeneous. With large numbers of a community proclaiming a new morality, with an end to shame, guilt and sentimentality, society is no longer a community. This leads to confrontations, and it is time to split apart into sub-communities, each sharing its own but differing common values. There can be no meeting of minds when fundamentally different views of the world are in conflict.

Breakdown of morality

The proof of the breakdown of morality is everywhere. The battles for women's rights are pitting old barbarian males against new women. Drug and alcohol abuse, gambling and pornography are frowned upon everywhere or banned, and yet they are found everywhere. Catholic priests are charged with child abuse: the Church can no longer keep the vices of its priests hidden. The religious taboo against abortion is breaking down. In Ireland abortion is illegal, and so there is a steady trade with women seeking the operation in Britain (Pollack, 26 May 1998). Morality is a business opportunity for the amoral (and the immoral), particularly in countries like Ireland where society is badly split over a particular issue, and passions ride high (Green, 9 July 1998). In Ireland, opponents led by the Catholic Church preach against sin, but in the United States there is a much more violent reaction. Anti-abortion and other hate groups are on the increase. In 1994 a doctor and a security guard were murdered at a clinic in Pensacola, Florida (*Reuters News Service*, 8 July 1998). In January 1998 a police officer was killed and a nurse seriously injured in the bombing of an abortion clinic in Birmingham, Alabama (*Reuters News Service*, 8 March 1998). In the religious terrorism of old barbarism, it is moral to kill and maim the immoral in the cause of morality.

However, it will never be moral to kill oneself. The right to die with dignity will pit the individual against the collective, for the collective claims the sole (and soul) ownership of the citizen, and insists on the right that the state and only the state may terminate the deed of ownership. Australia's Northern Territory legalized euthanasia for the terminally ill, provided some very strict conditions were met (Lee Martin, 12 April 1996). The 'pro-life lobby' was horrified – they foresaw an influx of 'one-way tourism' into Darwin of those who could stand their pain no longer. In that respect they were quite right; it could have been very big business. A minimum 'cooling off period' would have kept hospital beds full, and caring relatives (some not-so-caring, thinking of the Last Will and Testament) would give the hotel business an all-year-round trade. Uncharitable charities would be bloodsucking around the soon-to-be death-beds, gouging out last-gasp donations, all the while preying on the guilt of the bereaved. Darwin could have built up its commercial future on the terminally ill's perfectly reasonable yet 'immoral' craving to die in peace and with dignity. But that was all ruined when central government in Canberra repealed the local law.

At least proponents of euthanasia are honest. There is growing concern in Britain that, because of financial stringency in the national health service, terminally ill patients are having life-support facilities withdrawn in order to free up beds and reduce spending. The inference being that under financial pressure, life-support facilities are being withdrawn from coma patients. This battle is truly global. Countries each have their own Dr Death. In the United States, Dr Jack Kevorkian not only supports voluntary euthanasia, but also the subsequent 'harvesting' of organs for transplants. He has assisted in more than 100 mercy killings, and has been tried five times, being acquitted on three occasions, and a fourth judged a mistrial (Egan, 16 May 1998). He was finally sentenced in April 1999 to between 10 and 25 years in prison for assisting the suicide of Thomas Youk, who was suffering from motor-neurone disease (Whitworth, 14 April 1999). But his battle goes on.

Longevity and low infant mortality are often seen as measures of social progress. Hu Yamei, a deputy to the Ninth National People's Congress in Beijing, disagrees (*BBC Monitoring Service*, 12 March 1998). 'A modern society should have modern ethics.' She is approached regularly by retired revolutionary veterans who want to see a law on euthanasia enacted, and hospitals in Beijing and Shanghai used for medical trials. Only to be carried out on patients with incurable diseases, permission for the procedure would have to be granted by the patient, the family and most importantly the relevant government department. Hu blames feudal superstition in China for hindering the implementation of a euthanasia law. She is quite clear. This is a battle between the ancient and modern in society.

We could be seeing a demographically led change in attitude. Their own mortality is now staring the 'baby-boomers' in the face. Theirs is a horror of the advances in medical technology enabling the medical profession to keep patients wired up and 'alive', rather than admitting 'the failure of death'. Behind this 'moral' support for the undead there is a growing suspicion that to the hospital a dead patient is also a dead revenue stream. That cynicism is countered by the would-be beneficiaries of those expensively maintained in pain or coma.

Moralists don't just attack those who take life; they also attack those who create it. On 6 July 1996, 6LL3 (alias Dolly the sheep) was born near the Roslin Institute in Scotland. A product of asexual autonomous reproduction (cloning), Dolly unleashed a furious worldwide ethical debate. Fanciful newspaper articles talk about human cloning and the possibility of cloning Jesus (from the Turin shroud), Einstein or Hitler or a master race.

In November 1997, UNESCO passed a Declaration on the Human Genome and Human Rights that banned human cloning. The World Health Organization has passed a similar resolution. The Council of Europe sees cloning as contrary to human rights. Canada is considering a five-year jail sentence and substantial fines for anyone who dares to break this fundamental taboo (Faunce, 2 June 1998).

This is unrealistic. On announcing the birth of Dolly, shares in PPL Therapeutics, the company that undertook the cloning, rose by 16 per cent (Taylor, 25 February 1997). Governments are caught in a moral dilemma. Do they ban cloning, or do they support research that puts it to good use (whatever that good may be)? They have already identified politically correct uses for cloning: the preservation of endangered species and preventing Alzheimer's disease. Scientists at Mahidol University in Thailand are hoping to clone the rare white elephant from genetic material preserved from the last century (Sheridan, 3 January 1999). A number of research establishments are cloning cells so that everyone could have their own 'body repair kit': such blood, muscle, bone and brain cells could be transplanted into the body without fear of tissue rejection (Connors, 8 November 1998).

Do governments ban such experimentation under pressure from 'right-thinking' zealots, or do they share in a bonanza? Can there be any doubt? Governments will finally come down on the side of the money (with weasel word reservations). Whatever the rights and wrongs, there are plenty of people who will pay for cloning. Families who have lost loved ones through illness or accident have already approached Dr Ian Wilmut, the creator of Dolly, to resurrect them (Wilson, 26 June 1997). There is no shortage of egotists who believe the world needs more than one copy of themselves. Renegade scientists are already talking about setting up clinics to undertake such cloning. There are alternative 'moral majorities' elsewhere in the world, who see in cloning and other forms of genetic engineering, the possibility of eugenics, and hence the perfectibility of their society by creating more good members and destroying the bad.

The term eugenics, meaning 'well born', was coined by the English scientist Francis Galton, a cousin of Charles Darwin, who wanted populations graded, with the most able permitted to have more children than the inferior. Eugenics is the intervention in the evolutionary process aimed at improving populations by understanding their biological and sociological development patterns and then changing them. Note the adjective 'sociological' is in this definition. By adding the word 'understanding', the door to all the old barbarian moralities is opened. Think about eugenics and we immediately see the horrors of the Third Reich. Smug liberal and social democrats like to think that such atrocities could only happen in totalitarian socialist states, and certainly not in enlightened and highly moral Western countries. Yet between 1920 and as late as 1970, 100,000 'undesirables' were sterilized across Sweden, Denmark and Norway (Pallister, 26 August 1997). The Canadian province of Alberta spayed around 3,000 women between 1928 and 1972, and one US historian claims that 60,000 US citizens were forcibly sterilized in the 1930s (*Economist*, 30 August 1997). It is still happening. In Austria, more than a thousand mentally retarded young women have been sterilized since 1992 (Fullerton, 27 August 1997), and all 'in their own best interests'.

No doubt, the blame for such behaviour will be placed at the feet of new barbarians – but their sins are more likely to be ones of omission. It is the old barbarians who commit the sins of commission. New barbarians, be they individuals, families or close communities, may take eugenic decisions, but each case will be dealt with on its own individual merits, and only within the assenting group; the rest of the world can look after itself. The old barbarians, on the other hand, know what is good (moral) and right for everyone, and they will impose it on everyone regardless. There is always excess in any utopian political doctrine that preaches progress for 'the people'. For when the good of the masses is paramount, attitudes toward unknown individuals become impersonal, and the good of the individual must be suppressed. Once old barbarians manage to take away individual responsibility from every individual, family or close community, then inevitably the 'control freaks' will consider each citizen, not as an individual, but as an economic unit.

In their drive to economic viability of the human-ant colony, control programmes start with the recommendation of voluntary birth control, followed by its enforcement. Then it is only a short step to eugenics. The whole sordid history of that particular monstrosity will be conveniently ignored with the moral reassurance that 'it will be different this time'. And there have been fairly benign, even comic, attempts. Mensa, the organization for people with if not high intelligence then high IQs, has set up a sperm bank to help women give birth to 'genetically superior babies' (Rogers, 15 February 1996). But it is a slippery slope: such thinking was the basis of the eugenics movement in England in the early 20th century with worries that the 'lower classes' were outbreeding 'decent people', and this culminated in the death camp at Auschwitz. In the 1960s in India men were given transistor radios after a vasectomy, and in 1986 Singapore arranged to give pay rises to female graduates after they had given birth (Christie, 26 August 1997) and non-graduates were given housing grants if they agreed to be sterilized. Then in 1980 the People's Republic of China started its one child per family programme. It was readily accepted among urban Chinese, but not in rural communities. It did, however, have a sinister side-effect, not expected by government. Because families wanted their one child to be male, 97 per cent of abortions after ultrasound scans were of female foetuses (Mirsky, 29 August 1996). That government has gone even further and instigated a law on maternal and infant health, calling for the sterilization of couples with genetic defects to stop the prevalence of abnormal births. To the old barbarian, every infirm child is an economic drain, whether or not the family and friends are willing to support the child.

Moral cleansing

The old barbarian 'moral majority' will always find ways of getting rid of new barbarian troublemakers (sinners), from female foetuses to political freethinkers. At the very least, adult sinners will be expelled. For when sin (that is a different morality or amorality) is abroad, moral cleansing is soon on the agenda. Expelling individuals almost passes without comment, as when morality is equated with taxation. The banning by politicians of tax exiles from re-entering the United States is cheered by the moralizing masses, provided of course that a substantial sum is taken from the escapees before they leave.

Internal exile too is a tried and tested approach for dealing with malcontents. It is not just the gulags of the Soviet Union or the forced labour of Red China. In 1929 the British Labour government set up a network of more than 25 labour camps across the British Isles to house more than 200,000 unemployed men from the depressed regions of Scotland, South Wales and Northern England (Austin, 9 August 1998). Men who were unemployed for more than 12 months and who had 'lost the will to work' were not exactly forced to go to the euphemistically labelled 'industrial training camps'; however, refusal meant that they and their families would be denied social benefits. It also meant that by isolating potential troublemakers in bleak far-flung outposts of the British Isles, the possibility of organized social unrest was substantially removed (Urquhart, 18 July 1998).

However, when the dominant morality is based on racial or tribal membership, then moral cleansing gets very sinister and equates to enforced exile, either external or internal, to ethnic cleansing by murder, torture and starvation, or to civil war when the immoral group is too large to go quietly. The lessons of Yugoslavia and Rwanda are nothing new. History books overflow with similar examples: the Jewish diaspora, including the numerous pogroms and Hitler's heinous 'Final Solution'; Queen Isabella of Spain expelling the Moors in 1492; in Scotland the anti-Jacobite atrocities following the 1745 uprising and the highland clearances of the 18th and 19th centuries; the Irish potato famine of the1840s; St Bartholomew's Day massacre of more than 50,000 Huguenots in 1572; and Idi Amin's expulsion of the Asians from Uganda in 1972. It has been standard practice for powerful groups to expel (and worse) inconvenient ethnic, religious, philosophical or financial groups, but only after stripping them of their wealth. Sometimes wealth is the real reason for the violence, and morality is merely a plausible justification. 'Defender of the Faith' Henry VIII made a tidy profit when he decided to defend a different faith and dissolved the Catholic monasteries across England and Wales before seizing their land and valuables. These were all **moral** acts, a perverted morality, perhaps, but morality none the less. How else could the perpetrators live with their actions?

How long will it be before the notion of a brutalizing penal colony is reinvented: a new Devil's Island, a new Botany Bay? Britain has experimented with the old idea of a prison hulk: HM Prison Ship *Weare* is moored in Portland harbour, which gives a welcome source of income after the Royal Navy ceased to be a major employer there in 1993 (Grey, 8 July 1998). Western countries are having to increase prison places. It is becoming big business, particularly when whole sub-sections of society are being alienated and criminalized. In 1995 the United States spent more on building prisons than on building universities. In California the operating costs of prisons are more than double that of higher education, a complete reversal from a decade ago (*Economist*, 15 March 1997). However, with the jail population of the United States rising from 744,000 in 1985 to nearly 2 million in 1998, the prison business is set to become highly profitable (*Economist*, 16 July 1999). Already in the United States, some poor regions with no industrial employment potential have turned themselves into commercial penal colonies. Eastern Kentucky has seven private, state or federal prisons; it's the only job in town now that the coal-mines have gone (Mueller, 25 January 1999). The prisoners themselves will be expected to work to pay for their keep. Already Best Western, Microsoft (Allen-Mills, 25 May 1997), Marks & Spencer (Ford, 26 May 1995), Shelby Cobra sports cars and TWA (Cass, 4 September 1996) use prison labour.

Affluent states that don't want prisons in their back yard are paying to export their criminals. Jails in Texas house prisoners from Oklahoma, Wisconsin, Hawaii, Massachusetts, Idaho, Wyoming and New Mexico (Noriyuki, 5 August 1998). Distances soon become too far for families to visit their incarcerated loved ones. Once visiting ceases, why stop at placing your prison in the next state? Why not outsource prisons to Siberia, where they have gulags to spare and would offer very competitive rates? Their frozen wastes have the added advantage that, even without malice aforethought, many of the unwanted inmates wouldn't survive sub-zero temperatures. Why not dump criminals in mosquito-infested parts of Africa? Why think geographically? Narcotics could sentence criminals to an alternative existence.

Old barbarians will introduce the death penalty for all categories of violent crime, not just murder. Capital punishment has the advantage of reducing the huge costs of running jails. The necessary legislation should be easy to introduce, given that the bigoted democratic majority already want it, and are offended that their squeamish parliamentary representatives always vote it down. How long before violent offenders are seen as a source of corneas, kidneys and livers for human organ transplants? Why not use chemical sterilization on those guilty of rape? The same method could be extended as a general sentence for young offenders; that should keep the criminal classes from breeding. Why not subtly support the abuse of alcohol and narcotics among the unwanted underclass? Suicide too is quite an effective and guiltless way of reducing the number of depressives in society.

There we have it. The centre cannot hold, and community leaders will scramble in a ritual frenzy to the old moral high ground, trampling innocents in the rush. Innocence is no defence against the mob; mere accusation will be proof of guilt, just like the witchcraft trials of May–October 1692 held in Salem, Massachusetts. The charge will no longer be witchcraft, but the testimony of brainwashed children may still be sufficient to imply guilt. It took three years for Peggy McMartin Buckey and her son to be acquitted of charges of child molestation in their Los Angeles pre-school in August 1983, in a trial that cost taxpayers $15 million (*Reuters News Service*, 18 January 1990). Ludicrous accusations of satanic rituals and mutilation were enough for old barbarian 'therapists' to destroy the lives of the Buckeys. Across the Atlantic Christian bigots, who see Satan everywhere, have infiltrated British social services. They mounted dawn raids on homes in the Orkneys in 1991. Charging parents with child abuse and satanic rites, they seized nine children and placed them in care (*Guardian*, 23 August 1994). Although innocent of the charges, the families were destroyed by the storm-troopers of a religiously inspired state fascism. The bigots were wrong in both these cases, but they still feel justified in their actions because paedophilia has reached epidemic proportions across the world.

The excesses of old barbarians are limitless once a society has been compromised. Their morality can be used to justify any arbitrary action against anti-social elements, which is anyone who doesn't show them total obedience. China's Cultural Revolution (1966–76) forced 'intellectuals' to labour in the fields of far-flung provinces. Human rights and civil liberties will be seen as phenomena of the 20th century, and they will disappear along with their century. And that is the problem. New barbarians, children of the Enlightenment, cannot face going back to the superstitions of an old barbarian age, and to their pathetic rituals. What should new barbarians do when they know that they can no longer rely on democratic governments? What should new barbarians do, knowing that they live in a society where the official morality and the economic reality are out of synchronization? They must show no more sentimentality toward their community. If that community does not share their own personal values, then they must get out. They must recognize themselves as new barbarians, and find another community where they can belong.

Part VI

The winners

| 14 |

The making of a new barbarian

It is not just the old barbarians of religious, ethnic and political prejudices that the knowledge worker has to worry about. In business the old barbarians of Victorian capitalism are also on the move. For the past two decades financial capital has been aggressively pouring its resources into attempts to automate intellect. Automation has enabled capital to vanquish organized physical labour. Now factories are run by a few machine minders and security guards. Increasingly computerization is overcoming the in-person service workers by destroying (re-engineering) service and office jobs. There was a certain inevitability about owners of company equity looking to deskill intellectual labour by automating intellect. Capitalists were among the first to recognize the increasing power of new barbarian economic mercenaries, whose innovative skills ultimately create the profits of their companies. Having defeated all the other workers, they naturally wanted to avoid the indignity of having to pay 'danegeld' to their talented employees. Computer science, in particular artificial intelligence (AI), was the first choice for capital in its attack on the knowledge worker. But it will fail. For AI is merely a myth of the computer age. In fact every technological age has its myths about synthesizing intelligence. Mud-technology had Adam and Eve, clockwork had Coppelia, electricity had Frankenstein. Our age is no different.

Intelligence

Ironically within this myth, the computer, the seed of the Information Age, has reached the limits of its applicability. Computerization, the high point of the Machine Age, is at the same time its nemesis. Paradoxically, this ultimate automating technology, this destroyer of all jobs requiring physical strength, is totally dependent on intellectual labour. For the production of intellectual capital is the sole prerogative of the knowledge worker. These talented new barbarians are realizing their value, and they are learning to invest their capital wisely. They know that attempts to disembody intelligence through the application of mathematical models and then to automate it are doomed to fail. Mega-millions of dollars have been spent on research in a futile quest to categorize common-sense knowledge in this daft way. No machine can build generic common-sense structures without 'being there'. Knowledge workers know that intelligence is not a drab and inert collection of 'if-then-else rules' and 'structured queries' traversing synthesized knowledge stored in tree structures. This 'bubbleware', of circles and arrowed lines pretending to give meaning to the words scribbled alongside, is about to burst.

Yet naive technology supremacists still believe that the human mind is a machine, and that rigidly mechanistic and logical thought is virtuous. They are constantly irritated by an immoral humanity that was granted access to the true and wonderful enlightenment of logic, only for it to be squandered by 'human failings'. To them these failings can only be righted by the creation of an intelligent machine, untouched by original sin. Heaven on earth is possible, but only by imposing a synthetic intelligence on humanity. This may well be possible, but only by denying of humanity all that makes it human, by creating a hell on earth.

The Machine Age mind-set refuses to accept that humanity has been successful despite this rigid way of thinking, rather than because of it. New barbarians know better than to worship at the temple of the machine metaphor. They transcend logic. The talented know that there are occasions when it is intelligent to be illogical: to act, to react instinctively. 'The music is not in the notes' (Charles Ives); it is in the musician. Intelligence is not in the machine; it is in the mind and body of the symbolic-analyst. Information is not in the data, it is in our awareness of the wider meaning of the data. Intelligence is our ability to recognize the significance in what we know, and to understand, reason and learn to adapt to, and profit from, new situations. It must be emphasised knowledge workers are not 'computer buffs'. Computing is a mere support technology for human communication, and technocrats are merely the 'navvies' building the superhighway, and the 'greasemonkeys' servicing the vehicles that travel along it.

Intelligence is not something that can be tuned into. It is the contrived and coarse systematization of sense data and biochemical input that enables us to make our way in a hostile world. Intelligence dictates to our observations so that we can interpret and make sense of them. Human intelligence is what we do, how we think, how we cope – it is essentially us, and the emergent knowledge feeds back to reinforce and enhance intelligence. This feedback loop of understanding is entangled, not only in the uniqueness of each individual's experience, but also in an evolutionary spiral, genetically restricted and limited by 'the curriculum of an earlier mankind'. (The unascribed quotations in this chapter are all from Friedrich Nietzsche.)

There was no magic moment when, on the tree of human evolution, our progenitors were given the keys to the kingdom of knowledge. Intelligence has not been perfected into some state of grace. It is the result of feedback and the totality of effects, the choices made by, and the constraints imposed on, individual experience and on our ancestors, in humanity's quest for survival at every stage of development. Our means of thought was never its original function. Intelligence is a mere side-effect of the way we each deal with our environment. Ours is an island of reason, of rationality, of logic, concocted in the universal sea of the unreasonable. There is no knowing these alien waters, and there is no escape. We cannot reason with that universal, we merely interact with it. Hence new barbarians are not all atheists; however, their religion is not the dogmatic imposition of arbitrary beliefs and morality on others for political ends, but rather a personal expression of spirituality.

Our world is unknowable, yet variously interpretable. There is no one meaning behind it, rather a myriad of meanings, each an internally consistent form, although not necessarily mutually consistent. 'Only very naive people are capable of believing that the nature of man could be transformed into a purely logical one.' 'The world is logical because we made it logical.' We made it logical in the aeons of feedback that is life on earth. We are trapped in this mode of thinking, forced to build within a framework of cyphers that is knowledge, a cage set down before the dawn of intelligence. 'Just as certain human organs recall the stage of evolution of the fish, so there must also be in our brain grooves and convolutions that correspond to that cast of mind: but these grooves and convolutions are no longer the riverbed along which the stream of our sensibility runs.' We have merely developed upon the fishes' eye view of the world, and cultivated a more sophisticated schema. There is no knowing about knowing. 'How should a tool [our intellect] be able to criticize itself when it has only itself for the critique?' 'How can we look around our own corner?'

Intelligence has nothing to do with truth or reality, nor has information. Neither intelligence nor information can be separated from being; they cannot be captured in some inert symbolism. It is our willingness to compromise with the lie of intelligence that has made humanity so successful. What logicians perceive as failings are actually the critical success factors of humanity.

Logic

Logic is a fiction of intellect; it is a systematization of cyphers that prejudices us in the belief that our sensations show us the truth about things about 'reality'. Such delusions can be effective none the less. After all, the domination of logic over today's thinking is based on the authority of past usefulness. At each stage in the feedback of our development a logic was formed that was sufficient for the effective interpretation of sense data. 'Not to know but to schematise – to impose upon chaos as much regularity and form as our practical needs require.' Our cyphers describe things, and describe them well. They describe and designate in a way that is useful. But although useful, 'what convinces is not necessarily true, it is merely convincing'. What convinced us there and then need not convince us here and now, everywhere and everywhen. Yet these past-advantageous fallacies of logic are self-perpetuating. The dominance and ritualized authority of logic in our education (our conditioning) and in our social, political and economic systems is what makes it unassailable, not logic itself.

New barbarians do not find it necessary to convince themselves of any universal validity of logic merely in order to apply it appropriately. They know that the human brain created logic because it was useful, not because it was true – despite the theory and not because of it. 'Our intellect is a consequence of the conditions of existence', a culmination of feedback in this species' successful (to date) quest for survival. Human intelligence is tied to life; it is biological and genealogical rather than logical. Such intelligence cannot be separated from what is the human total. Logic is a product of intelligence, but the perverted causality of Machine Age thinking would have us believe that intelligence is a product of logic. Not so. 'True' and 'false' are merely artificial concepts born in a successful feedback themselves sometime-appropriate misinterpretation.

Logic contrives to make simple and consistent that which is not. The methods of science (or rather pseudo-science) so prevalent nowadays are not going to help us walk the tightrope stretched above the abyss that is the future. Their ritual application as a cosmic panacea means that their relevance to us has become as entangled as the Gordian knot. Like Alexander the Great, the new barbarian will not patiently try to untie the knot, but will slice it through with the sword of lateral thinking. Many of our rituals have evolved to be optimal in the Machine Age, but they will not help us cope in the Information Age. It is neurotic to want our world to be tidy, to reflect the virtues of a machine. It is crazy to try and banish all the 'evil spirits' by forcing tidiness on it with the magic wand of systematic, yet arbitrary, use of measurement, socio-economic classifications, performance measures, efficiency audits, cost–benefit analyses and knowledge management. It is absurd to think that the complexity of our world can be captured as a mere collection of numerical data – so-called absolute facts. 'A fact is like a sack – it won't stand up till you've put something in it' (Pirandello). Each fact really does depend on the context.

Numbers and measurement

Yet everywhere we still see the folly of forecasting techniques that are merely an assignment of numbers to the future. Such forecasts are a belief that controlling the future is a matter of labelling it with numbers. But the future is not some smooth trajectory of the past; the discontinuities implicit in change are forever pulling the future away from past trends. Searching for the right numerical label to represent the future is no different from numerology and astrology: it is the modern-day equivalent of 'reading the runes'. Is it any wonder then that despite computers, and perhaps because of computers, we face a world of increasing uncertainty?

Uncertainty does not conform to numbers and to a neat computational logic. It must be continually re-evaluated. I was once at a commercial conference entitled 'managing uncertainty'; one session was run by myself and a statistician. He talked for 45 minutes on distributions, expectations, functions, formulae and curves. Within five minutes eyes began to glaze over. After 10 minutes he was just talking to an audience of one: as I was on the stage, I had to listen. When it was my turn, I walked over to the podium, and just stood there… and stood there… and stood there. For a whole minute I just stood there. I fidgeted uneasily, and shot frantic and terrified glances at the audience. At first there was silence, then a few murmurs, then a growing rumble of concern. The chairman rose to help me, but when he was half-way across the stage I banged my fist on the table and said: 'Now that is uncertainty; it has nothing to do with statistics.'

When it comes to winning the argument, rhetoric is far more powerful than logic. You can even be wrong and still win an argument. After all, the use of numbers is itself dependent on an intellectual trick that we play on ourselves. That trick, the concept of comparison that pervades all pseudo-scientific thinking, is fundamentally flawed. 'The presupposition that there are identical things, that the same thing is identical at different points of time', the idea of 'sameness', the seed of equality and enumeration, and thus of logic, was merely **appropriate** in our evolution. New barbarians admit to being in the trap of evolution. They call themselves human, and accept 'sameness', and hence 'number', as a practical choice but with circumscribed appropriateness, while at the same time denying its universal validity. Such a stance is only a problem to those who insist that the logic of false opposites, grounded as it is in 'sameness', must be all encompassing. The logic of mathematics is just idiosyncrasy, and in analysing societal problems it has become mere self-indulgent over-sophistication. Mathematics is not universally appropriate. And artificial intelligence, the bastard child of logic, the last bastion against the barbaric knowledge worker, is just error compounded on error.

This insistence on measurement has spawned the idea of 'equilibrium' that underlies so much of the 'scientism' of modern economics and management theory, particularly now in their degenerate computerized forms, which capital tries to use against the knowledge worker. These are outdated rituals, merely comforting fairy-tales for those lost in the post-modern world. To paraphrase George Soros (1994), who many demonize as a bogeyman and the cause of so many of the world's economic woes: there is no such thing as a state of equilibrium, only the question of where we are in the perpetual movement between 'near-equilibrium' and 'far from equilibrium'. And today we are **far** from equilibrium. He says it will take very special people to succeed in the 'reflexivity' of this dynamic environment. Soros calls such people today's alchemists, those who can turn the base metal in the chaos all around us into the gold of success; in other words they are new barbarians.

A role for alchemy

Alchemists are strategic brokers; they use their information systems to broker the identification and solution of problems, and deliver ideas, procedures and applications that can succeed in the midst of social, political and economic upheaval. They know that a good technological platform, although necessary, is not sufficient for success. What makes the real strategic difference is the quality and integrity of the individual knowledge worker. The symbolic-analysts who succeed in this dynamic environment treat technology as only one element in a socio-technical system – an information system.

Alchemists know that the success or failure of their actions will be determined by unique context-sensitive social, economic and political factors – *Human, all too Human* (Nietzsche) factors – and that there can be no effective action without a vision that interprets the evidence all around, but which we tend to overlook in the panic of uncertainty. Alchemists have that vision, and they have the know-how and will to make it happen. They are pragmatists who do not promote false theories of scientific and technological truth, but who base their actions on what they believe to be procedurally successful.

These new barbarians bypass questions of why science should fail totally outside its ghetto of clearly circumscribed linear functionality. New barbarians don't care; they just get on with life as it is and with what they can make of it. They refuse to play by the rules of the logicians. They are confident in their own individual self-decided designations of 'appropriate' and 'inappropriate'. For ours is a world of delusions. Our institutions are delusions, and our values are delusions, but they are shared delusions maintained by ritual. Logic is only an internally consistent instrument inside some of those old barbarian delusions. However, there can be no logic **of** delusions. Whoever can break free of the shackles of those shared delusions can manipulate us. Alchemists practise the magic of seeing our delusions clearly, as delusions, and then accepting the complexities and ambiguities in the unknown and unknowable. Ambiguity is only a problem to those thinking about it within the cage of logic; for then ambiguity makes us rigid and we cease to function. But ambiguity is part of life. The people who need certainties, the miserable old barbarians, do so because they have no joy in life; new barbarians revel in it.

With an alchemical view, symbolic-analysts are supremely confident that there will be no automation of their intellect, no short cut to their skills. They know about people and the manipulation of people, which is far more important than knowing about technology. This cynical stance will make them invincible in the conquest of cyberspace. To them, cyberspace is not an off-planet experience; it is merely the delivery mechanism for cyphers that must add value. The high-tech medium has only changed the form and scale of that delivery. Technophiles claim to see these cyphers floating around in cyberspace, but there is no world of cyphers out there. The information content of cyphers does not exist in some mystical dimension. Information is the same as it always has been, something reserved for the planet-bound human brain, to communicate between people within human society, still very much down to earth. New barbarians know that their empires will be carved out of 'cypherspace' and not 'cyberspace', the same 'cypherspace' humanity has always inhabited, only now they have supercharged transport. The technophiles have inadvertently given the innovative knowledge worker the means to travel around at warp speed.

In this battle for dominance in the Information Age, every new barbarian (individual and industry) will need to maintain good relationships among their global human networks. We can forget what the technologists predict: impersonal electronic contact will **not be sufficient**! International travel, both business and social, will have to increase substantially to maintain these human networks. Many technocrats have silly ideas about the Internet, video conferencing and the like, taking away the need to travel. I predict a major expansion in travel. Everyone's motto must be: 'Act locally, but think globally and link globally.' Success will depend totally on the global network of contacts that is the virtual enterprise.

This means looking forward to a future of new communities and relationships, and not backward to the past. By all means be proud of the past, but there is no point in dwelling on it. The future is different. The future is a diversified set of societal patterns, formed by the competing forces of political, sociological, technological and commercial potentials. These potentials, supplied by companies, customers, suppliers, governments, cultures and society at large, are the components that are all brought together by intellectual, social and economic forces. These potentials are the contributing factors toward the evolving future, but not the causes of it. They push and pull against one other; and natural selection will eventually create the dynamic, self-organizing mosaic that is the future.

But this mosaic is no arbitrary pattern. Behind all potential there is design, and behind that design there is vision. I am not saying that we can see into the future. We can't; it isn't there yet. There can be no vision of the future, but there can and must be a vision **for** the future: a new barbarian vision. A future that isn't there yet can't be discovered. It is created by men and women of vision, who are faced with a very simple choice: to create their own future, or fall into somebody else's; to take control of their own destiny, or be at the mercy of another's whim.

There are choices that each of us will have to make when designing our own future, our own mosaic. The various components of this mosaic are being pushed and pulled away from their nice comfortable position fixed within yesterday's mosaic of the status quo. Innovators competing in society at large will be distorting this mosaic. And everyone involved will have his or her own vision for the future. That vision will bring in the bigger picture, which is truly global and touches all parts of every society. Everyone will have to take a global perspective if intending to be a winner. No one can be complacent about the future imperfect, nor can anyone be completely certain about it. We will all have to change. And yet so many people look on change as something to fear, which is why they turn to old barbarians for help. Winners, however, are certain that change means achievement, opportunity and progress for themselves. These new barbarians have a firm belief in themselves and in their abilities, and they are convinced of the viability of their ideas. 'The reasonable man adapts himself to the world: the unreasonable one persists in trying to adapt the world to himself. Therefore all progress depends on the unreasonable man' (Shaw, 1903).

With new technology raising the spectre of 'virtual' this and 'virtual' that, many people are wondering if there can be any future at all for anyone or anything that is earth-based. We needn't worry. All wealth creation revolves around a meaningful application of information, so that it adds value to saleable products. That value does not exist in some virtual reality, but in a very real reality, a reality of hot-spots all linked together by electronic and transport networks, a reality circumscribed by the ever-changing social reality described in this book. And the key to success? 'The more things change, the more they stay the same.' The three most critical success factors for every business are the 3Ls: location, location and location. Having links into a network in the right place at the right time is what will separate the winners from the losers in the Information Age. And the right place? A welcoming, safe, secure and fun location with a state-of-the-art technological and communication infrastructure, whose social, economic and political institutions sponsor and support innovation.

With rising unemployment and lower wages, profit margins in mass markets are becoming negligible. I am **not** saying there will be no markets, but that markets will be different. The economists' dream of converging mass markets will become a reality. Every company must now focus on transitory premium markets, where the real money is. This means that all commercial enterprises must move rapidly to be near any market as it appears, and leave it quickly as it fades. The company's manufacturing base must be transferred to where it can take advantage of cheap labour and 'regulatory arbitrage'. The company must anticipate market needs, and influence and manipulate them. This means networking with new barbarians in the global community. The virtual enterprise must broker counter-trade and transfer-pricing deals, so as to reduce the tax burdens of itself, its suppliers, customers and employees. Using the skills and knowledge of the new barbarians, and their innovation, companies will take advantage of the reduced regulation and financial incentives that governments are using to attract freewheeling employers.

The new barbarians don't just wait around until somebody else makes the decisions for them. They do not treat the future with a mixture of ignorance and indifference. They do not take their network of contacts and their community for granted. They get to know the human network; they care about it. Only then can they add value to the requirements of that new community. The future is the collision of visions and chance in the realm of necessity. New barbarians ensure that their individual visions and actions are there, fighting for a say. They refuse to be dominated by the will of old barbarians, be they religious, ethnic, racial, socialist, or capitalist.

By all means deny my particular truths, and ignore my predictions, but you must create your own truth to see by. There are many many more alternative visions out there pushing and pulling at the fabric of the future. Morality really is relative. This is **my** vision for the future, my version of truth about the play-off between the contingent and the unforeseen, my predictions of the winners and losers of natural selection. But ultimately it is you, and only you, who are responsible for your own future. If you end up a slave to old barbarians then you have only yourself to blame.

Mutation of the nation–state

In the future I am predicting, information technology will wash away the state-drawn barriers drawn up to confine the new barbarian 'economic mercenary', the uniquely skilled entrepreneur and individualist. These free-thinkers, who liberate themselves from collective control, are neither anti-social nor isolated. They too form groups, but coherent and cohesive groups based on trust, with a shared sense of enlightened self-interest, and a shared but different view of the world. The whole purpose of a community is to create an ordered society; new barbarians are no different from anyone else in seeking stability amidst all the turmoil. With the new modes of communication and a whole raft of possibilities given to them by other new technologies, they will set out to control their own destinies. They will form themselves into voluntary tribes, globally distributed commercial and philosophical leagues maintained by telecommunications.

New communities

The practical forms of governance for these states have yet to emerge, although many candidates are being proposed. No doubt a wide variety of possibilities will survive the battles of natural selection. Some, as suggested by Davidson and Rees-Mogg, could have a population of one: the *Sovereign Individual* (the ideal at the core of Ayn Rand's thinking) (1997). Indeed she asks: 'Is man a *sovereign individual* who owns his own person, his mind, his life, his words and its products, – or is he the property of the tribe (the state, the society, the collective) that may dispose of him in any way it pleases, that may dictate his convictions, prescribe the course of his life, control his work and expropriate his products?' Naturally, they are more likely to be reconstituted communities: enterprises, corporations, families, paternal or maternal groups, fiefdoms, towns, or colonies with a shared philosophical outlook. However the nation–state will not just roll over and let it happen. As a form of governance it has been making steady strides for the last century. The nation–state was the ideal form of governance to sustain the mobilization of the large numbers of people needed to support the factory metaphor of the Machine Age. In 1904 there were only 50 sovereignties in the world. Starting with Norway's secession from the union with Sweden on 7 June 1905, the number of sovereignties has now more than tripled and is well along the way toward quadrupling (Jacobs, 1993). Most have been the results of the break-up of empires. Now it is the turn of the nation–state to break up, because it no longer has a valid economic role. Now it is quality not quantity that matters. Nation–states, the champions of quantity and size, 'are dinosaurs waiting to die' (Kenichi Ohmae, 1995). National sovereignty is corroding because 'rapid capital flows can offset, negate or subvert government policies'. The nation–state can no longer proclaim itself to be the pre-eminent form of governance.

Meanwhile hard-working citizens are losing their faith in the nation–state, seeing it as a peculiarly 20th-century phenomenon that supports the profligate and penalizes the thrifty. For the state is failing to deliver its side of the Faustian pact, where the individual submits to the legitimate violence of the state in return for protection, welfare and security. Individual entrepreneurs and companies, the real generators of wealth, feel totally justified in rejecting their deal with the increasingly bankrupt devil state. National politicians still demand an unalienable right to allocate property rights and to exploit the human resources inhabiting their territory. The state has grown obese on this free-ride of imtimidation, hostage-taking and ransom demands (taxation) that is citizenship.

Yet for all this talk about conflict between the individual and the state, we all have to live in a community, with our feet firmly planted on the planet. However, that community need not be a nation–state. The fact is, the human individual has always lived in a multiplicity of overlapping communities, and we tend to forget this because the nation–state demands total dominance over all other loyalties. There are many candidates for the ideal community, ranging from utopian dreams to the more practical and pragmatic, all confronting each other in the battles of natural selection. The rules of engagement are very clearly described by Canadian author Jane Jacobs (1993). She categorizes humanity as possessing two radically different ways of dealing with its needs. Humanity either 'produces and trades' or 'scavenges and takes'. This dichotomy creates two radically different value systems. Jacobs calls them moral syndromes, which she categorizes as 'commercial', with occupations that produce and supply physical needs, and 'guardian', which protect. Commerce needs the symbiotic help of guardians to combat predators, and to mandate and enforce standards of honesty. Guardians are funded by the wealth created by commerce.

Each syndrome has a separate set of ethics (see box), some of which are mutually incompatible. A healthy society is one where the two syndromes are kept in balance. Jacobs says: 'You can't mix up such contradictory moral syndromes without opening up moral abysses and producing all kinds of functional messes.' She formalizes this in her 'Law of Intractable Systemic Corruption: any significant breach of a syndrome's integrity – usually by adopting an inappropriate function – causes some normal virtues to convert automatically to vices, and still others to bend and break under the necessary expediency'.

The commercial moral syndrome	The guardian moral syndrome
Shun force	Shun trading
Come to voluntary agreements	Exert prowess
Be honest	Be obedient and disciplined
Collaborate easily with strangers and aliens	Adhere to tradition
Compete	Respect hierarchy
Respect contracts	Be loyal
Use initiative and enterprise	Take vengeance
Be open to inventiveness and novelty	Deceive for the sake of the task
Be efficient	Make rich use of leisure
Promote comfort and convenience	Be ostentatious
Dissent for the sake of the task	Dispense largesse
Invest for productive purposes	Be exclusive
Be industrious	Show fortitude
Be thrifty	Be fatalistic
Be optimistic	Treasure honour

Source: Jane Jacobs, *Systems for Survival*

She gives numerous examples. The mafia practise commerce but in accordance with guardian precepts. Voluntary mutual agreements mean nothing, and its trading, involving intimidation and bribery, is 'a monstrous moral hybrid'. Practising guardianship under commercial precepts can also lead to ethical dilemmas, which is why the largesse of socialism always degenerates into cronyism. Problems always arise when the role of economic planning is placed in the hands of guardians. This results in commercial planning for guardian priorities, the classic problem of the now-defunct Soviet Union. There the apparatchiks provided millions of desirable non-jobs for the 'common good', but at the cost of dragging down viable production and commerce. 'They pretend to work, and we pretend to pay them' (Mikhail Gorbachev).

Likewise, the stressing of commercial priorities contaminates guardianship. Introducing performance measurements into the police force will corrupt officers. Illegal arrests and the 'fitting up' of suspects will be used to maximize perceived performance. The very best that can be expected is that the letter of the law, not its spirit, will drive behaviour. The most likely outcome will be incidents similar to the example quoted by Jacobs of officers from the New York Transport Police falsely arresting innocent African-American and Hispanic men in order to improve their arrests-per-working-hour productivity measures (Levine and Neuffer, 24 November, 1987).

Once the practices of any organization move away from the constraints of its syndrome and become institutionalized, then virtues become vices and vice versa. Then rituals, instead of giving meaning to the world, introduce confusion. Taking and trading are fundamentally different from each other, and even their derivative forms that exist in today's society still remain fundamentally different. Jacobs makes it totally clear that it is impossible to unify commerce and guardianship into single systems of morality. Attempts to do so will ultimately create colossal tensions, but not immediately. A series of tiny transgressions, each seeming obvious and harmless, beneficial even, are the first steps on the road to perdition. There are no alarm bells; life goes on, only with each infringement society becomes just a little more corrupt. Drip, drip, drip, until the floodgates open. The guardians, instead of setting standards and punishing wrongdoers, are corrupt and corrupting. Meanwhile the traders are making you 'an offer you can't refuse'. And who guards the guardians when morality collapses into vice?

We seem to have forgotten the rules of guardianship. In medieval times, no man whose parent, grandparent, or great-grandparent was a merchant would be admitted into an order of chivalry. As recently as the early 19th century any Polish aristocrat who dabbled in trade would lose his rank and privileges. This attitude toward business was well established in the Europe of the Middle Ages. Franciscus Gratianus, a medieval monk from Bologna, was clear: 'Business is nothing but the struggle of wolves over carrion, men of business can hardly be saved for they live by cheating and profiteering.' In Dante's *Inferno* usurers were placed alongside sodomites in one of the circles of hell. Quite independently, and a world apart, Japan and India both placed traders near the bottom of society. The levels of governance were defined by the dominant instigators of physical and intellectual violence, namely the soldiers and priests at the top. However, nowadays such differentiation cannot work in the world of trade in knowledge products. Knowledge workers insist on a say in the shaping of society. This means that the relative status of trade within society must change; although the forced separation between trade and guardianship is not negated.

With the freedoms delivered by new technology, voluntary agreements are essential. But voluntary agreements presuppose choice, and effective choice calls for free competition. Commerce can only flourish over an extended time when free competition delivers new products and services into the marketplace: that is new ways of producing, distributing and communicating. Supporting such initiative and enterprise is a practical matter. It requires a framework of trust, and trust is feasible only where honesty is the norm. Contracts must be upheld, and the social status of the parties to it must be irrelevant. Rank should not permit the holder 'to terminate a lease on a whim, evade a legitimate debt, welsh on a promise to deliver, withhold agreed-on wages, and so on' (Jacobs). Such honesty must be enforced by the courts. This requires guardian help, but from guardians who are not involved with trade, who do not meddle in its practice, and who do not force their beliefs on to traders. Guardians must deliver freedom to commerce, not slavery. When there is no such symbiosis between the two sides within the economic and political power structures of the time, then the relationship will inevitably fail.

Unfortunately that is our position today. The trend toward the growing power of knowledge workers is totally undermining the centralized power of state machinery and its ability to tax and regulate. Globalization has shown the James Bond myth that the state is good and global corporations (Spectre) are bad to be blatant propaganda on behalf of the nation–state, a morality tale told by tax collectors.

The nation–state is based on tribal virtues and the collectivist doctrine that the state owns the individual. We are all equal in that we are all property of the state, or rather of the leaders of the state. These leaders insist that the state can dispose of their slave-property as they see fit. The politicians want to enslave the knowledge workers, and confiscate the harvest of their intellectual labour in order to support all the idle poor in society who vote them into power. Governments have lost any sense of balance between income from work and taxation. It is not just the rich who are targets for this state theft; now anyone who works is targeted for the benefit of the parasites in society who expect the good life, free of effort. Today there is no job security, yet income is taxed as if there is. Worse, the unemployables see governments stealing from anyone who works; so they too think it is open season. Knowledge 'workers of the world unite, you have nothing to lose but your chains'. All is social injustice; there is no justice in equality.

Tribal leaders can no longer intimidate the entrepreneurial elite in their society. Knowledge workers want 'the equality to make themselves unequal' (Iain Macleod). They say with derision that the 'common good' isn't good; it is merely common. All taxation is theft. Taxation is the state obtaining money with menaces. Government is merely legitimate organized crime. That most cynical of politicians Richard Nixon knew this all too well: 'When the President does it, that means that it is not illegal.' It may not be illegal, but the abuse of power cannot be tolerated in a healthy society where commercial and guardian syndromes are in balance. Despite President Clinton's series of amazing escapes, special prosecutor Kenneth Starr's constitutional right to question the President shows that the United States has the procedures to pass this particular health test, which is more than can be said for secretive European countries whose political elites close ranks at the first sight of trouble. Ten per cent of the European Union's annual budget of £60 billion cannot be accounted for. The stench of cronyism and corruption hangs heavily over Brussels, the situation made worse when Paul van Buitenen, an auditor for the European Union, turned whistle-blower and was suspended on half-pay. Meanwhile, those responsible for the frauds were left in post (Grey, 17 January 1999).

New barbarians do not insist on the abolition of taxes, merely on a renewed understanding of what taxation is, namely that tax is the voluntary payment to the guardians in return for their delivery of security and standards. If the guardians are too greedy then the voluntary nature of taxation is compromised. In the modern global environment this means that the whole fiscal system will collapse. Thus, the very nature of the nation–state itself is mutating; increasingly in economic matters it will have to give up its dominant position of power. There will have to be a balance of, and a separation between, the guardians and commerce. Business meekly submitting to the will of the voters and their representatives is neither balance nor separation. In fact nations have always conspired in fraud against sections of their populace; national politics has always been a racket, but with delusions of morality. Now, as the smug and sanctimonious legitimacy of state disintegrates, all pretence of behaving morally will also disappear.

That the roles of governments and organizations have been converging was unconsciously highlighted in the *Guardian* (10 December 1993). It asked: 'What's the difference between Zambia and Goldman Sachs?' The *answer: 'One is an African country that makes $2.2 billion a year and shares it among 25 million people. The other is an investment bank that makes $2.6 billion... and shares it between 161 people. FAIR ENOUGH!' The liberals of the Guardian* whinge at the gross unfairness of it all, and make snide comments about 'Goldmine Sachs'. They fail to see that the symbolic analysts of Goldman Sachs earned that money, and earned it fairly, working in cyberspace. And they intend to keep it.

To the new barbarian knowledge worker, this call for fairness is the mere whingeing of failures and parasites. They say it is time to rid themselves of that backward-looking idea, that work involves physical effort. Of course labour is needed in physical space – but there is a world full of labourers out there. The Marxists' myth, that labour creates wealth, will be buried once and for all. It is that rare resource, human talent, that is the stuff of work in the cyberspace of tomorrow's world. Politicians must stop saying 'nanny knows best' and playing to the sentimentality of the herd. The guardians will have to right-size their communities, and cut back on their largesse, as traders will not stand idly by and watch their taxes squandered, just to buy votes for inept politicians. However, these same traders are willing to pay for government-supplied protection for themselves and their property. Consequently governments, like all other organizations, will have to survive economically on the efforts of an elite few – but no nation–state has an automatic right to exist.

If the state can convince the commercially attractive elite of knowledge workers and local entrepreneurial companies to stay, then a virtuous circle of success is ensured. For then, migrating global players and their wealth will also be attracted into that country. If, however, the state maintains a greedy collectivist and populist stance, under the defunct motto 'power to the people', then the entrepreneurial and knowledge elite will move on to more lucrative and agreeable climes. In the long term, the loss of this talent will leave that country economically unviable, composed solely of the unproductive masses, sliding inevitably into a vicious circle of decline.

Jacques Atali, former head of the European Bank for Reconstruction and Development, well understood this fact, and used the metaphor of a hotel to describe his country's plight. In his analysis the guardians are the hosts; wealth creators, the entrepreneurs and businesspeople, are potential guests. He says that like hotels, every country must make itself attractive to its guests, or they will find somewhere else to stay (Bodkin, Conradi and Lang, 23 November 1997). He claimed that unless it changes its ways, Hotel France will find itself empty because of high taxes and red tape. Already small businesses like bakeries and hairdressers are registering their businesses in Britain to save on social security, health and life insurance payments. This is hardly surprising when their taxes support the quarter of the French workforce employed by the state; that figure is one in six in Britain and one in seven in the United States and Germany (*Economist*, 26 April 1997). In France an employer pays the government 160 francs for every 100 francs it pays to an employee. The government then takes its cut of the salary, leaving the worker with 55 francs (Laughland, 28 May 1997). In Germany the cost of a worker to a company averages out at 2–3 times that worker's take-home pay (*Economist*, 3 May 1997), and in Italy the figure is around three times.

This profligacy with companies' and taxpayers' money can't go on. To a certain extent, countries already know it. They have to tread very carefully around credit assessment agencies, such as Moody's Investors Service and Standard & Poor. These highly secretive companies are answerable to no one and nothing but their own high standards of integrity on which their very existence depends. They arbitrate on the credit ratings of not only corporations, but also national, federal, state and provincial governments. What they are actually doing, when assessing different governments, is differentiating between their respective guardian elites in terms of their behaviour toward trade. Moody's devised the AAA to C notation that has become the accepted international standard. Governments play fast and loose with their ratings at their peril. On 1 July 1991, Moody's downgraded Italy from AAA to AA1, and then on 13 August 1992, to AA3. Each downgrading caused serious disorientation of the financial markets. The agency was questioning the financial viability of the Italian government: Italy withdrew from the European exchange rate mechanism (ERM) on 17 September 1992. Analysts did not believe that outside influences such as the Maastricht treaty and eventual monetary union could impose the necessary fiscal discipline on domestic politicians who attempt to bribe the electorate prior to the popularity contests that are democratic elections (*Economist*, 29 December 1992).

Agencies don't even have to go as far as a downgrade. Canadian finance minister Paul Martin was within a fortnight of delivering the national budget when he received a warning shot across his bows. Moody's cautioned a possible downgrading of Canada's AAA rating to AA1, and this precipitated a 7 per cent drop in the value of the Canadian dollar, short-term interest rates were raised and the bond market was badly hit (Ip, 17 February 1995). Although Moody's denied a link between timings of the budget and their report, the markets still made a connection.

As the nation–state mutates, its role is to produce the right people, with the right knowledge and expertise, as the raw material for global companies, to service these companies, and to provide them with an efficient infrastructure, a minimally regulated market and a secure, stable and comfortable environment. If a state cannot produce a quality 'people product', particularly new barbarian scientists and technologists, in sufficient quantities, then it must buy them from abroad.

Increasingly the nation–state will delegate market regulations to continent-wide bodies such as the North American Free Trade Agreement or the European Union. These in turn will use their economic muscle and conspire with local communities to undermine each member state. It will be inevitable that nation–states will fragment and mutate. The mutation is already under way in Britain. The European Union is pouring money into the margins in order to inspire self-confidence in areas like Scotland and Wales, thereby fuelling the clamour for independence under the umbrella of Europe, so subverting Westminster.

But the European Union is wasting its taxpayers' money. Rich areas are realizing the advantage of dumping poor areas: the Czech Republic has shown the way. The naïve nationalists of poorer Slovakia demanded their independence, and were shocked to be given it with very little fuss. This placed the Czechs in a far better position to face the transition to a market economy, because they saved themselves from having to subsidize their impoverished now-neighbours. Will Belgium break in two? What about Italy, Spain, France and Germany? What about the United Kingdom, which has never been truly united? In Britain much of the noise will actually come from England, particularly the soon-to-be-independence-minded Home Counties, which will realize the benefits of discarding that black hole for taxes north of Watford. What about the United States, now that certain states are cynically using tax perks to attract employers away from their neighbours?

Right-sizing

Such shakeout trends can be interpreted as downsizing of the state, a strategy that is being considered by most shrewd major corporations these days. The downsizing has already started, as the state realizes that it cannot afford to pay for large and moribund health, pension and welfare schemes out of its shrinking tax revenues. We have already seen similar and more ambitious schemes, which pander to a dependency culture, bring Sweden to the verge of bankruptcy. This caused a tax revolt, which, for a short while, brought an end to 40 years of socialist government. Predictably, the growing mass of frightened losers in the Swedish electorate brought the old barbarians back in the 1998 elections.

The areas that will be successful in the Information Age think differently. To protect their wealth, rich areas will undertake right-sizing, ensuring a high proportion of (wealth-generating) knowledge workers to (wealth-depleting) service workers and the unemployed; and 'delayering', getting rid of excessive state bureaucracy. Rich areas have to maintain and expand a critical mass of scientific and technological expertise, and use it to underpin an effective education system to regenerate the resource. The rich areas will reject the liberal attitudes of the present century, as the expanding underclass they are spawning and the untrained migrants they welcomed previously are seen increasingly as economic liabilities. 'Many too many are born. The state was devised for the superfluous ones.' With these pitiless words from the 19th century, Friedrich Nietzsche heralds the demise of the nation–state in its present form as we enter the 21st. Mass-production methods needed an oversupply of humanity. In a sense the Machine Age spawned the nation–state, but with its demise what is to be done with the glut as we enter the Information Age?

Newly emerging elitist global enterprises are rushing in to fill the economic and political power vacuum, and they are engaged in alliances and power struggles amongst themselves, to determine who will win the natural selection for dominance. To be successful, a geographical region has to have the intellectual infrastructure to generate its own elite. It has to reorganize if it is to entice the global corporations, by portraying itself as an ideal place to do business, while remaining a pleasant place to live. Therefore it needs major cultural, social and technological attractions, and it must support art, culture, science and education, not for reasons of altruism or philanthropy, but because it makes hard-headed business sense.

However, unquestionably, the first priority for a region is a substantial investment in a centre for global communication at the hub of international cable and satellite traffic, so that it can act as a focus for servicing knowledge-worker traffic. However, the region must also guarantee the safety of company employees and property. Increasingly the security of the rich (the knowledge workers), and the protection of their interests, property and independence (anywhere, anytime, anyhow), will become big business in the Information Age, perhaps the only legitimate growth industry. Lack of government funding may mean the end of the welfare state, but the rich will always find the money for their security. Without question, an effective and trusted police force is a very prominent competitive advantage for any region in its attempts at attracting migrating employers. The knowledge worker wants to live in a policed state, but **not** a police state. The police are necessary, the military and judiciary likewise, as well as public health programmes. They must be paid for from taxation. The natural order is reasserting itself: the police are there, not to protect the masses, but to protect the rich from the masses. The military are there to protect the rich from other countries' masses. The judiciary is there to settle property disputes. Public health officials prevent the spread of communicable diseases. But who guards the guardians? That's where we find the only role for politicians.

Private and public policing

Consequently there is likely to be much closer co-operation between local police forces and company security agencies, and the edges between the two groupings will become increasingly blurred. However, as Jane Jacobs has indicated, unless this is well managed it could well lead to corruption. Today in the United States there are nearly three times as many private policemen as there are public; even in Britain this figure is two to one (*Economist*, 19 April 1997). The eleventh biggest police force in the United States is that of the New York schools authority (McRae, 1994), and General Motors alone has more than 4,000 policeman (*Economist*, 19 April 1997). Every business will find itself involved in policing to a certain extent. The airline companies already have to process immigration data on passengers they fly into a country, or they find themselves faced with hefty fines for transporting illegal immigrants.

Furthermore, to protect supportive companies, states will impose draconian penalties, along the lines of the Swiss system, on the perpetrators of economic crimes and those who betray commercial secrecy. For example, in the 1970s Stanley Adams worked as a mole for the European Commission within Hoffman-La Roche to expose price-fixing within the pharmaceutical industry. He was arrested under Swiss law for espionage. Adams, however, was eventually given a suspended jail sentence and was awarded £500,000 by the yesterday's men of the European Court of Justice (Duce, 15 March 1994).

Such an act of gross sentimentality could not happen in the future of the new barbarians. Not that democratic government will disappear, rather it will become just another particular form of governance competing in cyberspace. People and not things will become the raw materials of industry. The role of government is to nurture, propagate and supply that quality resource: information has a very short half-life and so talented people have to be supported in their continual and continuous drive to re-skill themselves. When knowledge workers are not selling their information, they must be acquiring new. Democratic government, or any other kind for that matter, is merely the supplier and protector of property at the bottom end of the value chain that ultimately supplies wealth. This wealth, however, is not the product of labour, but of individual talent and determination.

In this future, some governments will lose their internal legitimacy and be ripe for a takeover by predatory organizations – look for example at the new imperialism of the United Nations. The UN is flexing its bully-boy muscles, albeit in a somewhat inept manner. Donning the mantle of policeman of the world, UN action has led to one shambles after another: from Yugoslavia to Somalia. Then consider the behaviour of the World Bank (WB) and the International Monetary Fund (IMF) toward some African countries. This emergent form of new colonialization is not a deliberate conspiracy; it is just the inevitable flow of events caused by organizational ideologies and practice that conflict with indigenous cultures. It is the juggernaut of our times running loose in cyberspace. Countries that seek aid-assistance find that they are confronted by a new imperialism – 'fiscal discipline', the ideological imperialism of money. Karl Marx saw this a century ago: 'Money is the universal, self-constituted value of all things. It has therefore robbed the whole world, human as well as natural, of its own values.' The free-market ideology of the aid agencies will soon dispel any silly ideas about the national sovereignty of a bankrupt state. 'Beggars can't be choosers.'

It is not only poor African countries that prostrate themselves before the IMF. Britain kowtowed in 1976, and Mexico in 1994. The long list has been extended by South Korea and some other Asian tigers who are facing the same indignity to their sovereignty because of the currency turmoil of late 1997. Both the IMF and the World Bank are themselves dependent on the funding of rich nation–states. For how much longer will countries be bailed out by the IMF? What happens to the IMF and WB when every nation–state is in trouble?

Most international groupings sooner or later start behaving with similar barbarity. Power corrupts. Even apparently benign groups like the international football organization FIFA, or the International Olympic Committee (IOC) get sucked into the power play and ultimately fall prey to Jacobs' Law of Intractable Systemic Corruption. When the guardians of FIFA and the IOC become involved in the commercial aspects of their community there is fertile ground for corruption. The bribery scandal surrounding the Winter Games in Salt Lake City and the Summer Games in Sydney were almost unavoidable (Mackay and Chaudhary, 25 January 1999). Furthermore, with the financial stakes so high, it was inevitable that leading administrators of sport would turn a blind eye to drug abuse among athletes, because sponsors and advertisers have too much money tied up in their stars to see it thrown away by a mere drugs scandal. It was no surprise then that Juan Antonio Samaranch, president of the IOC, should announce to the Spanish newspaper *El Mundo* that he is not averse to the use of performance-enhancing drugs in sport 'provided that they do not adversely affect the athletes' health' (Brown and Millward, 27 July 1998).

The vainglorious administrators have themselves become addicted to the trappings of wealth and power that have been tainting their jobs as guardians of sport. Only very strong aristocratic personalities are immune to the inducements made by towns and governments to sweeten the International Olympic Committee in the hope of 'landing' the Games; and the same applies to FIFA and soccer's World Cup. Because of the spin-offs, a region can gain much by hosting such events, in terms of tourism and other business.

There is quite a temptation to better the odds of being chosen. In such a climate it is easy to see the boards of the IOC and FIFA as a hybrid of guardians and trade.

Add into the equation a herd of other non-governmental organizations and supra-governmental bodies, and the situation becomes one of excessive complexity and uncertainty. It can only get worse. Dealing with the chaos will necessitate some very shrewd strategies, from the leaders of both guardians and commerce. This requires an adequate strategic understanding of the socio-economic properties that emerge from the reflexive interaction between business and its social and political context. The effectiveness of the strategy of any particular community will depend on its vision, its integrity or wholeness, the sense of identity and trust within it and how it deals with change. This will require understanding, both within commerce toward the importance of the state in the delivery of a trading environment, and within the state of the freedoms needed as the fundamentals of trade. The rituals of today's states reflect the understanding of the power relationships of yesterday. Tomorrow is going to need a totally new understanding, totally new rituals, totally new forms of governance and hence a totally new type of state.

| 16 |

The flight of the information rich

In 1863 Jules Verne wrote *Paris au XXème Siècle*, a prediction of what Paris would be like in 1963. Far too gloomy for that technologically optimistic time, the book had to wait until 1993 to be published. Verne's Paris of 1963 had become a drab and dismal city, a city of machines, fit only for machines. Not Verne's best work by far, it took the pessimism pervading our own *fin de siècle* to trigger its publication.

Whatever that particular book's literary merits, or otherwise, in one giant intellectual bound Verne had managed, indisputably, to leap right over the technological optimism of both his and the twentieth centuries, to land fairly and squarely in today's gloom. He had beaten Fritz Lang's *Metropolis* by over half a century. But even those doom-laden scenarios pale into insignificance when compared to the 'new age' mythologies embedded in today's popular collective psyche. The *Mad Max* films, *Blade Runner* and numerous imitators show a junkyard of rusting technology, the Götterdämmerung of the new millennium, economic and social collapse, death and destruction. Nostradamus, the ex-champion of one-upmanship in the prediction game, fixed on July–August 1999 as the date of Armageddon, a lesson for all of us who dare describe *The Shape of Things to Come*.

The most successful 'futurologists' have, like Verne and H G Wells, steered a middle course, avoiding both utopia and dystopia by extrapolating knowledge of already-apparent technologies and making shrewd guesses about their social impact. However, the futurologists of today have one advantage over the ancients: with a whole armoury of useful new expressions being delivered by such insights as chaos theory and complexity theory, we have a battery of new excuses for getting it wrong.

Am I predicting the future, or only reinterpreting the present in a different light? After all, for most of the world's poor, dystopia is here and now, as it always has been. A fifth of the world's population live on less than a dollar a day. They have '…no society; and which is worst of all, continuous feare, and danger of violent death; and the life of man, solitary, poor, nasty, brutish and short' (Thomas Hobbes). The debacle that is Africa throws up a legion of examples. Robert D Kaplan's chilling article in *Atlantic Magazine* (February 1994) makes it all too apparent. He quotes a description of a coup in Sierra Leone: 'One of the coup's leaders, Solomon Anthony Joseph Musa… shot the people who had paid for his schooling "in order to erase the humiliation and mitigate the power his middle-class sponsors held over him"… What we have now is… the revenge of the poor, of the social failures, of people least able to bring up children in a modern society… The boys who took power… in three months… confiscated all the official Mercedes, Volvos and BMWs and wilfully wrecked them on the road.'

This a world run by those who cannot build, only destroy and worse, those who take pleasure in that destruction. The *Mad Max* scenario is not fiction, and it is not the future – it was yesterday in Sierra Leone; tomorrow it could be anywhere, everywhere, here. Only in films are there Mad Maxes to defend the innocent and the not-so-innocent against the mindless viciousness of virtuous victims intent on righting imagined wrongs in an orgy of violence. 'In Liberia the guerrilla leader Prince Johnson didn't just cut off the ears of President Samuel Doe before Doe was tortured to death in 1990 – Johnson made a video of it, that has circulated throughout West Africa' (Kaplan, 1994). When it is always someone else's fault, or someone else will pay, the ruination of the society is inevitable. Wishy-wash Liberals, when they help free the victims of violence, are always surprised at the mendacity of these ex-prisoners, who behave just as despicably toward their opponents whenever they take charge. The fact is, some political prisoners deserve to be prisoners, whoever the prison guards are. Mad dogs always bite the hand that feeds them. The reality of the human condition is that charity, to ward off the guilt of past sins, or the paying of danegeld to ward off an invasion of the poor or the aggressive, simply doesn't work.

Brain drain revisited

The new barbarians are not going to sit around at the mercy of a pre-modern anarchy. They refuse to apologize for whatever real or imagined past sins have been perpetrated by their forebears against the anarchists. Nor will they put up with the purposeful violence of totalitarian old barbarians who are forcing order on to the revolting masses with messages of religious, ethnic or ideological superiority. However, the new barbarians won't fight this take-over. They will vote with their feet, and quietly leave one country, taking their money and their brains with them, to be **invited** into another – a complete reversal of old barbarisms. They will escape the tyranny of the masses by running away. The great escape has already started. It was denounced in his final book by the well-known American liberal, Christopher Lasch, as *The Revolt of the Elites* (1996). Lasch is typical of liberal and social democrats of Western societies in the way he mixes up cause and effect. The freedom in democratic societies that they hold so dear was not delivered by democracy, democracy was delivered in the feedback of those expanding freedoms. However, the very success of democracy and the spirit of the Enlightenment are now degenerating into the old barbarism of populism, of the many against the few, of the tribe against the individual. The liberals can bleat all they like, but chasm is opening up between the information rich and the information poor; between the knowledge workers and the rest; between the post-modern, and the modern and pre-modern. The generators of wealth will not stand idly by and see their wealth stolen, so that some of it can be spread (too) thinly among the poor, with most of it going to the fat cats of government and their cronies. 'You cannot help the poor by destroying the rich' (Abraham Lincoln). Tax exile, the solution of only the super-rich today, will soon be the act of choice for every knowledge worker.

We will witness a brain drain on a scale that will dwarf previous examples. In the 1960s knowledge workers abandoned socialist Britain in large numbers for the advantages of the United States. The grass was certainly greener there: better salaries, better working conditions, better equipment and less tax. Today's disaffected knowledge workers can ponder this successful precedent of the United States plundering the British knowledge base, and its even greater forays into other countries. Having had their eyes opened, now knowledge workers must scan the globe looking for 'smart regions' where their intellectual capital will be valued, and where in return they will be treated as individuals and given the intellectual and financial freedoms to prosper.

Such a brain drain is not new. During the 1851 Great Exhibition, that outpouring of British industrial vanity, agents of foreign countries such as the United States, France and Germany came, apparently to admire, but they enticed skilled individuals away, and took the blueprints of valuable products with them. Earlier still, between the 16th and early 19th centuries, the financial success of the City of London was built on commercial expertise attracted away from Germany, Holland and northern Italy.

The brain-drain issue regularly resurfaces in the politics of many countries as a measure of a state's overall economic health, although always in a most partial way. Most commonly, jingoistic politicians invoke the rhetoric of treason when they describe knowledge workers who leave to follow their own self-interest. Given the trends predicted in this book, the numbers of brains drained in the past will seem negligible when compared to the global exodus that is about to happen. However, the highly politicized and subjective descriptions of previous brain drains confuse the issue and hide the real trend. Statistics on mass movements, which are carefully collected by national governments, really do not help in the understanding of the phenomenon. These measurements, fixed in Machine Age thinking, are answering the wrong questions. It is the loss of an elite few that damages a nation's wealth creation; the loss of the non-productive masses is in many ways an advantage.

Increasingly the nation–state is unable to control its own affairs or that of its citizens. Globalization is exacerbating the never-ending tension between the individual and the collective, between personal ambition and societal demands. Most service workers still believe that their continued well-being depends on the 'nanny state' and that 'nanny knows best'. But power has swung away from the guardian leaders of the state and in favour of the elite not-so-few traders, the knowledge workers. Meanwhile, an increasing number of service workers see their leaders, whether in parliament or in the trades unions, becoming sidelined by events, and their disillusion is rapidly turning to resentment.

The global nature of business and instantaneous worldwide telecommunication has aided the knowledge workers in subverting the power of the nation–state. Information technology has made national boundaries increasingly transparent, and has limited the ability of the state to use its borders as a barrier to the free trade of goods and the free movement of an individual's wealth. Nowadays most knowledge workers speak American English, the international language of business. Those with saleable skills, who resent their treatment by the nation–state of their birth, will simply drain away. Speaking English, they can 'hit the ground running' in their chosen destination.

Wealth is created by the free. This is no new observation. Writing in the 1830s, Alexis de Tocqueville observed: 'I do not know if any single trading or manufacturing people can be cited, from the Tyrians down to the Florentines and the English, who were not a free people also. There is therefore a close bond and necessary relation between these two elements, freedom and productive industry' (1990). A free people is a collection of free individuals, not the self-important masses who are free to intimidate the individual. De Tocqueville saw such freedom in a youthful and self-confident United States, a freedom that would transform a post-colonial backwater into the most powerful nation on earth in just over a century.

Today such freedom implies that knowledge workers will no longer be coerced by a government claiming as its sole legitimacy the representation of the mass of service workers. Knowledge workers can always flee, or sell their intellectual products on an international electronic black market, or they can refuse to engage in intellectual effort. If this weren't such an intellectual as well as a commercial disaster, it would be funny to see the position of Russia, Poland and most former communist countries in their transition to a market economy. Formerly they treated their scientists and artists as jewels of the state and gave them the best available resources in state-run elite institutions, although they stopped well short of giving them ownership of the wealth they generated. Now that these countries have become 'democratic', they put the wishes of the masses (that is the voters) before any intellectual (and hence elitist) resource. Consequently the very best entrepreneurial scientists and artists, but only the very best, are being seduced abroad. The second division, who none the less have much to offer, have instead joined an internal brain drain, finding that they can make a better living driving taxis or growing cabbages than by following intellectual pursuits. The rapid loss in the skill base will in the long term be a national disaster. They will eventually realize that they have to compete for wealth creators to replace those they so thoughtlessly wasted.

Knowledge workers demand a fair return on their intellectual labours. It is an interesting historical note that the late Ayn Rand foresaw today's brain drain in her famous pre-1960s polemical novel *Atlas Shrugged* (1957). This morality tale of the conflict between the 'men of mind' and the 'moochers and looters' manages to be highly prophetic of the Information Age. 'Wealth is the product of man's capacity to think... You cannot have wealth without its source: without intelligence... You cannot force intelligence to work.' And most perceptively: 'The highly skilled will... become more mobile – top talent... in the world's fastest growing professions, such as... financial services, can choose where to locate itself... it will mean creating societies in which mobile talent wants to live... Society is... individuals acting... rationally in their own self-interest... To an economist, there is no... society, only individuals who constitute it... Disunited, thirsty for power, undisciplined and disloyal... no loyalty or inducement' can keep them.

Incredibly these words were written before the advent of instant international telecommunications and global financial services. Nevertheless, her call to arms is clearly a rallying cry to today's knowledge worker. 'I have taught them [the men of mind] that the world is ours, whenever we choose to claim it.' Today the men of mind, the knowledge workers, are claiming it. The governments don't like it, and they will try to fight back. But Rand warned of the flight of innovators from research and development whenever there are adverse societal and political pressures. As innovators are both increasingly regulated in their pursuit of production, and over-taxed on the profits of their risk taking, they will either give up totally ('downshift'), or seek new business opportunities on the margins of government interference. Free of government meddling until very recently, the information technology industry has consequently managed to flourish in the United States relatively unscathed. The government didn't quite know how to deal with it, and so left it alone. However, it doesn't matter how the goose that lays the golden eggs was raised; eventually all governments end up trying to kill it. Bill Gates should have seen the US government antitrust action coming.

Rand recognized that the pull of intellectual freedom built into the 'American Dream' would prove far too tempting for most dissatisfied foreign scientists. However, she and a few other American critics were, and some still are, warning that the United States too was 'going down the drain'. *Atlas Shrugged* describes the final collapse because of anti-elite 'brotherhood of man' prejudices. Rand hinted at a growing collectivism, the sentimental promotion of mediocrity born in an increasingly intolerant Christian fundamentalism that was denying the Enlightenment tradition that gave birth to the US Constitution. No doubt she would claim that 'political correctness' is merely the latest of a long line of self-righteous prejudice, including the Sherman antitrust laws and Prohibition.

Government action

Today in the United States, the Republican Party is trying to reverse the vast raft of government legislation put in place to control social behaviour and economic activity. They need to, or else the United States will find, as Rand predicted, that its finest brains, individualistic adventurers and entrepreneurs will escape government repression of individual freedoms, and board their own *Mayflower* to set sail for a New World of tax-free ports in cyberspace. But why bother with cyberspace? There is already talk of escape on the high seas. Florida engineers and businesspeople are planning a 2.7 million-ton vessel, the *Freedom Ship*: freedom from taxes that is (Austin, 15 March 1998). It will circumnavigate the globe once every two years, and never stop anywhere long enough to incur tax liabilities. A rival company, World City Corporation, also has plans for a 250,000-ton ship called *America World City*. 'Prince' Lazarus Long, an American millionaire and latter-day Captain Nemo (Jules Verne's anti-hero of *Twenty Thousand Leagues under the Sea* who had a pathological hatred of so-called civilized nations), is planning to build New Utopia in the Caribbean, 100 miles from the nearest country (Barot, 30 August 1998). Concrete pillars will be set in the seabed 20 feet from the surface, and building platforms laid on top, 10 feet above sea level.

The principality of New Utopia is meant to be a totally new country that will be a tax haven and offshore banking centre. All three schemes share a fatal flaw in that they are all engineering solutions to the problem of tax flight. They cannot possibly work, because they are mechanisms, not organisms; they are parasitical and are not underpinned with the metabolic systems necessary for long-term survival. What they do demonstrate, however, is a growing resentment with the tax policies of the nation–state, and they point the way to enlightened and viable states on terra firma realigning themselves to service this demand. A city-state already extant is far more likely to succeed than some oceanic pipe-dream.

Rand's critics say she was wrong and point to the fact that her prediction of the collapse of US and other societies in the 1960s just didn't happen. Rand's analysis of the United States in *Atlas Shrugged* (1957), and the general insights of others, were not wrong. Rand saw in the United States a spreading 'rust belt' and dramatic expansion of its national debt, as well as the general worldwide collapse in confidence in various systems of government and political leaders. However, the most dramatic predictions of decline and fall have been merely postponed by the rise of information technology and its effect on the global nature of capital and labour. She was convinced of the inevitability of the tyranny of the masses, which in Britain precipitated the brain drain and a slow but inescapable industrial decline, climaxing in the unionized anarchy of the 'winter of discontent' of 1978/79. That decline, only postponed by wasting the riches of North Sea oil and a fleeting flirtation with Thatcherism, is again picking up momentum under the social democrats of New Labour.

What Rand and her like did not and could not see was the engine of growth of the relatively unregulated information technology sector. It was unregulated simply because of its newness; the politicians didn't know what they were dealing with. This freedom of action spawned the Information Revolution. Driven by massive and unrestricted profits, sucking in entrepreneurial talent from around the world, this revolution has generated unprecedented wealth, effectively camouflaging the 'internal brain drain' of the United States' best talent, who were leaving productive pursuits in their droves and entering accountancy, law, administration, politics and other parasitical callings. In the United States between 1968 and 1995 the median annual salary levels for engineers with 10 years experience had actually dropped by 13 per cent (Luttwak, 6 May 1996). Much of the scientific and engineering talent that drove the new technological revolution in the United States had to be imported from abroad. For example, in its early days nearly half of Intel's graduate staff of physicists and engineers came from Taiwan, Israel, India, and Pakistan (Large, 1980).

However, if the US government, like most governments, cannot stop itself from meddling on behalf of the 'public good', then the brain drain will start up again. But it will be in the opposite direction. Information technology has now made it far easier for the knowledge worker to escape, either as individuals marketing their expertise on the Net, or as groups hitching a ride on the back of transnational companies. These companies now think globally because they can communicate globally! Increasingly, the world headquarters of important business units will be transferred abroad. Transnational corporations are moving despite risking a loss of control, because they have to operate near key customers and tough rivals in the dynamic markets, far from what used to be home. Companies recognize that they can no longer run a global operation from one single location. They must compete with the other new barbarians already out there.

Meanwhile, politicians stuck in the Machine Age still feel they have the right to interfere. President Clinton complained that foreign companies were not paying their 'fair share of taxes'. The more enlightened in Washington pointed out that the amount of direct taxes to be gained from corporations would be much less than the benefits derived from their presence and activities. The United States will have to face up to the fact, as Britain did a decade ago, that the question is not whether it should tolerate and tax transnational corporations, but how to attract and keep them, and just as importantly how not to lose (what used to be called) US transnationals to the seductive signals from more enlightened countries.

Yet the United States does have enormous advantages. Under its current tax regime, it is a natural choice for footloose companies. Compared to other industrialized nations, the US labour force is inexpensive with a good productivity record. This is why both BMW and Mercedes have chosen to move production facilities from Germany to South Carolina. But by raising taxes and increasing regulations that hurt foreign transnationals, by adding a xenophobic resentment to the spectre of a 'litigation culture', and by increasing medical costs, these companies will leave just as easily as they entered. And what will states like South Carolina do if they find that their hard-won competitive positions are continuously being undermined by Washington to the advantage of other states: secede from the Union? Texas has the legal right in its constitution to withdraw from the Union, so Washington must tread carefully. At present only a few 'loonies' from the Texas separatists are demanding out, but when the imposition of the central fiscal regime becomes too much for Texans, who knows what will happen? What about the Confederacy? Perhaps the 'South will rise again'. The Southern Party was launched in 1999 with the Asheville Declaration, 'dedicated to limited government, low taxes, maximum individual liberty, a free market and self-determination for Dixie' (Whitworth, 9 August 1999). What do the good burghers of Seattle feel about the US government persisting in its attempts to break Microsoft up by use of antitrust laws? Perhaps the idea of Cascadia (Washington, Oregon and British Columbia) is not so silly.

Information technology has changed the whole scale, scope and complexity of the brain drain. Governments now have a big headache. Not only must they worry about individuals fleeing the clutches of their tax collectors; now whole corporations can desert, throwing entire communities out of work. The example of Ericsson considering the abandonment of Sweden shows that politicians can no longer intimidate transnational companies. For it is not just the market for a company's products that is spread around the globe; now its shareholders, its executive and its employees are also an international community. Head office is just the focal point of executive control.

In Germany, there is growing unrest among the trades unions over major corporations that react to excessive employment regulations by moving their factories abroad, to Hungary, the Czech Republic and far further afield. But not only factory jobs flee. Companies in the southern Indian city of Bangalore have developed a thriving business offering a highly trained skill base and top quality work at low cost, all available in a commercial environment with minimal regulation. The Tata company is delivering software systems to companies as diverse as London Transport and AT&T. Many Western companies see enormous opportunities in such 'hot-spots', and are opening subsidiaries and joint ventures there. Their competitors cannot risk isolation and must follow suit.

Eastern Europe too has the highly skilled personnel needed to take advantage of the trend, but only if their governments refuse to follow the advice of the Western-government-sponsored 'transition' consultants who swarmed into their countries following the collapse of communism. Already we are seeing countries that, in introducing Western-style (and hence highly complex) cost, tax and regulation infrastructures, have undermined the very foundations of the business they so badly need. Some of the more astute leaders are questioning the motives behind this advice, fearing that it is merely a cynical ploy to protect jobs in the donor countries. The town of Sopron in Hungary near the Austrian border is showing the lead. With a population of only 55,000, it boasts 85 dental clinics that charge far less for their services than do their Austrian equivalents. Naturally, visiting Austrians also spend money while in the town, and this has totally revitalized the local economy (Hooker, 20 October 1993). Such medical tourism is spreading. Opticians in Bratislava are now reporting a thriving trade with Austrian visitors.

Everyone is at it, from crooks to the men in grey suits – and no country is immune. Tax evasion cost the New Zealand treasury more than $3 billion in 1994, and the black economy was running around $9.6 billion annually, equivalent to 11.3 per cent of the GDP. There was a 60 per cent increase in both tax evasion and the black economy between 1970 and 1994 (Lilley, 8 May 1998). The Australian government is losing $14 billion annually from their alternative economy (Fergusson, 9 May 1998). The Australian Financial Review claims that a dozen of Australia's top multinationals paid no tax at all in 1997 (Carr, 13 May 1998), and that the number of companies paying no taxes is more than half (*Independent Business Weekly (NZ)*, 8 April 1998). However, their most damning claim is that over half of the world's trillion dollar a day trade is not trade at all, but transfer pricing.

'The internationalization of markets... will have large effects on some [tax bases] (financial capital), marginal or no effect on others (land, already installed capital, unskilled labor), and intermediate effects on others (skilled labour)': so says Vito Tanzi, director of the fiscal affairs department of the International Monetary Fund. In his book, Tanzi (1995) focuses on financial capital – he could have gone much further and made more dire predictions for the information capital tax-base, of which financial capital is a mere subset.

Organizations are freeing themselves everywhere by mobilizing and globalizing, integrating themselves into a global economy as they move rapidly, unshackled from the chain-gang of national boundaries and barriers. These newly independent and highly mobile companies of the future, their management elite and key knowledge workers are on the move to more responsible countries offering better deals, with lower pay levels, less stringent legal requirements and more advantageous employment and tax regulations. Archetypical knowledge workers, Mick Jagger and the Rolling Stones, cancelled a tour of Britain because new tax laws meant an increased total tax bill for everyone concerned of around £12 million (Atkinson, 13 June 1998). The British chancellor Gordon Brown proved once again that politicians haven't a clue about the growing internationalization of the workforce. 'I won't be lectured on tax by tax exiles.' He had better listen, and quickly, or his actions are likely to increase the number of tax exiles from British shores, thereby reducing the tax take rather than increasing it. Where will they go? Offshore? Off-planet?

Off-planet commerce

It bears repeating: freedom of movement is a real competitive advantage for any 'virtual enterprise' with a moveable centre of gravity; and for those 'economic mercenaries' who are willing to trade their expertise in an electronic marketplace. They still have to be based somewhere, but how long before their information wealth leaves tribal grounds and moves to the deregulated common grounds of space? Satellite companies have spare capacity and they are actively looking for synergistic extensions for their mass-media businesses. The virtual reality of off-planet commerce beckons. At first glance such trade looks like a silly idea. All it would take to stop it is for every state to embargo trade with satellite-based business; but even if it was in every state's interests to ban this trade, it is very doubtful whether they could agree. However, many poorer countries can gain substantially by supporting this offspring of the 'flag of convenience' and 'pirate radio'. For with off-planet trade any country, developed or underdeveloped, can enter the hi-tech business. Even with only the most rudimentary telecommunications infrastructure a state can still get into the action – it merely acts as a tax-haven and data-haven for footloose organizations.

There are no barriers to entry; this is hi-tech business by proxy. Previous societal disadvantages of the Third World, like bribery, corruption, incompetence and political instability, are obstacles no longer since, except for a brass plate, a company has no physical presence there – business is all off-planet. The big boys of the developed world and their G7 cartel can no longer use their technological superiority to keep the rich pickings for themselves. The Third World no longer has to plead for crumbs; it can take the whole loaf. The OECD is already decrying the 'unfair lowering' of tax rates and a 'race to the bottom' that could lead to 'fiscal degradation'. 'They ain't seen nothing yet.'

Off-planet commerce will service any (information) product that can be dematerialized. Pop records, films, books, newspapers, sporting events, software and money are all just strings of binary bits. Payment can be by credit card (or soon digital cash), just like products advertised on CNN, which are sent by mail from warehouses based in low-tax countries to minimize price and cost. There will be no more paper, cardboard boxes, shrink-wrap, vinyl, compact discs, floppy disks or video tapes in the mail – data will be delivered directly and instantaneously from a satellite to a desktop or portable computer (no more waiting two weeks for delivery). Already many Europeans buy goods over the Net from the United States; the *Amazon.com* online bookstore is leading the way. How many customers actually pay the required VAT sales tax? Such trade has only just begun – and why should it be based in the United States? With effective voice-activated systems just around the corner, even the telesales component of this business, in fact of every business, will be up in space. Cyberspace is no mystical dimension. It is extra-planetary and extraterritorial.

'We need banking, we don't need banks!' So why not off-planet banking? A satellite can act as a depository for digital cash, with hand-held personal computers linked to 'transceivers' moving cash anywhere, any time. It will be secure because customers send not only their digital cash and other information capital, but also the digital safe that secures it – and they hold the only key. This potential will not be lost on hawala bankers (see Chapter 3) in their schemes to bypass national currency regulations. These pressures will make a mockery of national and international regulations on the transfer of money and data. Under the smokescreen of its money-laundering laws aimed at chasing narco-dollars, the United States is using its extraterritorial muscle to track down tax-flight dollars in Switzerland and Grand Cayman. Germany wants to staunch the haemorrhage of deutschmarks to Jersey, Guernsey and the Isle of Man. Between 1992 and 1994, $300 billion left Russia (Kerry, 1997). Politicians, businesspeople and gangsters don't leave their money in an unstable country; especially not in countries run by the gangsters themselves.

The battle has only just begun. Soon under-reporting of taxes will snowball into the total migration off-planet of a state's taxation capacity. It should come as no surprise that tax officials are talking of a 'bit tax'. The only way they can swindle their share of this trade is by taxing data flow by volume, as if it were whisky. Their problem is that the value of information does not correlate with volume. A Hollywood film, delivered to a television, accounts for around a gigabyte of data, whereas commercially valuable data would be a tiny fraction of that size. The European Union is now insisting that all transactions over the Net should be charged the VAT sales tax (Lavin, 25 June 1998). They say it is unfair to normal retail outlets. The new barbarians have news for the EU: all taxation is unfair. Slowly companies and knowledge workers are waking up to the fact that their predicament is unjust.

In a rapidly integrating world economy, a country's borders no longer deliver freedom of manoeuvre for the tax collector. Politicians cannot control the arbitrage pressures, the exploitation of price, tax and regulation differentials that form spontaneously within markets. 'Disintermediation' and 'dematerialization' are the two key words they should heed. Strapped for cash, governments can only steal (tax) products that have a solid form and that move physically across their jurisdictions. When they learn this lesson, then taxes on fuel, food and clothes will inevitably rise. What could be more immobile than property? Hence property taxes will be increased: in 1913 60 per cent of US tax revenues came from property; today it is 10 per cent (Economist, 31 May 1997). In 2013 will it be back at 60 per cent, and consequently will property values fall? Sweden levies a property tax of 1.5 per cent per year. It was 1.7 per cent (Goldsmith, 19 May 1998), but when the government gets squeezed they will inevitably put the rate back up again.

Dematerialized e-cash is the ultimate in liquidity. Along with all other information products, it will slip through politicians' grasp. If income and sales are taxed at 'source', then that source will find its lowest tax level – somewhere else, when levels are high. If that tax is based on 'residence', then it can be collected only if the authorities have global access to data on international flow of money and other information capital. However, off-planet commerce will purge itself of the intermediaries who meekly report their audit-trails to governments. When there is a direct link between buyer and seller, as in the black economy, both sides have much to gain by keeping their transactions to themselves.

Look to the horizon; through a sky full of laundered and untaxed dollars the Information Age is dawning. The Age of Aquarius has finally arrived, when the information rich (but only the information rich) individual is finally free of the grasping and ungrateful tribe.

Part VII

How to become a winner

Winning through: a strategy for survival and success

The number of those who need to be awakened is far greater than that of those who need comfort.

(Bishop Wilson, an 18th-century cleric)

When I started writing this book, it was going to be about information technology, and how this technology was changing modern society. However, very soon I realized that new technology wasn't the only driver of change. Information technology is just the last straw that broke the camel's back. That last straw is having a magnifying effect on the many other important factors in play: unemployment, overpopulation, starvation, disease, mass migration, limited natural resources, religious intolerance, ethnic and racist bigotries, mindless violence, narcotics and so on. The backs of all camel institutions born in the Industrial Age (the age of the machine, the age of the masses) are being pressurized by these debilitating factors, and they are now breaking under attacks by throwbacks from an earlier age.

The message of this book is quite simple. It is a restatement of the Marxian view that economic forces drive societal development. The way that a society organizes economic production feeds back and reshapes that society. The inescapable fact is that information technology, amplified by the other destructive forces mentioned above, is deconstructing production and hence societal development. The impact that it is having on the subsequent creation of wealth implies that today's institutions must either mutate or die. 'Institutions are the rules of the game in a society or, more formally, are the humanly devised constraints that shape human interaction. In consequence they structure incentives in human exchange, whether political, social or economic. Institutional change shapes the way societies evolve through time and hence is the key to understanding historical change' (North, 1990). (I accept totally Douglass C North's meaning of the term 'institution' to indicate society itself and any political, social or economic grouping within it.) The institutions of our industrialized society are facing a contagion of uncertainty and self-doubt. As products of the Machine Age they may have no place in the coming Information Age. 'What is at stake is the compatibility of technical progress with the very institutions in which industrialization developed' (Herbert Marcuse) and vice versa. A spectre haunts these institutions (and the whole of society): perhaps they are artefacts of the 20th century with no place in the next. Can they change and confront the challenge, or will they hang on to the past and face extinction?

Today's institutions, national and organizational, along with the ritualistic behaviour that supports them, are failing. 'Neutron Jack' Welch, chairman of GE, captured the mood at a shareholders' meeting in 1989: 'Ahead of us are Darwinian shakeouts in every major marketplace, with no consolation prizes for the losing companies and nations.' 'Get better, or get beaten.' It will be evolution of the most brutal kind. Strangely, many people think evolution is less threatening than revolution, and even have ideas about evolution being controllable. Revolutions may kill large numbers of individuals, but evolution makes whole species extinct!

We are facing evolutionary forces, although not necessarily all of the Darwinian variety. There will be a neo-Lamarckian element involved: a transmutation involving blended inheritance or acquired characteristics. This is evolution by social acquisition that is begetting a sub-speciation of humanity, an ethnogenesis (Gumilёv, 1990) of new barbarians. The constituent parts of this evolution are not arbitrary genetic mutations, but are the result of conscious choices, where human judgement and preferences are exercised by individuals and communities in the quest for social, economic or cultural goals, which are then communicated to succeeding generations. It is purposeful; each culture is itself a phase of continuous Lamarckian evolution, where the environment triggers human action that acts directly on social structures.

Old barbarians

Apart from the new barbarians, another, and to begin with a more powerful, group is also entering the fray. These are the old barbarians, throwbacks, who by dint of their past momentum have managed to survive up to and into the present. Not totally destroyed in the present, they now see their chance to retake control in society, as the forces that formed the present power structures collapse, and as, in fear and uncertainty, members of society look inward and backward on a misremembered past for help. Beware the fifth column of old barbarians in our midst. They are everywhere; look carefully and the signs are there for all to see. More than half the members of the US Congress do not hold passports; they have never left their country and have no intention of ever doing so. The Henley Centre has shown that two-thirds of British people still live within five miles of where they were born and brought up (Mulgan, 30 January 1995). Every modern Western state can boast similar statistics. Like Savonarola, the throwbacks will call for a 'Bonfire of the Vanities'; to them all the aspirations of post-modernity and internationalism are vanities. They will call for a new spiritual age among the losers thrown up by the new economic conditions. They will unleash the tribal mass in a stampede of inferiority. From there it is only a small step from the 'first among equals' and *e pluribus unum*, to *Animal Farm* where 'all animals are equal, but some animals are more equal than others'.

The old barbarians have the strength of their past glories. The new barbarian mutations, whether of a genetic Darwinian or a systemic Lamarckian form, are initially much weaker. The newcomers have no history with which to sway their society. They may not even recognize themselves as newcomers. Only the success of their present action along a different path will bring self-recognition, and convince their society of their benefits. However, being different and extraordinary, they are immediately seen as dangerous. They can only survive initially in isolated communities (in cyberspace?), possibly in hiding within the larger communities. The masses have the size to dissipate the energies of anyone different. Isolation ensures that the inertial force of old barbarian bigotries, which grows to dominate the mass of society in times of uncertainty, is not apparent in the isolated outpost. These new forms emerge with new solutions for profiting from societal uncertainty. They will not all succeed, but those that do will be copied, and will survive and prosper. The old barbarians, who are busy taking over the centre, at first won't care about and may not even know of the existence of these transmutations. Consequently the old barbarians won't try to destroy the new until the innovators have managed to claim a foothold in some areas and can then defend themselves.

Meanwhile anyone who, in desperation, sides with the old barbarians will find that the old ideas won't see off the impending chaos, although they may just hold it back for a little while longer, for the old barbarian position is founded on failing ritual and morality. Morality does not endow power. Morality merely follows power. Morality is the prejudice of yesterday's power. Therefore, any society whose stability depends on its morality, and not on power, is doomed. There can be no permanent being in control of any society that is continuously evolving and emerging, or of any of its institutions. The imposition of standardized and standardizing old barbarian rituals comes with the inevitability of long-term damage. Control only exists in the sense of purposefully formulating and precipitating actions or intentions. But this is not being in control of consequences. Increasing entropy, the gradual running down to disorder, is the natural condition of all mass cultures. Collapse is inevitable, and holding back the inevitable will only make the final disintegration even more painful.

The future

In evolution, the future is nothing if not uncertain. Even the use of the word 'evolution' is highly misleading: it is used as a shorthand description for the effect on one particular category of an explosion of localized co-evolution of one particular category (specie). Yet nothing evolves independently. Survival or extinction depends on the particular conditions existing in the location, and every small change in what is being categorized will impact on that local environment and trigger a feedback that changes other uncategorized entities, and so on, and so on. Even what we perceive as the rules of arbitration underlying natural selection will themselves change along with the transmutation of species. Such rules can only be vague generalizations. We glean them from experience, from observations of things we chose to identify as a category, within a locality we have arbitrarily designated. However, these are things that will co-evolve into things different from the original categorization and designation. Hence, every categorical description is an error of choice, an irrefutable error accepted as truth by force of ritual, and a choice, made habit by orthodoxy.

'Error is a condition of observation in general.' We possess merely 'a convincing criterion of reality in order to misunderstand reality in a shrewd and advantageous manner', and 'what convinces us is not necessarily true, it is merely convincing' (Nietzsche). The only question of importance is whether the errors we make are appropriate or inappropriate. Winning and losing will often depend on uncategorical conditions local to the conflict. There will inevitably be substantial variety within the broad categories of co-evolving old and new barbarians, because there are significant variations in the localities where the punctuation mark of evolution is situated. A particular form of new barbarian will win in one place, of the old in another, until the next time. It is a continuous process.

It is not possible to identify who will win and where, to claim access to that which will be necessarily so, to the universal. 'We interact with the universal, we don't view it' (Nietzsche). We cannot get at the essence of the universal as 'a mere shadow, time, marches forward'. We use our socio-economic institutions as the means of seeing abstract patterns in the way we interact with the universal. We understand by interpreting the interaction between our institutional systems and whatever is being considered. Such meaning-full structures are, however, mere orthodoxies fixed in yesterday. As the shadow of time moves on, the resolution of our observation changes, and so do the abstractions we perceive in the universal. Old meanings lose their meaning. The only constants are Power and the *Will to Power*, but this we forget because we are blinded by the rituals of old powers that insist on denying any other.

In learning to live with this uncertainty, societies cannot deny inevitable ambiguity and vagueness. Unless each culture can reinvent itself and become revitalized by exposure to new mutations, then chaos is inevitable. Here we see clearly the difference between Darwinism and Lamarckian evolution. The latter doesn't leave human future to chance. We don't simply stumble into that future; it is conjured up by the alchemy of ideas and vision mixed liberally with determination and the magic of institutionalized ritual. Since all categories are errors of choice, there can be no scientific construction of a society's future. Alchemy, however, is different. Whereas method of science is predicated on accepted truth, alchemy is based on the appropriateness of admittedly false patterns that accommodate us to the world. By sheer insistence, by convention reinforced by contrivance of ritual, members of society can be made to see that the pre-chosen categories of its alchemical vision are appropriate for their society. Alchemy conjures up a world made different by the incantation of idea, ideas that are made tangible by innovation; innovation made inevitable by force of will. Provided any magical explanation of socio-economic reality does not vastly contradict that which is necessarily so, then the alchemical creation can survive. It will prosper if, barring accidents, the arbitration of natural selection resolves that its particular vision, in its particular context, at some particular time, is more appropriate than competitor alchemies. In this way the society does not become rigid with indecision; it is given a way through, a way forward. However, truth has nothing to do with it. All that matters is which vision, despite the error rather than because of it, is least damaging and/or most beneficial (most appropriate) along the way.

Based in error, all alchemies will eventually fail, as what is appropriate in their local context changes. Hence societies must leave individuals free to experiment and deal with the increasing ambiguity of their position. As the old power bases collapse all around, new power-brokers create new alchemies, new orders of things, through novel, imaginative, opportunistic and often simplifying interpretations of complex situations. They are less dogmatic than the leaders of their society (the high priests of the failing ritual) when contemplating the future. Free individuals, that is those not shackled to past interpretations, are more productive, identifying the issues and trends that will be of far more fundamental use in future. These are necessarily symbolic-analysts, who will broker the identification and solution of the problems endured by their community, and then turn these into new rituals, procedures and applications that can succeed in the midst of social, political and economic upheaval.

Hence, and paradoxically, societies need the variety delivered by new barbarians in order to cope with the social, political and economic changes occurring in the wider world around them. The masses, on the other hand, are an inertial grouping. They are always in decline, and yet perversely they believe exactly the opposite. In fact the masses are likely to blame their problems on the new mutations, rather than on the failings of the old ways. 'But what more oft, in nations grown corrupt, and by their vices brought to servitude, than to love bondage more than liberty – bondage with ease than strenuous liberty – and to despise, or envy, or suspect, whom God hath of his special favour raised as their deliverer?' (This quotation, taken from *Samson Agonistes* by John Milton, has pride of place in the foyer of the Chicago Tribune building, put there by editor 'Colonel' Robert R McCormick, who saw his role, and that of his newspaper, as limiting the excesses of governments and politicians. He attacked Prohibition, the New Deal of Franklin D Roosevelt, the Fair Deal of Harry S Truman, and the Marshall Plan.)

At last we arrive at the underlying theme of this manifesto: the enduring conflict between the individual and the collective, between freedom and coercion, between the new and the old barbarians, all within the necessity of balancing order and chaos. Either way, my advice is clear: be a barbarian, not a victim. Come to recognize the ritualized pyramidal pecking order of compulsion and submission that is the modern nation–state and the modern institution, merely an unstable compromise between the modern and the pre-modern in society. The problem is that emerging post-modern conditions have seriously complicated matters. This new three-body problem means that a harmonious compromise will be far more difficult. Ayn Rand's prediction of social and economic collapse has started – 50 years late, but it has started. No one is taken in any more by governments claiming to have ever increasing access to resources. Soon the pensions, health service bills, the costs of public works and the salaries of state officials will not be paid; worse, rivers will run dry, and fuel and food-stocks will run out. For how much longer will the creators of wealth allow the losers in society to choose the government? For how much longer will they pay for the government's failure to keep the ship of state afloat? The nation–state may continue to exist for a little while longer, but with ever decreasing power.

Collapse is inevitable. We live in a society that has lost its way and its will. The promise of progress has proved to be a lie. The barbarians are at the gate, and in our degeneracy we have two choices: follow the new barbarians and advance to an uncertain future, or obey the old barbarians and return to the rigid permanence of a false past. Be warned, the old barbarians will eradicate all the hard-won benefits of the status quo. Intellectual women, in particular, have the most to lose. A century of progress will count for nothing against revitalized male chauvinism. Homosexuals, immigrants, non-believers, in fact anyone who is different had better choose the new barbarian way, or suffer the wrath of old barbarians. There will be no consolation prizes for those who are trapped by the impending societal breakdown: their individual talent and worth will count for nothing.

Thankfully the success of the old barbarians is not certain. However, the new barbarians will have to organize if they are to survive the fallout and not be left at the mercy of the throwback masses led by old barbarians who are intent on destroying the culture of the Enlightenment that has dominated Western thought for the past 300 years. It is the Enlightenment that underpins the culture of individualism that is fundamental to the new barbarian approach, whereas old barbarians manifest authoritarian collectivism and *The Road to Serfdom*. Old barbarians preach the social glue of fundamentalism as a reaction to the failing modern world. The price of saving society from what they see as perversions of religious and political beliefs is a loss of freedom for the individual unbeliever. Enlightenment is the freedom of the individual innovator to trade in being different. In doing so everyone benefits. However, this seems to have been forgotten, as is evident in today's perverse popular mass-delusion that the ant-hill of labour is the creator of wealth.

Increasingly, the new barbarians represent the winners in the new economic reality, leaving the losers to circle their wagons around old values and rituals, easy prey for the old barbarians. New barbarians see individuals; old barbarians see body counts. Old barbarians talk of management, command and control; the new talk of husbandry and trust. Old barbarians profess a philosophy of difference; the new barbarians a philosophy of variety. Old barbarians are intolerant of other views; new barbarians are permissive.

Consequently, the new barbarians must escape to safe communities where the illumination of the Enlightenment still shines. Otherwise they too will be dragged into the dying of the light by the pious commentators of old barbarian rituals, forced to conform to bigoted extremes or suffer the consequences. The Marxist–Leninist labels of 'reactionary' or 'counter-revolutionary' will be used to justify old barbarian excesses toward anyone and everyone different. There will be no discussion. Events in Iran, Iraq, Afghanistan, North Korea, the Balkans and Northern Ireland should be a warning to us all. Even the mob can be terrorized into compliance. Such is the end of Enlightenment.

The first sign of the old barbarian advance will be seen in the collapse of the modern nation–state. Rapid international travel and global telecommunications have complicated the concept of spheres of influence and are undermining the state's attempts to defend its borders by keeping some people in and others out, either physically or electronically. Telecommunication technology will further limit the state using its boundaries as a barrier to trade. Even the United States is under attack from all sides. Senator John Kerry is convinced of this fact, and in his book *The New War* he warns of 'The web of crime [and terrorism] that threatens America's security'. The very core of the United States is being poisoned by a degeneracy induced by the narcotics cartels and other criminal organizations. Similar things can be said of most other nation–states.

However, what is more sinister is that individual barbarians with a grudge believe they can declare war on any nation–state. Many national politicians agree with Dr Mahathir Mohamad, prime minister of Malaysia, in concluding that speculation in the money markets is already tantamount to a declaration of war against nation–states. We are used to hearing about mercenary gangs taking over countries in Africa, but now ideologically and religiously inspired individuals such as Osama bin Laden (Byrne, 26 December 1998) are declaring war on the most powerful nation–state on earth, the United States. Images of body-bags returning to the United States are traumatizing US citizens. Their government is incapable of mustering the political will to defeat even a minor warlord like Mohamed Farah Aideed on the streets of Mogadishu in October 1993 (Dowden, 5 October 1993). The only military action the voters will stomach is a clinical air-strike made from a distance, preferably with unmanned missiles and stealth bombers, as the long-drawn-out confrontation with Saddam Hussein demonstrates. That particular old barbarian learnt the lesson of the Vietnam War, that any tyrant, who was willing to accept a rising body count of his own citizens with impunity, could successfully wage a war of attrition against the West. Saddam recognized the inability of Western democracy to deal with the sentimentality in its citizenry. He knows that power is not about holding weapons. It is about being willing to use them without forever justifying your actions. He knows that a willingness to use his chemical weapons makes him stronger than the West, which cannot bring itself to use its greater bio-chemical or nuclear arsenal.

As the modern liberal democratic state degenerates, slowly the leaders of such states will take the all-so-reasonable first step toward old barbarian ide-ologies. Christian fundamentalism is wielding increasing political power in parts of the United States. All across Europe, from the Atlantic to the Urals, socialism is again rearing its ugly head. Racial purification is on the cards everywhere. The mob of losers insists that the collective owns the individual, and that all wealth belongs to the tribe, and must be redistributed at the behest of the tribal leaders by fair(?) taxation. What they fail to understand is that they can no longer impose their will on the real generators of wealth – the new barbarian entrepreneurs, individuals and companies. The new-found power of the new barbarians is actually causing the breakdown of their society. To the new barbarian, democracy is a conspiracy of the mob against the creators of wealth. The new wealthy will vote with their feet, and leave the thieves (governments) to their own devices. They insist on a politi-cal–economic framework in which the 'men of mind' can trade the products of their intelligence, ingenuity and talent without the threat of government coercion. Because of information technology, now more than ever before, the power relationship has swung dramatically in favour of the few who can excel in commercially lucrative endeavour, provided that they grasp that power and use it.

Every technology creates alienation. This book is all about alienation, both alienation of the elites from the masses, and alienation of the masses by technology. When governments, in their drive to placate the voting masses, place undue restrictions upon the exercise of individuality, or limit the rewards that knowledge workers expect in return for their enterprise, then talented individuals will no longer take part in production or they will migrate to more agreeable conditions. Yet still the majority of the tribe believe that power lies with their leaders, and that their very continuity as a cohesive group depends on that leadership, sanctified as it is in the ethics and morality of the state. Meanwhile, the new barbarians, whose talent and knowledge mean that they can take full advantage of cyberspace, know that the power relationship has swung dramatically in their favour.

Yet if they are to survive and prosper, new barbarians must organize. It is time for them to come in from the cold and confront the old. For there is a shift of power from the centre to the political margins. The margins are a state of mind, but they have coalesced into smart regions such as Chicago, New York, southern California, Seattle, Hong Kong, Singapore, Dubai, Bangalore, Shanghai, Amsterdam and London(?), where people are creative and live to trade. These places are full of restless and risky businesses, in contrast to the rotting political centres such as Beijing, Brussels, Tokyo and Washington, whose immobility is reflected in their dependence on hierarchy and ostentatious ritualistic displays of yesterday's power. Nowadays, the politically marginal hot-spot is the place to be. These are the locations where institutions are based on knowledge, experience, exchange and innovation, rather than those still obsessed with territory and continuity.

All of these pressures are driving us toward a discontinuity, a punctuation mark between successive equilibria in human societies. However, there can be no certainty in predicting whether the old or new barbarians will win or lose. By its very nature, such a discontinuity is a denial of past trends. The problem is not predicting a discontinuity, but recognizing it after it has happened. For then new barbarians can take advantage by forcing their vision for the future on to society, attempting to precipitate a Lamarckian evolution, with the new society acquiring the preferred social characteristics and values that promote the protection of the property and physical safety of the information rich. There are no guarantees, but one thing is certain: the status quo is finished despite all the denials of self-righteous modernists, secular liberals and democrats.

New worlds

Robert Cooper (1996) is one clear-thinking predictor of what follows the present discontinuity. He divides the world into three zones: the pre-modern, a zone of chaos; the modern, an ordered zone of strong states; and the post-modern zone with order maintained through national transparency and transnational interference.

I too see three zones, similarly drawn along the fault-lines of modernity. In the pre-modern zone, the third world, the various modes of governance will be based on fear, where might is right. There is no underlying political philosophy – it is all repression by rabid ritual. This is a world of chaos, run by gangsters, perpetually on the edge of 'anarchic implosion'. What masquerades as government will be toppled at regular intervals by alternative gangs of thugs and warlords – just like the Third World of today.

The second world, of the modern, is an uneasy compromise between old barbarities and modern technology. That society is maintained by rational scientific methods and processes, but overseen with an excess of ritual ceremony and irrational value systems demanded by rule-based old barbarian ideologies. The mode of governance will be fixed in the all-consuming rights of the collective. Hence there will be a vicious streak of fundamentalism: religious, nationalist, socialist, capitalist or racist. There will be an uneasy tension between the old barbarians and those knowledge workers who either haven't managed to escape, or are ambivalent about both their status and state bigotries. The creators of wealth will not be free and will have to pay lip service in support of these bigotries. They will not be trusted by the state, and will continually have to prove themselves good citizens before the spies of the state – just like it is in the Soviet model that still drives most of the Second World today.

The post-modern first world is the realm of Ayn Rand's 'men of mind' – new barbarians. It will be a world born in trust. The mode of governance is Enlightened and libertarian, with institutions supporting the rights of the individual, not of the tribe. The Enlightenment can only continue in a first world held together by information technology. Their answer to aggressive second world state power is subsidiarity, embracing variety and diversity by distributing power and function to a maximum degree. In tomorrow's first world, decisions will be taken at the lowest appropriate level, which increasingly means the local community, be it county, town, suburb or even street. For not much longer will the nation–state claim the authority; it will leave responsibility to the local community, very much in line with the original American model.

The regions comprising tomorrow's first, second and third worlds will not necessarily be the same groupings as today's three worlds. Already parts of Europe are sliding toward second world status, if not worse. The first world will be balanced, where pragmatic guardians see the sense in protecting the property rights of the new barbarian. There always have to be guardians, because someone has to be in charge of territory and protect property rights. In the second world there are too many guardians; it is a world with too much emphasis on beliefs and mass ideologies. The third world is anarchy. Putting it simply, the three worlds are open society, closed society and no society. In the first world there is a harmony between trade and guardians; in the second the guardians are in control; and in the third the guardians are out of control. Disease (such as malaria and HIV) will be a major barrier to much of the third world. Also the rich of the second and third worlds will place their wealth in the first world. Consequently the two inferior worlds can never be financially successful. That wealth will be made increasingly liquid by new technology, and hawala bankers will offer a ready conduit for the outflow, no matter what regulations are imposed by the guardians there. Conversely, the first world will involve itself with the second and third worlds only via trading posts. If these three physical worlds were mapped on to cyberspace, then the first world would appear as a coastal trading region, and the second world its hinterland, a buffer against the blighted and benighted interior third world. Transnational enterprises from the first world will mount mercenary armies to protect their interests, to extract raw materials, and to collect food, fuel, water and, especially, young talent.

Individuals trapped in the two lesser worlds will be under threat from the masses. They face the mind control of religious, political and racist bigotry, and the physical threat of gangsters. There is only one sensible action: evade the tidal wave of ignorance by fleeing to economic hot-spots or smart regions, thereby escaping the oppression of the old world. They must reach the freedom of hot-spots in the new world where they will find the civilized support of civic pride. There the majority of people are happy and willing to give to society (within reason), rather than expecting only to take. This was the situation in most of yesterday's liberal democracies, but it did not last. For what happens when the majority want to take? The givers become disillusioned, and decide to leave. Such is the end of liberal democratic regions, and unless they can transmute into libertarian democracies, they will face serious economic problems. The libertarian time bombs of capital flight, data flight and the flight of intellectual property and talent, whether offshore or off-planet, will surely soon explode the smugness prevalent in today's democracies.

Where are the welcoming hot-spots? They won't be nation–states. To the new barbarian founding fathers, the nation–state is the enemy. The hot-spots already exist as smart cities and smart regions. They must already exist and be of a substantial size, as no village could survive the subsequent change of scale. They will not be the urban sprawls of Calcutta, Rio de Janeiro or Mexico City. These are tinderboxes, not smart city–states. New barbarian communities will be 'the rich man in his castle, the poor man at his gate'. I have already indicated some likely candidates above: Chicago, New York and so on. I am pinning my hopes on the emergence of an independent London Region. It is up to us new barbarians to make it happen.

The populations of these elitist smart regions are not groups of rabid individualists, uncaring and devoid of charity. Such regions cannot be solely composed of knowledge workers; to be viable each must be a balanced community of knowledge workers, service workers and a caste of guardians. There will be an understanding of those who are not creative. Charity and philanthropy will be encouraged, but as an act of choice, not of coercion by the state. And everyone will be expected to add some value to this right-sized community. In this way the first world will be composed of communities of trust, where individuals themselves take on the responsibility of their society. New barbarians, escaping from second and third worlds must choose their destinations carefully, because each hot-spot will have its own peculiar cultural idiosyncrasies. If we have to run, we should run sooner rather than later, and choose a culture compatible with our own. We can call on our personal global network for advice, for we must fit in. This shouldn't be too difficult because all trading cities are cosmopolitan. They will form global coalitions; after all because of telecommunications, distance is no longer a barrier to forming and maintaining relationships.

However, this brave new first world of libertarian freedoms won't just happen by accident. So what alchemy, what social glue and what types of organizational structure are needed to hold these marginal places together and make them tomorrow's centres of civilization? We should take a lesson from the early days of the modern nation–state, in particular the early days of German nationalism that culminated first in 1867 with the Prussian-led North German Confederation (of Germanic states north of the River Main) formed after their victory in the Seven Weeks' War against Austria, Bavaria, Hanover, Saxony and some minor states; and then in 1871 with the merging of the southern states (minus Austria) into the German empire to fight the Franco–Prussian War that was precipitated by the guile of Otto von Bismarck.

It would be wrong to think that this unification came about simply because of treaties following the Prussian or German victories in battles such as Königgrätz and Sedan, or at the Siege of Paris. It is not the final acts of unification that should be of interest to us here, but the groundwork that prepared the national consciousness and made such developments possible. We should look back more than 50 years earlier to when Wilhelm von Humboldt and Johann Gottlieb Fichte set down an education system (in particular the founding of the University of Berlin in 1810) that prepared the ground for a German national consciousness. Fichte in particular, who became the University's second rector, in his *Address to the German Nation*, was responsible for stressing the need of a sense of patriotism over individualism, cultivated via a completely reorganized education system run by the state and paid for by the state.

Fichte was convinced that children should be educated in a 'separate and independent community', free of parental influence. What is this but the social engineering of Lamarckian evolution, where the acquired characteristics for each new generation are passed on via the rituals implicit in the socialization and education of the young? What is this but alchemy, forcing a vision on to society in order to change its future? By interfering with (designing) these rituals, the evolution within society can be redirected. Fichte preached that young impressionable minds should be convinced of the virtues of nationhood. Such a proposition was only to be expected. Those who are bent on the ideal herd know they must first contrive the ideal herd-animal. Designing social ritual to throw evolution into reverse has always been, and always will be, a fundamental alchemy of old barbarians, be they nationalists, Christians or communists. The Jesuits have a maxim: 'Give us a child until it is seven and it is ours for life.' Lenin is credited with: 'Give us the child for eight years and it will be a Bolshevik for ever.'

Preaching a gospel of individual academic freedom (but on behalf of the state), Berlin University soon attracted the greatest radical minds of German-speaking Europe. The elite of German youth naturally rushed to Berlin for their education. These young men, destined to be the future leaders and civil servants of the fragmented Germany of the day, were consciously or unconsciously taught the virtue of a united Germany, having already been softened up by the state-inspired secondary education system. Paradoxically, and despite its espoused heterodoxy, the University of Berlin soon became a leading player in the unification of Germany. Most universities across Germany followed suit. After a few false starts, it took the disciplining of two whole generations of German youth to enable unification. The brainwashing, delivered by a primary and secondary school system, and by the perversion of the Enlightenment in the tertiary education system, proved so successful that the model was eagerly copied globally. It now forms the basis of state-run school and university systems in countries all around the world. Of course, such an expensive loyalty-making machine was all made possible by the state invention of income tax, imposed on the very parents of the raw material that the state machine needs to churn out good little citizens.

So how can new barbarians worldwide undo nearly 200 years of indoctrination? They don't need to! The old model no longer wields its mind-control for two reasons: firstly, state systems are becoming degenerate, and secondly, the state now has powerful competition. The strategy of using the school system to spread nationalism has degenerated into pandering to the masses, whose support is needed by politicians. In Britain, the grammar school system, which espoused the highest intellectual standards, has been systematically dismantled. It has been replaced by a comprehensive education that has banned failure. Wealth creation in the Information Age requires the very best, and yet the disposition of British education is to deliver a 'mediocracy' with aspirations that cannot possibly be realized.

However, of a far greater threat to the status quo is the competition posed by new technology. In the original German, Jesuit or Bolshevik model, parents handed over the raising of their children to the state, priest or party. Today pressurized parents place their children in front of the television set. Children are still being brainwashed, but not cynically with a clear-sighted ideological purpose, but rather arbitrarily with the hedonism of popular culture. A generation of couch potatoes, with few or no communication skills, are bombarded with mind-numbing pop music, turning many of those remaining into nihilists. These children, no longer controlled by state machinery, now snarl at their teachers. Instead of swearing allegiance to the flag, they are more likely to don it as underwear. Yet an intellectual elite from among this set are able to transcend their nihilism, and become individualists – new barbarians. Quite unknowingly, the individualistic values of

America's founding fathers, via the popular culture of Hollywood films and rock music, have come to the rescue of the few.

To succeed the new barbarians must take advantage of the opportunities presented to them, and prepare the ground to spread their message. What better way is there than to follow the well-tried old barbarian model? However, instead of influencing children in schools, they must use the media to create a new barbarian consciousness among the world's elite. The young are already committed to the technological media. They already get much of their education from television and film, and from multimedia computers and the anarchic Internet. The young are resentful that state schools turn them into 'just another brick in the wall'. In the words of revolt from the anti-school song *The Wall* by Pink Floyd: 'We don't need no education. We don't need no thought control.' The nation–state will continue to use the same media to push their message on to the young bricks, but the state has lost its monopoly of programming. Youth culture itself ridicules politicians who, in attempting to appeal to the young, line up at award ceremonies and pander to celebrities from the sport, film and pop industries. Official propaganda now has competition from more anarchic, more exciting and better quality material. New barbarians can access impressionable proto-barbarians via this alternative 'education', by ensuring that the hidden agenda is an assertion of the knowledge workers' *Will to Power*. They must take the Socratic position, that education is the 'corrupting' of young minds, in the denial of state-inspired indoctrination.

It is time to spread the word that the battle against the state, for the hearts and minds of knowledge workers, can be won. It won't be easy, and it too may take two generations. Many of today's knowledge workers simply cannot break themselves free of the brainwashing implanted by state-inspired education. They still feel subservient to their has-been political masters, showing gratitude for the merest crumbs thrown from the taxpayers' table, forgetting that it is they who pay an excess of taxes. It's not too late. Now is the time for new barbarians to organize. Now is the time for them to realize the economic power in their group, to organize that power and to demand political power for themselves. Now is the time for knowledge workers to put their first world first, and then let the natural selection of history take its course.

The new barbarians must use the new technological media to set up a delivery network that will spread the gospel of individual freedom among all ages. They must grasp the initiative from the false prophets of state propaganda, and return it to the individual. Wean the elite individual away from the influences of the nanny state. Stress the merits of the global cosmopolitan elite. It can happen, but it is clear that the initial impetus can only come from new barbarians living in the United States. The United States in general, and its leading establishments of higher education in particular, are the major hope. Like in the Second World War, yet again freedom-loving individuals from Europe and around the world will be calling on the United States to rescue them from attacks by totalitarian states. The whole of the short history of the United States has been about allowing new barbarian business practices the freedom to create the future with a minimum of state intervention. Even occasional old barbarian outrages, such as the McCarthy witch-hunts between 1950 and 1954, were all eventually banished by the dominant culture of civil liberty and individual freedom. Paradoxically, the Cold War helped to destroy any lingering aspects of McCarthyism. In battling the old barbarian menace of the communist 'evil empire' for half a century, the United States needed to be largely free of a collectivist philosophy, in order to attract the very best scientists and entrepreneurs from around the world.

The same cannot be said for the other side of the Atlantic. In its search for stability, Europe, always glorifying its past and yet terrified by past mistakes, is sinking into socialism, some of it of the most vicious nationalist and racist variety. That continent has lost the nerve, vigour, vitality, virility and vision required to prosper in their increasingly collectivist world. There are very few European universities that can independently develop the necessary will to support the global intellectual elite: they are mostly far too busy creating the ideal herd-animal for the state.

Most of the top universities in the world are now based in the United States, and they are all almost independent of state charity. A subset of this elite group could join together using telecommunication technology, possibly with junior partners selected from prestige local universities from elsewhere around the world, and break totally free of the stranglehold of state funding. Such a global network would be a first division virtual university with the credibility to deliver an attractive new barbarian education across all three worlds. Supported by virtual primary and secondary education, they would spread the word that mediocrity will no longer be tolerated. Hot-spots need a hotbed of talent. This independent global system would be set up specifically to examine the world's intellectual elite by judging them against the highest educational standards. Intellectual talent uncovered in this way would then be offered employment in the economic powerhouse of the first world – capital and intellect in a partnership that delivers opportunities to all irrespective of family, connections, race, colour, sex or creed.

This attitude is necessary if first world societies are to maintain a balance between the guardians and trade. The new barbarians will pay for the police, military, judiciary and public health. They need the guardians to protect their property and health rights. Payment is the libertarian choice of tribute, not taxation. There is even a role for politicians in that someone has to maintain the balance. They guard the guardians. Society will be a true partnership, not the form of today's collective rhetoric, pretending that we are all equal, and using societal ritual to paper over the cracks in the hope of making the differences disappear. There will be a unity of purpose held together by the power of rituals, but these rituals will be rational for tomorrow's world. The traders, who ultimately pay for the basic mechanisms of social unity, do not depend on their place of birth, the status of their families, their race, sex or religion. They depend solely on their abilities as individual knowledge workers. There will be many different attempts to strike this balance in the various differing ritualized communities around the first world. However, there is no guaranteed utopia. Natural selection alone will decide winners and losers in the coming battle. Be warned!

A spectre is haunting the Globe – the spectre of New Barbarians. All the Powers of the old world have entered into a holy alliance to exorcize this spectre of enlightened self-interest: churches and monarchies, capitalists and socialists, populists, totalitarian nationalists, militarists, and spies for the state.

Where is the party in opposition that has not been decried as self-interest by its opponents in power? Where the Opposition that has not hurled back the branding reproach of self-interest, against the more advanced opposition parties, as well as against its reactionary adversaries?

Two things result from this fact:
I. The New Barbarism is already acknowledged by all World Powers to be itself a Power.
II. It is high time that New Barbarians should openly, in the face of the whole world, publish their views, their aims, their tendencies, and meet this nursery tale of the Spectre of New Barbarians with a Manifesto.

(With apologies to Karl Marx and Friedrich Engels, authors of
The Communist Manifesto.)

The new barbarians are organizing to face a future that won't be easy and that won't be nice. Orson Welles sums up the situation most succinctly in *The Third Man*, the 1949 film set in the rubble of post-war Vienna. Justifying his barbarian actions he says: 'In Italy for 30 years under the Borgias they had warfare, terror, murder, bloodshed, but they produced Michelangelo, Leonardo da Vinci, and the Renaissance. In Switzerland they had brotherly love, they had 500 years of democracy and peace. And what did they produce? The cuckoo-clock.' ('The cuckoo-clock was actually invented in the Black Forest in Germany, but there is no need to let that fact spoil a good quotation.)

How will we cope in the rubble of the coming conflict? That future is a war of cultures, and hence a war of alchemies. Cultural treasures are legitimate targets. These treasures in themselves do not exist free from cultural overtones, and this seals their fate. The greatest treasure of our culture, individual freedom, the freedom to be different, is now at risk. That is why I stress the importance of our education systems in spreading the new barbarian message, the message that places individuality above the wishes of the mob. Schools and universities have a cultural role to play. Their task is not to produce the wealth of the Information Age. I am quite sure that most 'talent workers' do not need intellectual talent. Much of the wealth of the Information Age will not be classified as intellectual in any way whatsoever. However, it will take the intellectual drive of new barbarian equivalents of Fichte and von Humboldt to make sure that the wealth generators are conscious of the need to defend their individual freedoms, and that the ground is prepared so that talented individuals can survive and prosper for the benefit of all.

Are we willing to defend those freedoms? Do we have *The Will to Power* and, more importantly, are we willing to use it? If the answer is yes, then what must we do? In the long term, we must look to our talents and intellectual assets, and invest in an elitist training and education for ourselves and our families. We should attend (physically or electronically) only the most prestigious academic or training establishments, preferably those with a minimum of state interference. Education is not only what we learn, but also the subtle mind-games that the institution plays as it indoctrinates its students. Then there are the doors it opens, who we meet there, the networks we form and the status it invests us with. The designer label on our qualifications says a great deal about who we are: are we haute couture or charity shop cast-off? However, a label by itself is not enough. The new barbarian aristocracy is a talented elite, not the ill-educated crumbs from a disintegrating upper crust.

So much for the medium to longer term, but in the short term we must secure our financial assets. We should join in tax revolts to maximize our wealth, and put as much of it as possible into liquid assets. Spread it around the globe, so that neither the dying state nor their old barbarian successors can confiscate it. Then if we need to fly off to a 'hot-spot', our wealth elsewhere will ensure a soft landing. Be ready to flee at a moment's notice. However, if we find it impossible to abandon our fixed assets then we are well and truly trapped. We should never own an asset that we can't walk away from. Property is the very first asset the dying state will seize. British governments of every political shade have been very keen to promote Britain as a home-owning democracy: if we have all our assets tied up in property, we can't escape. As part of our escape plan, we should become knowledgeable about international travel and telecommunication systems. We should get to know the smart regions, the economic hot-spots. We should expand our personal network of international contacts, human and corporate. Thanks to telecommunication technologies, distance is no longer a barrier to forming new global relationships and maintaining old ones.

But where are these emerging hot-spots? First and foremost is the United States (or rather parts of it), a beacon of hope for the Enlightened, although even the United States is not totally secure, which is why this book has concentrated so much on the very real dangers to its archetypal smart regions. For 50 years liberal intellectuals have been denigrating 'the American Dream', a vision that is at the very core of the new barbarism. The country has the serious internal threats of religious, racial and ethnic fundamentalism, and the arbitrary and unstable 'redneck' militias, topped off by the circus of control-freaks and 'fixers' in Washington. But countering these liabilities is a vigorous capitalistic and individualistic work ethic, a 'can-do' culture of self-sufficiency, and a mode of state governance that increasingly stresses subsidiarity, with political power being held at the local level. It is certain that most of the rich US states and cities will hold on to the intellectual high ground of enlightened self-interest. And they have the military might to back it up. Thankfully, US society is totally free of the most insidious virus, the corrosive sentimental socialism that has terminally corrupted Europe. Europe itself will fragment, but some hot-spots like Greater London may well escape. Aligning themselves with other globally distributed cosmopolitan smart regions, the escapees will join the enlightened first world under US leadership. It is becoming increasingly evident that the 20th century is not 'the American century' as many defeatists would have us believe; that honour is being reserved for the 21st century of new barbarians.

If we are unable or unwilling to run to an existing hot-spot, then the best we can hope for is that our community will become a smart region. But that won't happen by accident. It takes alchemy. It takes vision. We must organize, network, spread the word and make it happen. It's our future and our choice.

Welcome to the future. Welcome to the brave new world of *The New Barbarian Manifesto*.

References

Accountancy, December 1987, Former champion jockey Lester Piggott was sentenced to three years

Acey, Madeleine, Internet 'bit tax' proposed by EC, *Network Week*, 25 March 1996

Alexander, Garth, Asia crashes, *Sunday Times*, Business Focus, 31 August 1997

Allen-Mills, Tony, Prisoners put to work on the phone gang, *Sunday Times*, 25 May 1997

Anderson, Benedict (1983) Imagined Communities, Verso, London

Anderson, Sarah and Kavanagh, John, Corporate power isn't discussed, *International Herald Tribune*, 23 October 1996

Atkinson, Dan, Hooked on drugs money, *Guardian*, 5 November 1997

Atkinson, Dan, Can't get no satisfaction, *Guardian*, 13 June 1998

Atkinson, Dick (1995) *The Common Sense of Community*, Demos, London

August, Oliver, Gates, 42, contemplates a long retirement, *Times*, 8 July 1998

Austin, Mark, Titanic tax haven to sail with 65,000, *Sunday Times*, 15 March 1998

Austin, Mark, Revealed: 'slave camps' of Labour's first New Deal, *Sunday Times*, 9 August 1998

Authers, John, Expansion taxes higher education, *Financial Times*, 20 March 1995

Barker, Paul, The end of the job for life?..., *Independent on Sunday*, 26 May 1995

Barnett, Anthony, New Labour's old subsidy dilemma, *Observer*, 23 November 1997

Barot, Trushar, New Venice rises to save tax in the sun, *Sunday Times*, 30 August 1998

Baudrillard, J (1994) *The Illusion of the End*, Polity Press, Cambridge

BBC Monitoring Service, 3 September 1994, Khmer Rouge issue 'communiqué' on immigration law

BBC Monitoring Service, 12 March 1998, NPC deputy says 'high time' for euthanasia debate trial run

Bell, Daniel (1976) *The Coming of the Post-industrial Society: A venture in social forecasting*, Basic Books, New York

Bell, Susan, Disgraced mayor plans Nice comeback, *Times*, 2 August 1994

Bild, Peter, Steffi in clear as her father gets 3 years, *Daily Telegraph*, 25 January 1997

Blackstock, Colin, By 2000 there'll be 200,000 millionaires, *Independent on Sunday*, 3 August 1997

Boadle, Anthony, Canada taxes cigarette industry to combat smuggling, *Reuters*, 8 February 1994

Bodkin, Wayne, Conradi, Peter and Lang, Kirsty, Jospin offers young 'joke jobs', *Sunday Times*, 23 November 1997

Boseley, Sarah, Samaritan rock drummer blows his cover in plea to suicidal young people, *Guardian*, 25 June 1998

Boyes, Roger, German tax men target Becker in raids, *Times*, 30 July 1998

Brady, Simon, Is Italy going down?, *Euromoney*, 15 October 1992

Brittain, Victoria and Elliott, Larry, United Nations: dollar-a-day losers in the global economy, *Guardian*, 12 June 1997

Brown, Andrew, Kings of the wired frontier, *Independent on Sunday*, 30 April 1995

Brown, D and Morse, L (1997) *Cybertrends*, Penguin, London

Brown, Tim and Millward, David, Olympic chief backs drug use, *Daily Telegraph*, 27 July 1998

Brynjolffson, E *et al* (1989) Does information technology lead to smaller firms?, *Sloan Working Paper*, No. 3143–90, Sloan School of Management

Burke, J and Leppard, D, British drive to lure millionaire foreigners flops, *Times*, 5 February 1995

Burt, Tim, Ikea rated among Sweden's top three businesses, *Financial Times*, 6 July 1998

Business Times Singapore, 29 December 1992, Farewell to frontiers

Byrne, Paul, Bin Laden in 'avenge Iraq' plea, *Mirror*, 26 December 1998

Cairncross, Frances (1997) *The Death of Distance*, Orion Business Books, London

Campbell, Duncan, 'Eccentric' firm may handle police files, *Guardian*, 30 June 1992

Campbell, Matthew, Heston stars in US gunfight, *Sunday Times*, 14 December 1997

Canada Newswire, 9 June 1998, Symantec sponsors telecommuting Web site

Carr, Simon, Cyberspace threatens to devour tax gatherers, *The National Business Review (NZ)*, 13 May 1998

Carvel, John, Quarter of teachers over 50 in rush for early retirement, *Guardian*, 14 December 1996

Cass, Julia, State prisons diversify their work load, *Philadelphia Enquirer*, 4 September 1996

Casson, Mark (1998) *Institutions and the Evolution of Modern Business*, Frank Cass, London

Cathcart, Brian, Reporting restrictions have been lifted – by the Internet, *Independent on Sunday*, 19 February 1995

Chen, Edwin, Campaign reform on ballots of 6 states, *Los Angeles Times*, 2 November 1996

Chote, Robert, Aid to poor nations falls to 18-year low, *Financial Times*, 8 April 1999

Christie, Bryan, Victorian cradle of master race dream, *Scotsman*, 26 August 1997

Clark, Tim, Dealing in danger – the growing business in used and counterfeit aircraft spares, *Daily Telegraph*, 13 July 1996

Coase, Ronald H (1991) The nature of the firm, in *The Nature of the Firm: Origins, evolution and development*, ed O E Williamson and S G Winter, Oxford University Press, Oxford

Cohen, Nick, Murdoch's tax – Labour has, er, nothing to say, *Independent on Sunday*, 3 December 1995

Congress Daily, 20 July 1998, Past dirty dozen targets say listing did not hurt them

Connors, Steve, Doctors plan 'genetic twin' for every child, *Independent on Sunday*, 8 November 1998

Cooper, Robert (1996) *The Post-modern State and the World Order*, Demos, London

Cope, Nigel, Stores fight ban on cut-price designer goods, *Independent*, 17 July 1998

Cornwell, J (1996) *Harm: Mind, medicine and murder on trial*, Viking, New York

Cornwell, Rupert, Clinton bars the Cuban boat people, *Independent*, 20 October 1994

Cornwell, Rupert, FBI sets sights on far-right US groups, *Independent*, 22 April 1995

Cornwell, Rupert, Muslims guilty of bombs plot, *Independent*, 6 September 1996

Courtenay, A, Money laundering: washed and brushed up, *Banker*, 1 October 1996

Coyle, Diane, Access to the Net, *Independent*, 12 July 1999

Currid, Cheryl, Are you prepared to make the move from your office to cyberspace, *Windows Magazine*, 1 October 1995

D'Arcy, David, A look at what makes this continent attractive to chip firms, *Electronics Weekly*, 20 November 1991

Daily Mail, 11 September 1997, Sweet-tooth tests on mental patients

Daily Mirror, 12 July 1996, Greedy B'stards

Daily Telegraph, 1 March 1995, Immigrant tax

Dalrymple, Theodore, Bored to death by an empty existence, *Daily Telegraph*, 26 August 1994

Davidow, W H and Malone M S (1992) *The Virtual Corporation*, HarperCollins, New York

Davidson, J D and Rees-Mogg, W (1997) *The Sovereign Individual*, Macmillan, London

Davies, Hugh, Passport fraud nets £216 million, *Daily Telegraph*, 5 February 1990

Davies, Hugh, Waco disaster – Waco ends in suicide inferno, *Daily Telegraph*, 20 April 1993

Dawson, Stella, Government says many new jobs pay well, economists disagree, *Reuters News Service*, 15 April 1992

de Tocqueville, Alexis (1990) *Democracy in America*, vol 2, Vintage Classics, New York

Denny, Charlotte, Threat to central banks, *Guardian*, 27 August 1999

Desai, Meghnad, Corporations rule the world, letter to the *Independent*, 24 October 1995

Donegan, Lawrence and Smithers, Rebecca, Tory MP to fight party over deselection, *Guardian*, 31 January 1997

Douglas, Mary (1984) *Purity and Danger: An analysis of the concepts of pollution and taboo*, ARK Paperbacks, London

Dowden, R and Castle, S, Who are we in the world, *Independent on Sunday*, 26 March 1995

Dowden, Richard, Mogadishu raked by ferocious street battles, *Independent*, 5 October 1993

Drohan, Madeleine, Investor immigrant rules to be tightened much to the annoyance of Quebec, *Globe and Mail*, 22 August 1990

Drucker, P (1992) *Post Capitalist Society*, Butterworth, London

Duce, R, Whistle-blower given 10 years for murder plot, *Times*, 15 March 1994

Duval Smith, Alex, French seamen call off blockade for talks with British firm, *Guardian*, 28 February 1995

Duval Smith, Alex, France battles for welfare, *Guardian*, 20 November 1995

Eaglesham, Jean, Mardi Gras bomber pleads guilty to blackmail, *Financial Times*, 8 April 1999

Economist, 2 May 1992, Cross frontier broadcasting: and nation shall speak guff to nation

Economist, 29 December 1992, Farewell to frontiers

Economist, 21 May 1994, Welcome to Cascadia

Economist, 11 February 1995, A world without jobs

Economist, 29 April 1995, The politics of blame

Economist, 6 May 1995, Encryption, secret plans

Economist, 17 June 1995, Democracy and technology – e-lectioneering

Economist, 22 June 1996, Feds 1, Freemen 0

Economist, 18 January 1997, The year down-sizing grew up

Economist, 15 March 1997, An unhealthy silence

Economist, 15 March 1997, Just desserts

Economist, 29 March 1997, The changing dream

Economist, 19 April 1997, Campaign clipboard

Economist, 19 April 1997, Policing for profit

Economist, 19 April 1997, Welcome to the new world of private security

Economist, 26 April 1997, It's wise to deindustrialise

Economist, 26 April 1997, Mr Clean

Economist, 3 May 1997, Campaign clipboard

Economist, 3 May 1997, Light on the shadows

Economist, 31 May 1997, Disappearing taxes

Economist, 30 August 1997, Nordic eugenics

Economist, 13 December 1997, The virtual gambler

Economist, 20 December 1997, Rising tide, falling boats

Economist, 16 July 1999, Where the jailbirds are

Eddy, Paul, True defective stories, *Sunday Times Magazine*, 10 August 1997

Egan, Mark, Doctors less inclined to assist suicide, *Reuters News Service*, 16 May 1998

Ellis, Virginia, Poverty rates among state's children rises sharply, *Los Angeles Times*, 10 July 1998

Etzioni, A (1994) *The Spirit of Community*, Simone Schuster, London

Faunce, Thomas, Human cloning – why prohibition will fail, *Canberra Times*, 2 June 1998

Fergusson, John, Risking a fortune, *Herald Sun*, 9 May 1998

Financial Post, 9 April 1992, Ottawa scraps export tax on cigarettes

Financial Post, 6 November 1992, Kick the tax habit – tobacco products

Financial Post, 11 February 1994, Cigarette tax cut an 'interim' plan

Financial Times, 16 November 1995, Chung Hwa Picture Tubes – to build a £260 million cathode ray tube plant in Scotland

Financial Times, 31 May 1997

Fineman, Mark, Military can't outflank rebels in war of words, *Los Angeles Times*, 21 February 1995

Fleming, Thomas, 13 things you never knew about the American Revolution, Parade Magazine, *Boston Globe*, 23 November 1997

Flynn, Sean, The case of Ray Burke, the sheikh, £20 million and 11 Irish passports, *Irish Times*, 4 October 1997

Ford, R, Government defends £1m entry fee for immigrants, *Times*, 25 May 1994

Ford, Richard, Prisoners gain foothold at M&S, *Times*, 26 May 1995

Ford, Richard and Lee, Adrian, EU treaty blamed for gypsy influx, *Times*, 21 October 1997

Fran, H R and Cook, J P (1995) *The Winner-Take-All Society*, Free Press, New York

Francis, Diane, Slashing liquor taxes would kill smuggling and bring back jobs, *Financial Post*, 13 December 1994

Fukuyama, Francis (1992) *The End of History and the Last Man*, Penguin, London

Fullerton, Elizabeth, Austria still sterilizes mental patients, *Reuters*, 27 August 1997

Gartland, Peter, Be a card: buy your own bank, *Times*, 18 July 1993

Geddes, Ashley, Alberta cracks down on tobacco smuggling, *The Financial Post*, 6 May 1994

Ghazi, Polly and Jones, Judy, The future of work revealed, *Independent on Sunday*, 28 September 1997

Gilard, Michael, SFO enters the inner sanctum, *Observer*, 24 September 1995

Gimson, Andrew, Kohl pledge to stay on despite poll catastrophe, *Daily Telegraph*, 28 April 1998

Goldberg, Andy, Israel seals Gaza as Hamas vows to avenge its dead hero, *Sunday Times*, 7 January 1996

Goldsmith, Belinda, Swedish leaders give in over homes tax cut, *Reuters News Service*, 19 May 1998

Green, Richard, State intends to introduce abortion in one bold move, *Irish Times*, 9 July 1998

Green, Sue, Territory's people undeterred by new Australian scheme, *South China Morning Post*, 22 February 1992

Grey, Michael, Portland comes to life again, *Lloyd's List*, 8 July 1998

Grey, Stephen, Community of the corrupt, *Sunday Times*, 17 January 1999

Guardian, 23 August 1994, Give me my kids back – Orkney child abuse scandal

Guest, Robert, Gangsters held on Kobe quake fraud, *Daily Telegraph*, 16 March 1995

Gumilëv, Leo (1990) *Ethnogenesis and the Biosphere*, Progress Publishers, Moscow

Gurdon, Hugo, Washington in fear of Barry's fifth-term plans, *Daily Telegraph*, 2 January 1998

Ham, Paul, Outback militia awaits 'Asian horde', *Sunday Times*, 19 July 1998

Handelsblatt, 4 October 1992, Mercedes-Benz officially announces location of new plant in Alabama

Handy, Charles (1994) *The Empty Raincoat*, Hutchinson, London

Hawkes, Nigel, Every day, 12 Britons commit suicide, *Times*, 22 May 1993

Hayek, Friedrich A (1944) *The Road to Serfdom*, Routledge, London

Hayek, Friedrich A (1976) *The Denationalization of Money*, Institute of Economic Affairs, London

Henning, Christopher, In the event of my death…, *Sydney Morning Herald*, 9 May 1998

Herald Sun, 7 July 1998, Women play supporting roles in pay race

Herrnstein, R J and Murray, C (1994) *The Bell Curve*, Free Press, New York

Hind, John, The good news: Lloyd Webber's off, *Observer*, 22 February 1997

Hoffman, Bruce, American right-wing extremism, *Jane's Intelligence Review*, 1 July 1995

Hogben David, B C to grant immigrant status to 100 rich investors, *Vancouver Sun*, 29 December 1995

Holmes, Stanley, Boeing machinists take up labor's top cause – job security, *Seattle Times*, 23 August 1999

Hooker, Lucy, Dental wars erupt as Hungarians 'poach' Austrian clients, *Guardian*, 20 October 1993

Hoover's Company Profiles, August 1999, Lucasfilm Ltd

Hotten, Russell, Rover seeks grant aid of £70 million, *Independent*, 19 October 1995

Hughes, David, Pensions tax on the self-employed, *Daily Mail*, 4 July 1998

Hugill, Barry, Tax – a vicious circle that won't be squared, *Observer*, 9 April 1997

Independent Business Weekly (NZ), 8 April 1998, ATO focuses on multi-nationals tax-paying

International Herald Tribune, 19 August 1996

International Labour Office, Geneva, *World Employment 1996/97*

International Money Marketing, 15 March 1996, Belize passports for sale – US~$50,000

Investors' Business Daily, 24 October 1996, The Economy Perspective

Investor's Business Daily, 11 December 1996

Ip, Greg, Moody's warning rattles C~$, *Financial Post*, 17 February 1995

IT Times, 4 September 1997, Just churning out millionaires

Ivison, John, Murdoch cuts NI's effective tax rate to 1.2%, *The Scotsman*, 28 November 1995

Jacobs, Jane (1993) *Systems of Survival*, Hodder & Stoughton, London

Jacobson, Philip, Sweden is rocked by scandal of forced lobotomies, *Sunday Telegraph*, 12 April 1998

Jago, Richard, Graf finally gets a break on the tax front, *Guardian*, 13 June 1997

Jones, M, Conradi, P and Lang, K, Unravelling of the euro dream, *Sunday Times*, 1 June 1997

Kane, F and Oldfield, C, Maurice versus the beancounters, *Sunday Times*, 15 January 1995

Kane, Frank, Levy, Adrian and Haynes, Steve, Seychelles – crook's paradise, *Sunday Times*, 14 January 1996

Kaplan, Andrew, State imposes 200% tax hike on cigarettes, *US Distribution Journal*, 15 December 1995

Kaplan, Robert D, The coming anarchy, *Atlantic Magazine*, February 1994

Katz, Ian, Staten Island burns its ferries, *Guardian*, 8 June 1995

Kelly, Rachel, Stars in Irish agents' eyes – property, *Times*, 6 August 1994

Kennedy, P (1993) *Preparing for the Twenty-first Century*, Fontana, London

Kerry, John (1997) *The New War*, Simon and Schuster, New York

Key, Ivor, Officials pocket £600m given to rebuild Bosnia, *Daily Mail*, 18 August 1999

Kirkbride, Julie, Liberal democrat conference – attack on human waste – unemployment, *Daily Telegraph*, 22 September 1993

Kirschbaum, Erik, Taxin' Jackson? Germans lighten up, *Daily Variety*, 23 May 1996

Kwan Weng Kin, Why intelligent young Japanese join the sect, *Straits Times*, 4 June 1995

Lambert, Angela, Cold comfort when the pension runs out, *Independent*, 1 December 1994

Landler, M, Are we having fun yet? Maybe too much, *Business Week*, 14 March 1994

Large, P (1980) *The Micro Revolution*, Fontana, London

Lasch, Christopher (1996) *The Revolt of the Elites: And the betrayal of democracy*, W W Norton, New York

Lavin, Paul, The cyber VAT man cometh in Europe, *Newsbytes News Network*, 25 June 1998

Lawson, Mark, Putting trust in a foreign country, *Australian Financial Review*, 23 July 1996

Lee Martin, Geoffrey, Euthanasia to be legalized by Australian state, *Daily Telegraph*, 12 April 1996

Leger, Kathryn, Campeau gets tough, *Financial Post*, 10 May 1998

Lesher, Dave and Weinstein, Henry, Prop. 187 backers accuse Davis of ignoring voters, *LA Times*, 30 July 1999

Levine, Richard and Neuffer, Elizabeth, New York transit police officers accused of unlawful arrests, *New York Times*, 24 November 1987

Levy, Adrian and Burrell, Ian, Anarchists use computer highway for subversion, *Sunday Times*, 5 March 1995

Lilley, Ray, IRD challenged on tax report, *National Business Review*, 8 May 1998

Linton, M, http://www.gulets.u-net.com, 1999

Luttwak, Edward, Your job can be safe again – here's how, *Independent*, 6 May 1996

Lynn, Mathew and Olins, Rufus, Harmony restored as Michael sheds Sony, *Sunday Times*, 16 May 1995

M2 Presswire, 17 April 1998, Congestion makes case for integrated transport policy

McCarthy, Terry, Death becomes a top seller, *Independent*, 14 October 1994

McCrystal, Cal, California reels from stench of poverty, *Observer*, 21 April 1996

Mackay, Duncan and Chaudhary, Vivek, Bribes scandal forces Olympics shake-up, *Guardian*, 25 January 1999

Mackenzie, Colin, Tax time bomb, *Daily Mail*, 6 January 1999

McMenamin, Brigid, Follow through – your papers please, *Forbes*, 16 June 1997

MacMillan, Robert, Se. Phil Gramm plans hi-tech visa bill, *Newsbytes*, 2 June 1999

McRae, H (1994) *The World in 2020*, HarperCollins, London

Maingot, Anthony P (1995) Offshore secrecy centers and the necessary role of the state, *Journal of Interamerican Studies and World Affairs*, **37** (4)

Mandel, M J, Landler, M and Grover, R, The entertainment economy, *Business Week*, 14 March 1994

Marckus, M, Salaries and the emperor's new clothes, *Times*, 21 January 1995

Marsland, David, Tories take on the pension time bomb, *Daily Mail*, 6 March 1997

Martin, J (1978) *The Wired Society*, Prentice Hall, Englewood Cliffs, NJ

Martinez, Andres, Reforms opened up by lobbying game to more law firms, *Pittsburgh Post-Gazette*, 28 November 1995

Marx, K and Engels, F (1967) *The Communist Manifesto*, Penguin, London

Masuda, Y (1980) *The Information Society: A post-industrial society*, Institute for the Information Society, Tokyo, Japan

Mathur, L K, Mathur, I and Rangan, N, The wealth effects associated with a celebrity endorser – the Michael Jordan effect, *Journal of Advertising Research*, 1 May 1997

Midgley, Carol and Sherman, Jill, BBC may end radio poll after cheating, *Times*, 27 December 1996

Minford, Patrick, Unlocking the secret of capitalist growth, *Daily Telegraph*, 6 September 1993

Mintz, Bill, Target of FBI probe dies, *Houston Chronicle*, 14 October 1996

Mirsky, Jonathan, Peking drive to halt 'inferior breeding', *Times*, 29 August 1996

Moore, R H Jr (1994) Wiseguys: smarter criminals and smarter crime in the 21st century, *Futurist*, **28** (5), Sept/Oct, pp 33–37

Mueller, Lee, East Kentucky counties look for boost from prisons, *Lexington Herald*, 25 January 1999

Mulgan, Geoff and Murray, Robin (1993) *Reconnecting Taxation*, Demos, London

Mulgan, Geoff, Beyond the lure of off-the-shelf ethics, *Independent*, 30 January 1995

Muradian, Vago, Russians killed Chechen leader with a precision guided missile, *Defense Daily*, **195** (25), 5 May 1997

Murray, Ian, Passports for sale to Hong Kong at £500,000, *Times*, 10/8/90

Naisbitt, John, reported by (1994) *Global Paradox*, William Morrow, New York

Naughton, John, Why you can't fight cyberporn by raiding the newsagent, *Observer*, 7 June 1998

Negroponte, N (1996) *Being Digital*, Coronet Books, Hodder and Stoughton, London

Neligan, Myles, Concern grows over pornography and racist propaganda, *European Voice*, 25 June 1998

Nelson, Jack, Grappling with crime wave on the Web, *Los Angeles Times*, 30 November 1997

Nietzsche, F W (1967) *The Will to Power*, tr W Kaufmann and R J Hollingdale, Vintage, New York

Nietzsche, F W (1968) *Beyond Good and Evil*, tr R J Hollingdale, Penguin, London

Nissé, Jason, Woods in $90 million deal with Nike, *Times*, 25 August 1999

Noriyuki, Duane, Rent-a-cell trend at jails not always key to revenue, *Los Angeles Times*, 5 August 1998

Norris, D, Great call of China, *Daily Mail*, 7 February 1995

Norris, David, Firm's crate escape, *Daily Mail*, 22 February 1999

North, Douglass (1990) *Institutions, Institutional Change and Economic Performance*, Cambridge University Press

Nuki, Paul and Rufford, Nicholas, Channel smugglers spread net of organized crime, *Sunday Times*, 2 August 1997

O'Brien, Tim and Brown, Aaron, Disenfranchised prisoners, *ABC transcripts*, 25 October 1998

O'Reilly, Judith and Carr-Brown, Jonathon, Drop-out rate of 40% hits New Deal jobs, *Sunday Times*, 25 October 1998

Ober, Tracey, Spanish state blamed for 1981 health disaster, *Reuters News Service*, 2 October 1997

OECD 1994 Jobs Study, reported in A world without jobs, *Economist*, 11 February 1995

Ohmae, Kenichi (1995) *The End of the Nation State*, HarperCollins, London

Openheim, Carey, Must the child always suffer, *Guardian*, 27 September 1995

Orwell, George (1948) *Nineteen Eighty-four*, Penguin, London

Orwell, George (1998) *Animal Farm*, Penguin, London

Pallister, Marian, Secret pursuit of a pure species, *Herald*, 26 August 1997

Palmer, Mark, Life on the other end of the phone, *Times*, 27 January 1999

Pollack, Andy, 5,300 had abortions in Britain in 1997, *Irish Times*, 26 May 1998

Poole, Teresa, The great Chinese clean-up, *Independent*, 25 June 1998

Popper, K (1945) *The Open Society and its Enemies*, vol 2, Routledge, London

Popper, Karl (1992) *The Open Society and its Enemies*, Routledge, London

Porter, Michael (1998) *Competitive Advantage of Nations*, Macmillan, London

Poulter, Sean, Jobs threat as Rover is hit by strong pound, *Daily Mail*, 8 July 1998

PR Newswire, 11 October 1994, Study shows that costs of tobacco prohibition equal to that of natural disasters

PR Newswire, 25 May 1995, Tax means crime

Pratt, Kevin, Blair sparks offshore rush, *Sunday Times*, 19 May 1996

Private Banker International, December 1996, Lafferty Publications

Purnell, Sonia, Euro food destroyers, *Daily Mail*, 22 June 1998

Purnell, Sonia, Three men richer than 43 nations, *Daily Mail*, 13 July 1999

Puttnam, R D et al (1994) *Making Democracy Work: Civic traditions in modern Italy*, Princeton University Press

Rand, Ayn (1957) *Atlas Shrugged*, Signet, New York

Rand, Ayn (1964) *The Virtue of Selfishness*, Penguin, New York

Rand, Ayn (1967) *Capitalism: The unknown ideal*, Signet, New York

Rand, Ayn (1984) Faith and force: the destroyers of the modern world, in *Philosophy: Who Needs It*, Signet, New York

Rauch, Jonathan (1994) *Demosclerosis: The silent killer of American government*, Times Books, New York

Reich, R B (1991) *The Work of Nations*, Vintage, New York

Reuters News Service, 18 January 1990, Chronology of the longest trial in US history

Reuters News Service, 29 May 1992, Birth is a political issue in Yugoslavia's Kosovo province

Reuters News Service, 29 March 1993, Withdraw bank deposits, League tells Italians

Reuters News Service, 13 July 1993, Canadian tobacco exports soar on smuggling boom

Reuters News Service, 26 July 1994, Smuggling threat seen in high tobacco excise levels

Reuters News Service, 22 March 1996, German railway unions in deal to safeguard jobs

Reuters News Service, 2 December 1996, Whispers – Los Angeles is leading the fight against Proposition 218

Reuters News Service, 13 December 1996, Moody's lowers City of Los Angeles's general obligation rating from AA to AA1 citing Proposition 218

Reuters News Service, 27 August 1997, Activists say tobacco firms promote smuggling

Reuters News Service, 8 March 1998, US abortion clinic bomb hidden in plant

Reuters News Service, 25 June 1998, Key facts about China

Reuters News Service, 8 July 1998, Acid attacks on Texas abortion clinics

Reuters News Service, 12 October 1999, Austrian far right, conservatives share second place

Rhodes, Tom, White House woes increase with tax harassment claim, *Times*, 23 September 1997

Rider, B (1993) The financial world at risk: dangers of organized crime, money laundering and corruption, *Managerial Auditing Journal*, **8** (7), pp 3–14

Rifkin, Jeremy (1995) *The End of Work: The decline of the global labour force and the dawn of the post-market era*, G P Putnam's Sons, London

Rogers, Lois, Mensa sperm bank set up to create 'superhumans', *Sunday Times*, 15 February 1996

Ross, Sherwood, The art of cutting bureaucracy studies, *Reuters News Service*, 11 April 1994

Rougvie, James, Dispute at Timex ends with cries of betrayal, *Scotsman*, 15 October 1993

Santamaria, B A, The lost jobless, *Australia*, 15 November 1997

SAPA news agency, 13 October 1998, Survey finds increase in xenophobia since 1994

Sapsted, David, Plan to tackle soaring suicide figures in US, *Daily Telegraph*, 22 October 1998

Schloss, Glenn, Passport trade worth billions, *South China Morning Post*, 19 August 1996

Schumpeter, Joseph A (1991) *The Economics and Sociology of Capitalism*, Princeton University Press

Sebastian, Tim, Fugitive from justice, *Observer*, 3 November 1996

Shaefer, Sarah, A mixture of beer garden and panto, *Daily Telegraph*, 9 January 1997

Sharkey, Alix, The land of the free, *Guardian*, 22 November 1997

Shaw, George Bernard (1903) *Man and Superman*

Sheridan, Michael, Army runs China's smuggling boom, *Sunday Times*, 2 August 1998

Sheridan, Michael, All the white elephants you want, *Sunday Times*, 3 January 1999

Silverstein, Stuart, Other initiatives detract from campaign to raise minimum wage, *Los Angeles Times*, 26 October 1996

Simao, Paul, Czech gypsies discover harsh reality in Canada, *Reuters News Service*, 29 August 1997

Smith, David, Black economy booms ahead of Clarke's April tax rises, *Times*, 13 March 1994

Smith, David, Three tax-free cheers for the black economy, *Sunday Times*, 30 November 1997

Smithers, Alan, Rise of higher education sets hard questions, *Sunday Times*, 5 March 1995

Smithy, David, France blames 'London gnomes', *Sunday Times*, 8 October 1995

Soros, George (1994) *The Alchemy of Finance*, Wiley, New York

Soros, George (1998) *The Crisis of Western Capitalism*, Little Brown & Co, London

South China Morning Post, 26 July 1993, Nations ready to offer passports for sale in HK

South China Morning Post, 20 May 1995, 'Crown Prince' accused of bank fraud

South China Post, 15 April 1994, Ideology getting in the way of GATT

Steele, Jonathan, Child labour, child danger, *Guardian*, 31 October 1997

Straits Times, 2 August 1995, Changes made to New Zealand's immigration rule

Sunday Mail, 29 October 1995, Passports for sale – world probe – Scots official suspended

Sunday Times Insight, 2 August 1998, Spies on the run

Syal, R, Mobile millions Britain missed, *Times*, 29 May 1994

Tanzi, Vito (1995) *Taxation in an Integrating World*, Brookings, Washington

Taylor, Jeff A, National issue – the duelling ballot initiatives, *Investors' Business Daily*, 30 October 1996

Taylor, Jeff A, Rejecting burdens on business, *Investors' Business Daily*, 11 November 1996

Taylor, Richie, They've got loadsa yummy, *The Mirror*, 7 April 1997

Taylor, Roger, PPL shares climb as Dolly says hello, *Financial Times*, 25 February 1997

Taylor, Roger, More software companies look overseas, *Financial Times*, 8 April 1999

Tendler, Stewart, Straw backs police chief's plan to license private street patrols, *Times*, 17 July 1998

Times editorial, 9 May 1996, Vanishing tax cuts

The Grocer, 28 January 1995, Smugglers take their toll

Thoreau, Henry David (1849) *Civil Disobedience*

Toczek, Nick, Over-taxed and under siege, *Independent*, 21 April 1995

Toffler, Alvin (1980) *The Third Wave*, Collins, London

Toffler, Alvin and Heidi (1995) *Creating a New Civilization*, Turner Publishing, Atlanta

Turner, Clive, Why we must cut the price of cigarettes, *Observer*, 22 June 1997

United States Business Wire, 10 February 1997, Dual Star Technologies Corp. completes the first residential cyberbuilding system in New York City

Urquhart, Conal, Labour put jobless into depression work camps, *Scotsman*, 18 July 1998

Usborne, David, Mastermind burns evidence of world's biggest insurance swindle, *Independent*, 29 November 1999

Vallely, Paul and Wolmar, Christian, How to beat the rail strike, *Independent*, 18 July 1995

van der Zee, Bibi, Parts of the problem, *Guardian*, 2 July 1998

Vander Weyer, Martin, Do we really want to be a nation of Del Boys?, *Daily Mail*, 27 May 1997

Varadarajan, Tunku, Unabomber seeks book deal by post, *Times*, 25 June 1998

von Mises, L *et al* (1981) *Theory of Money and Credit*, Liberty Fund Inc., New York

Wavell, Stuart, A blonde bombshell for Sweden, *Sunday Times*, 30 November 1997

Webster, Justin, EU hits £230 million tobacco fraud, *Sunday Telegraph*, 15 March 1998

Whittell, G and Rhodes, T, We fight or starve, says migrant, *Times*, 11 November 1994

Whitworth, Damian, Doctor Death smiles at jail term, *Times*, 14 April 1999

Whitworth, Damian, Dixie's crusaders aim for secession, *Times*, 9 August 1999

Wiener, Norbert (1961) *Cybernetics*, 2nd edn, MIT Press and Wiley, New York

Wilkinson, Beth A, Victims' rights – a better way, *Washington Post*, 6 August 1999

Wilkinson, Paul, Bizarre remedies worried chemists, *Times*, 18 June 1992

Williams, Martyn, Jailed Chinese engineer given Internet free-speech award, *Newsbytes*, 16 February 1999

Wilson, Patricia, Family asks Dolly lab to clone dead daughter, *Scotsman*, 26 June 1997

Winnett, Robert, From tiny acorns new currencies grow, *Sunday Times*, 26 March 1995

Wolf, Martin, Corruption in the spotlight, *Financial Times*, 16 September 1997

Woods, Bob, Interesting Net facts, *Computing*, 21 October 1996

Index